W. Norman & R. Davies

Sept. 1996.

SINGAPORE

Publisher:	Aileen Lau
Editor:	Vivien Kim
Design/DTP:	Sares Kanapathy
Layout:	Rebecca Fong
Illustrations:	Parvathi N. Narayan
Maps:	Andrew Chan
Cover Concept:	Eh Ee Neh
Cover Artwork:	Susan Harmer

Published in the United States by
PRENTICE HALL GENERAL REFERENCE
15 Columbus Circle
New York, New York, 10023

PRENTICE HALL and colophon are registered trademarks
of Simon & Schuster, Inc.

ISBN 0-671-87916-2

Titles in the series:
Alaska - American Southwest - Australia - Bali - California - Canada - Caribbean - China - England - Florida - France - Germany - Greece - Hawaii - India - Indonesia - Italy - Ireland - Japan - Kenya - Malaysia - Mexico - Nepal - New England - New York - Pacific Northwest USA - Singapore - Spain - Thailand - Turkey - Vietnam

USA MAINLAND SPECIAL SALES
Bulk purchases (10+copies) of the Travel Bugs series are available at special discounts for corporate use. The publishers can produce custom publications for corporate clients to be used as premiums or for sales promotion. Copies can be produced with custom cover imprints. For more information write to Special Sales, Prentice Hall Travel, Paramount Communications Building, 15th floor, 15 Columbus Circle, New York, NY 10023.

Printed in Singapore

SINGAPORE

Text by Marcus Brooke

With contributions from:
Vivien Kim
Lee Geok Boi
Bina Maniar
Geeta Mirchandani
Sheila Mirchandani
Ilsa Sharp
Morten Strange
Tan Tarn How

Editor
Vivien Kim

Prentice Hall Travel

New York   London   Toronto   Sydney   Tokyo   Singapore

C O N T E N T S

C O N T E N T S

The city offers close

different kinds: witness a dragon dance, a boisterous affair; or enjoy the sound of bird-singing.

poreans are a serious lot, true colours

Amidst accusations that Singa-

city youths shine through at National Day – a carnival commemorating independence day.

Pleasing pagodas at

Chinese Garden and figures on the roof of the Hindu

Sri Mariamman Temple – garish evidence of the multiracial society splashes across town.

and something beautiful –

Something old, something new

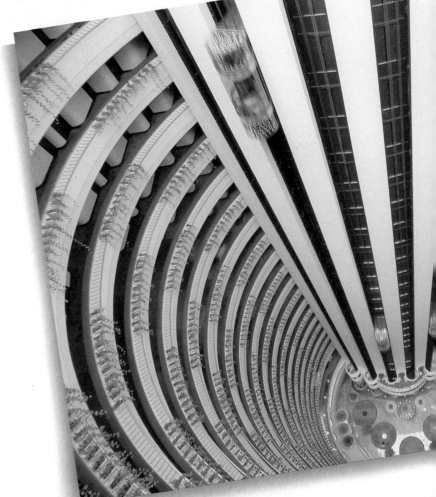

window-dressing at a kampung house in Sembawang,

modernity at the Glass Hotel, and pretty orchid blooms.

When night falls, silhouettes dominate the city skyline. Modern town apart-

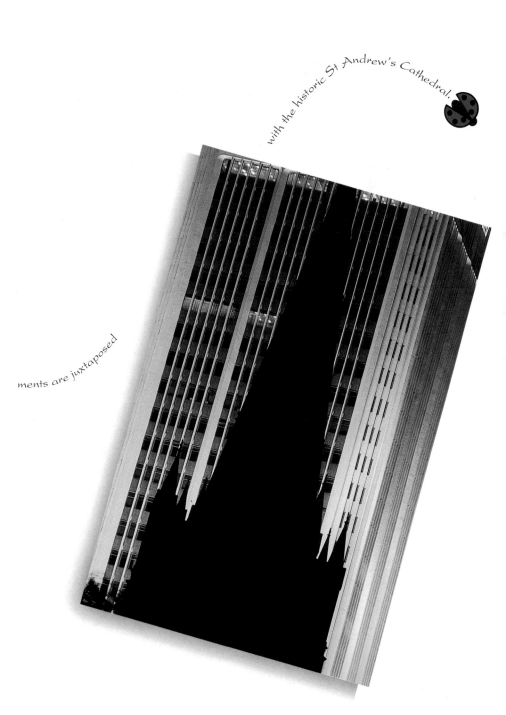

with the historic St Andrew's Cathedral.

ments are juxtaposed

I

t is often claimed that to qualify to write a travel guide to a country one must live in that country for either a few days or a lifetime. I fail to meet either of these criteria. I first visited Singapore in 1972, and have popped into it on innumerable occasions since then.

Each time, I have noted the remarkable progress made by Singapore. It is this progress, and consequent pristine beauty, that so disturbs many visitors, especially the young, who expect Singapore to be a seedy colonial city saturated with ethnicity, straight from the pages of a Graham Greene novel. In fact, if they stayed a little longer than the average three days, they would find the occasional ethnic vignette. By and large, however, I'd say they have arrived late.

Few realize that the golden age of the serious traveller in search of different cultures was in the 1960s and early 1970s. Before then, travel was the prerogative of the rich and the intrepid. Jet aircraft now makes it possible for almost anyone to travel vast distances in a very short time – London today, Singapore tomorrow, with even the most remote of places accessible by an airstrip. In the ASEAN

Never too young to bear the flag: nationalistic fervour as demonstrated by this young lass at the National Day celebrations (9 August).

Introduction

1

Singapore is considered the Switzerland of Southeast Asia,
not for its mountains of which it has none, but for its economic success
despite its lack of natural resources.

(Association of Southeast Asian Nations constituting Brunei, Indonesia, Malaysia, Philippines, Singapore and Thailand) alone, a score of new airports have been built in the past 10 years.

The result is that even the most remote places are affected by other cultures and lose a little of their own. The dilution of culture began here as early as the 1950s, and it is now almost complete. But not quite. It is still possible to find Chinese mediums who pierce their flesh with skewers that leave no mark when removed, and who enter trances and speak in tongues that are unknown to them. It is possible to find Indian devotees who walk on burning embers with no apparent injury to themselves.

Despite the ubiquitous use of English, the visitor should not be deceived into believing that this is a Western city. The Chinese Singaporean who steps from his Mercedes in the latest designer wear may have studied at Harvard Business School, but he is still influenced by traditional Confucian tenets. And this is why Singapore is so successful. Leaders are respected and heeded, and government campaigns to promote courtesy or to plant trees (to name but two) meet with an enormous response.

Personally, I prefer security to danger, hygiene to squalor, integrity to corruption. Because I am a Capricorn (and a water dog, according to the Chinese horoscope), I am occasionally dismayed by the rigidity of Singapore society and the apparent lack of humour, but – damn it – Singapore works!

– *Marcus Brooke, Singapore*

The Singapore River with Thomson Bridge, c. 1849–1853.

T

he name of a city some-
times gives a clue to its antiq-
uity. Although the modern
history of Singapore began as
recently as 1819, the San-
skrit origin of the name
"Singapura" suggests a far older past.
Singa means "lion" and *pura*, "city", and
the Lion City has been so called since the
early 15th century.

Even earlier, it was known by the
Malay name Temasek, meaning "sea
town". Third-century
Chinese accounts
mention a P'uo-luo-
chung (probably a
Chinese rendering of
the Malay "Pulau
Ujong" which means "island at the end
[of the peninsula]"). It may have been
the Chiamassie ("a large and noble"
city) referred to by Marco Polo at the end
of the 13th century, and it was almost
certainly the Tan-ma-hsi (a corruption
of Temasek) described by Chinese
trader Wang Ta'Yuan in the
first half of the 14th century.

The *Sejarah Melayu*, or
Malay Annals, a colourful
account of Malaya history
composed in the 17th cen-
tury, relates the story of Sri
Tri Buana (or Sang Nila
Utama, as he is better
known), ruler of the great
Srivijaya empire, who was
shipwrecked and cast ashore at

Personalities of the past: Top left, tigers used to roam freely – this one was sighted at Bukit Timah in the 1880s; bottom left, coolies at pepper plantations; bottom right, Sir Stamford Raffles.

History

7

the mouth of the Singapore River, then known as Kuala Temasek. There he saw a strange beast resembling a lion, but with a red body and a black head. Considering this encounter auspicious, Sri Tri Buana established a town on the site and named it Singapura.

The subsequent rise to power of Singapura as a trading centre, as described in the *Malay Annals*, appears to have little or no base in fact, but the stories nevertheless were set around a core of historical truths even though some of them sound more like mythical legends. It seems likely that there was a small riverine town, on the site of modern Singapore, during the period of Srivijaya's ascendancy in Southeast Asia. Buddhist Srivijaya held sway for some 300 years from its capital Palembang, in southern Sumatra, before power in the region was disputed by Thai expansion and the growth of the Hindu Majapahit dynasty in Java.

Towards the end of the 14th century, a Palembang ruler known to the Malays as Iskander (a corruption of Alexander), and to Portuguese historians as Parameswara, attempted to restore Srivijaya's former glory in the face of powerful opposition from Majapahit. A complex tale of intrigue ended when he settled briefly in Singapura, from which he was eventually driven by Thai forces in about 1398. The use of the name Singapura dates from about this time (both Srivijaya and Majapahit were Indianized kingdoms strongly influenced by Indian cultural and aesthetic ideas), and it has been suggested that Iskander changed the name from Temasek to Singapura to symbolize his attempted reconstitution of the "lion throne" of Srivijaya.

Iskander, fleeing before the Thai invaders, travelled north and founded the Muslim sultanate of Malacca (modern-day Melaka), which rapidly became the dominant trading centre of the region, with the tiny settlement of Singapura as one of its many vassals. The fall of Malacca to the Portuguese in 1511, and the subsequent retreat of the Malacca sultans to southern Johor, saw the final decline and dissolution of the Singapura settlement. It soon became a haven for the *orang laut*, or sea nomads, who lie in wait for vessels sailing through the straits transporting trade items between the east and the west. By the start of the 19th century with the reestablishment of the Johor empire, Singapura became home to a motley population under the control of the Temenggong, one of the two chief ministers of the Sultan of Johor.

Enter The British

And so it remained until the arrival of Stamford Raffles on 29 January 1819. His determination to make Singapore a successful free port appropriately earned him the status of "founding father" (see box on page 9). Nevertheless, it was the on-the-spot determination of Colonel William Farquhar as first Resident and John Crawford as second Resident (1823 – 1826) that pulled the infant settlement

Sir Stamford Raffles

In 1819, the English East India Company had a settlement in Penang and another on the southwestern coast of Sumatra at Bencoolen (Bengkulu). Most of the Indonesian Archipelago was in the hands of the Dutch, who also controlled the once powerful port of Malacca on the western coast of Malaya. Relations between the two European nations were strained: The English wanted greater control over the strategic Straits of Malacca in order to protect their trade with China, while the Dutch were as anxious to protect their own interests.

The Lieutenant-Governor of Bencoolen at the time was Thomas Stamford Bingley Raffles. The British government and its East India Company were losing interest in the company's possessions in East Asia (diverting most of its energy to India), but Raffles was adamant to resist Dutch intrusion in southwestern Sumatra and to secure the Straits of Malacca for trading vessels. In 1818, Raffles received the support of the Governor-General of India, Lord Hastings, on the latter point, and went on to designate Singapore island as the ideal post, commanding as it did the southern end of the Straits.

Raffles' knowledge of the area was encyclopedic. He spoke fluent Malay, was well versed in Malay history and culture, and was an ardent liberal in an age of political conservatism. He had joined the East India Company as a temporary clerk at the age of 14, had risen rapidly through diligence and application, and, in 1805, at the age of 24, had gone to Penang as assistant secretary. In 1811, he planned the invasion of Java, served as its Lieutenant-Governor from 1811 to 1816, and became Lieutenant-Governor of Bencoolen in 1818.

Then he attempted to plant another thorn in the side of the Dutch. Stretching the licence given to him by Hastings, and moving against considerable opposition in London and Penang itself, he looked first at the Riau Islands but found them under Dutch control. He turned to Singapore and some deft manoeuvring with the Temenggong and the elder son of the Sultan of Johor, in which he was greatly assisted by Colonel William Farquhar, who had acted as Resident of Malacca from 1803 to 1818.

On 29 January 1819, Raffles and Farquhar landed at the mouth of the Singapore River and met the Temenggong. Negotiations proceeded apace, and on 6 February an agreement was reached permitting the establishment of an East India Company commercial base in return for an annual payment to the Temenggong.

Raffles left Singapore the following day, leaving Farquhar behind as Resident. He returned for a month at the end of May. For the next three years he remained in Bencoolen, but the deaths there of his three children broke his spirit and forced him to retire. He visited Singapore in October 1822, stayed for eight months, returned briefly to Bencoolen, and departed for England in February 1824. He never saw Singapore again, dying of an apoplectic attack on 5 July 1826 at the age of 45.

through its precarious early years.

Farquhar lost no time in clearing the grounds and in encouraging trade by imposing no duties. In less than six weeks, more than a hundred Indonesian craft had called at the harbour. The port grew into a cosmopolitan town and Farquhar encouraged all who called to settle and by 1821 there were 5,000 inhabitants. Singapore owes its early success to its strategic location and this free-trade policy. Although pleased with Singapore's progress, Raffles objected to many of Farquhar's pragmatic measures and was angry that some of his instructions had not been carried out.

Farquhar and Raffles quarrelled bitterly during Raffles' last visit to Singapore, and Farquhar was relieved of his post. Raffles took over the responsi-

Japanese was a compulsory subject at school
during the Occupation (1942-1945).

bilities of Resident himself and set out to draw plans for the physical layout of the town and to install administration regulations. On his final departure Raffles appointed Dr John Crawford as the new Resident. During Crawford's tenure Singapore experienced booms in population, trade and revenues.

In August 1824, at Crawford's instigation, a further agreement was reached with the Temenggong and with Sultan Hussein Mohamed Shah of Johor, "whereby he ceded to the East India Company and its heirs perpetual title to Singapore and all islands within ten miles of her shores".

In 1826, the town, with Penang and Malacca, became one of the three Straits Settlements, which in turn became a British crown colony in 1867, when control was removed from India to London.

There had been a population of perhaps 1,000 on the island in 1819. By 1824, the population had reached almost 11,000, and was twice this figure in 1832 when Singapore replaced Penang as the centre of government of the Straits Settlements. Although the apparent promise of agricultural exploitation was never realized (the soil was not conducive to cropping, other than gambier and pepper), trade flourished. There were booms, and there were recessions, but by 1867 Singapore was one of the most successful trading ports in the British Empire.

This success was maintained for almost 80 more years, with Singapore

World War II Landmarks Revisited

World War II veterans and history buffs will not want to miss a tour of famous landmarks in the battle for Singapore between the British-led Allies and the Japanese, almost 50 years ago. The tour is divided into three modules, each of which lasts six and a half hours. These are "Memories of Changi", "The Attack" and "The Defence of Singapore".

"Memories of Changi" takes the visitor to a replica of Changi Chapel, museum and prison, St Luke's Chapel (in which there are murals inspired by biblical scenes painted by an Allied prisoner-of-war) and the remains of Selarang Barracks, in which 32,000 Allied servicemen and their families were interned.

"The Attack" focusses on the Japanese attack and the surrender by General Percival, the Allied commander in Singapore. The tour covers Kent Ridge Park, where fierce hand-to-

hand battles took place; Alexandra Hospital, where patients and staff were massacred; and the old Ford motor factory in Bukit Timah Road, where the Allied surrender took place.

"The Defence of Singapore" recounts the the Japanese surrender. It takes the visitor to City Hall, where the surrender was signed, an underground bunker in Fort Canning Park, and Fort Siloso and the Surrender Chamber on Sentosa Island. Visitors can choose to cover all three modules in four or five days, or any of the three modules in a single day.

Other World War II historical sites that may be of interest include Kranji War Memorial, in northern Singapore, which honours members of the Allied forces who were sacrificed during the war, and War Memorial Park and Lim Bo Seng Memorial, both near the Padang in downtown Singapore, the latter commemorating the eponymous general who was brutally tortured and killed by the Japanese.

For details of these tours, refer to the Trav' Tips (page 285).

Wax figures in the Surrender Chamber on Sentosa vividly reenact the Japanese surrender at the close of World War II.

relishing its role (in Raffles' prescient words) as "the emporium and pride of the East". Major world events in the last quarter of the 19th century provided the impetus to even further commercial development. The opening of the Suez Canal in 1869 established the Straits of Malacca, which replaced the Sunda Straits, as the major waterway between

Europe and the East; and heavy colonization by other European powers in Southeast Asia (the French in Indo-China, the Spaniards in the Philippines) led to an expansion of trade in the region. The extension of British protection to the Malay states and the arrival of the steamship replacing the sailing-ship were events that further propelled Singapore into being the major *entrepôt* port on the leading east-west Straits of Malacca. During the spiralling world demand for motorcars and rubber tyres, Singapore provided a convenient port for Malaya's rubber exports which represented more than half the total world supply.

By 1911 Singapore was Asia's most cosmopolitan city with more than 185,000 inhabitants – Chinese, Malays, Sumatrans, Javanese, Bugis, Indians, Arabs, Jews, Eurasians and Europeans.

World War II

Then, on 15 February 1942, the unthinkable happened: "Fortress Singapore" was surrendered by Lieutenant-General A E Percival to General Tomoyuki Yamashita, only nine weeks after the Japanese had started their drive southwards down the Malay Peninsula.

For the next three years Singapore, renamed Syonan-to, or "Light of the South", by the Japanese, was terrorized by secret police who tortured and killed both soldiers and civilians. Japanese was taught in the local schools, where the day began with the singing of the Japanese national anthem. Life was a nightmare: food supplies were scarce and the currency depreciated rapidly. Living conditions deteriorated and people were dying of malnutrition.

But as suddenly as it had begun, the war ended when the Japanese formally surrendered to the British on 12 September 1945, and the Union Jack, hidden all the while in Changi Prison, flew once more over City Hall.

Independence

The Japanese surrender saved Singapore from the devastation of a liberating invasion such as the one that almost destroyed Manila, but the return of peace did not bring back the good days of pre-war tranquillity. The victories of the Japanese in the east had added fuel to the fires of nationalism in East Asia, and the goal of independence from colonial rule became tangible. The Malays in British Malaya, and the overwhelming Chinese majority in Singapore, had become ever more active politically.

Without detailed plans for her post-war administration, Singapore underwent a period of social and political turmoil following the abrupt ending of the war. Secret societies flourished, labour strikes were rampant, there were widespread unemployment and a growing communist movement led by guerrilla commander Chin Peng. Events moved swiftly. With the formation of the shortlived Malayan Union in 1946, Singapore became a separate crown colony. In 1959, it became self-governing, with a fully elected assembly, although foreign affairs and defence remained under British control.

Meanwhile, progressive Singaporeans had no wish to contend with colonial rule forever. Trade union activity was on the rise and several political parties were formed in the early 1950s

Members of the People's Action Party – the only ruling party the island has
known – gathered on the steps of City Hall after its first victory in 1959.

including the PAP (People's Action Party) established in 1954 by Lee Kuan Yew, a young Chinese lawyer armed with a degree from the Cambridge University. The PAP fared well in the 1959 elections, winning 43 of the 51 seats. Lee Kuan Yew became the prime minister. He held that post until 1990 (see page 19).

Independence was achieved in 1963, when Singapore became a member of the new Federation of Malaysia which included the Peninsular Malay states and the states of Sabah and Sarawak. The marriage was not to work out, however, mainly due to the anxiety of Malay elements about the possible takeover by the ethnic Chinese. So the island state left Malaysia, and on 9 August 1965 Singapore proclaimed its full independence and assumed full sovereignty over its territory. The new nation was immediately recognized as an independent republic within the Commonwealth, and was admitted to the United Nations in September 1965.

The way the tiny republic overcame apparently inevitable hardships since post-independence years has earned it the admiration of many in the west. Singapore became increasingly identified with Lee Kuan Yew who emerged as a prominent international figure with his outstanding personality. The achievements of Singapore since independence have been considerable – surprising to outsiders, perhaps, but in tune with the dedicated pragmatism of its small but prosperous population.

The opening of Parliament by President Wee Kim Wee.

Government

The Republic of Singapore is a parliamentary democracy, with an elected president as head of state. The first locally-born president was Yusof bin Ishak, who, after his death in 1970, was succeeded by Dr Benjamin H Sheares. President Sheares died in 1981 and was succeeded, in turn, by C V Devan Nair, who resigned in 1985. Singapore's current presidential head of state is Wee Kim Wee.

Parliamentary elections, on the basis of universal suffrage, are normally held every five years. Government is in the hands of a parliamentary cabinet presided over by a prime minister, who must be an elected member of parliament and command the support of the majority of its members. The prime minister is appointed by the president, while the other cabinet ministers are appointed by the president in accordance with the advice of the prime minister. The cabinet is collectively responsible to parliament for policy. Parliament has the responsibility of electing the president.

The People's Action Party (PAP) contested the elec-

Prime Minister Goh Chok Tong sworn into office in November 1990.

17

tion of the first wholly elected Legislative Assembly in 1959, and won 43 of the 51 seats. Lee Kuan Yew, as PAP secretary-general, was appointed prime minister as a result of that election, and remained the chief executive in Singapore until 1990. The PAP has dominated all subsequent elections, the most recent of which was held in August 1991, when the PAP won 77 of the 81 seats. Lee Kuan Yew stepped down as prime minister in 1990, and Goh Chok Tong was sworn into office on 28 November 1990.

Life After Lee

Governing by planning and social engineering has been very much the PAP's way. It analyzes problems in perspective and carefully calculates probabilities. The meticulously planned and gradually implemented political suc-

cession to Lee Kuan Yew is a good example of this policy. For it was Mr Lee himself who started a more than two-decade long systematic and deliberate plan to groom a crop of successors. Described as a "non-event" by Mr Goh (because there was no break in continuity), the succession was smooth. This took place amidst traumatic events around the world (including neighbours in Asia like India, Myanmar, Philippines and South Korea) when fierce demonstrations and riots almost always accompany each change in leadership.

Uncertain political succession can be destabilizing in a young nation whose ability to survive its founders is yet untested. Singaporeans now want continued stability as provided by the PAP government as well as opposition in Parliament. It is perhaps early to tell how Goh's government will cope with the new demands. However, the values stressed by the new government remain

National Emblems

The Singapore flag consists of two equal horizontal sections, red above white. In the upper left canton is a white crescent moon beside five white stars arranged in a circle. Red symbolizes universal brotherhood and equality of man, while white stands for pervading and everlasting purity and virtue. The moon represents a young nation on the ascendant, illuminated by the ideals of democracy, peace, progress, justice and equality, as signified by the five stars.

The Singapore coat-of-arms (see illustration on page 17) consists of a shield emblazoned with a white crescent moon and five white stars against a red background. Supporting the shield are a lion on the left (symbolizing the island

itself) and a tiger on the right (the island's historical links with Malaysia). Below the shield is a banner inscribed with the motto *Majulah Singapura* (Let Singapore Flourish).

Lee Kuan Yew

Prime Minister for 31 years before he stepped down to Senior Minister's position in 1990, Lee Kuan Yew is the visionary power behind modern Singapore's outstanding success.

Lee Kuan Yew was born in Singapore in 1923. Although his forefathers were Hakka immigrants from China, his mother tongue was English, and he only became proficient in Chinese and Malay after he entered politics.

After World War II, Lee read law at Cambridge University in England, where he headed the honours list with a double first. He also married Kwa Geok Choo, another brilliant law student from Singapore, and became a socialist. Rather than practise as a barrister on his return, Lee entered politics and quickly outshone two political veterans – David Marshall, a lawyer who later became first chief minister and is today Singapore's ambassador to France, and Lim Yew Hock, a trade unionist who succeeded Marshall as chief minister.

In 1954 Lee became secretary-general of the People's Action Party (PAP), and after the PAP won the 1959 election he became prime minis-

ter. Unlike an ageing prize fighter who continues to fight in order to win another battle, Lee remains on the political stage because he fears what will become of his child once he abandons it. He did step down finally in 1990, but at the request of the new government leaders, he continues to serve the nation as senior minister.

Lee's philosophy has changed since his socialist days at Cambridge. "If in the name of socialism redistribution of wealth goes too far", he argued in a speech in 1990, "it will stifle the motivation to compete and to do one's best. Then socialism will become a failure... Winners must be well rewarded. Non-winners must also share in the gains, but not to the same extent."

Lee Kuan Yew is a very private man, and he abhors the cult of the individual. It is likely that he will not want a monument or street in his honour. But why toy with such trifles when an entire nation stands as a monument to him?

On The Campaign Trail

Singapore's so-called "draconian" S$500-a-throw anti-litter law is probably as famous as Singapore Airlines. In fact, litter-bug fines are seldom so heavy: $50 is nearer the norm. And the island is definitely not crawling with officials on the lookout for people dropping fag ends onto the street.

The anti-litter statute shows how the government typically solves social and other problems in Singapore: conduct a big campaign to educate the people about the problem, and if necessary, pass legislation to drive the message home. Hence, the litter-bug law is a by-product of the long-standing **Make Singapore a Clean and Green City** campaign. There have been anti-mosquitos campaigns, anti-jay walking campaigns, pro-environment campaigns – all with corresponding laws enacted – and productivity campaigns, you name it.

Many foreigners dub this "social engineering"; the government calls it "making things work". Singaporeans usually just shrug philosophically – but not always.

Non-smokers will particularly appreciate the continuing **No smoking** campaign. There are few public places left that do not have the almost ubiquitous red-X-over-the-cigarette sign. Cinemas, restaurants, lifts, government buildings are now all smoke-out places. Duty on tobacco is high, cigarette advertising is not permitted, and smoking is being snuffed out.

Further, no-one can miss the signs in public toilets proclaiming a $150-fine for not flushing. These come from the **Clean Toilets** campaign. A dozen or so men were fined in a blitz against those who refuse to pull the chain (how they were caught in the first place became an intense national debate). The press had a field day tracking down the "Ten Foulest Loos" in the country, publishing photos and stomach-churning accounts. The management of these – misnamed – conveniences quickly cleaned up their act.

So campaigns work, but sometimes so well

that they backfire. Twenty years ago, for example, population explosion fears sparked the **Stop at Two Children** and **Marriage Can Wait** campaigns. Mothers who ligate after their second child were given benefits, including priority in picking their children's school. But the two-child policy plus rising affluence led to an excessive drop in births: not enough babies were being born. The small family campaign was reversed and now the jingles heard on government-sponsored TV ads are variations of the "Families are fun" theme. Hefty tax rebates are given for having three and four children. Maternity wards are busy again.

The **Speak Mandarin** campaign, an annual month-long affair, was one campaign that was greeted with more than a philosophical shrug when it was first launched. Although their written language is the same, the Chinese speak a variety of dialects at home. The snag is that the "official" dialect, Mandarin, is taught in school, and so children ended up poor in both Mandarin and mother tongue – in other words, masters of neither. The government thought it could lick the problem with a campaign urging the Chinese to junk their beloved dialects in preference to Mandarin. This sparked off a huge outcry, particularly from the older Chinese who have a strong dialect pride and identity, accusing the government of trying to kill the Chinese culture. Despite the pressure the government did not stand down. And since then, the dissent has largely died now because, as Mandarin became more widely spoken, Singaporeans are discovering the benefits of a lingua franca.

During the annual courtesy month, the use of please's and thank you's reaches a seasonal peak and everyone becomes more polite. At other times, hotels and restaurants generally rate high in courtesy, but unlucky tourists still encounter a nasty case of the old boorishness, especially from commission-paid shop assistants denied a sale. This campaign will probably have to go on for a while yet.

The imposing colonial facade of the Parliament House, where parliamentary debates result in the implementation of new policies and laws.

unchanged: the resilience, the hard work and the thrift of the Victorian era combined with appropriate Asian traditions now equated with Confucianism in a loose sense (filial piety, duty rather than rights, respect for hierarchy). With such values small wonder Singapore is viewed by others as "a good citizen of the world community".

Judicial Power

Judicial power is vested in the Supreme Court and the subordinate courts. The Supreme Court consists of the Chief Justice and other judges who may be appointed from time to time. There are constitutional safeguards for the tenure of office and the independence of judges in the Supreme Court.

Visitors may view the court and some of the other government buildings. The older buildings, dating from colonial times, are located downtown (see map on page 122). These include the City Hall, the Supreme Court, the Parliament House, the Attorney-General's Chambers and the Empress Place (once a government office but now an exhibition centre). Other newer government buildings include the Ministry of the Environment Building in Scotts Road, the Ministry of Labour Building in Havelock Road and the Treasury Building in Shenton Way. The grounds of the Istana, the president's official residence, are open on some public holidays.

Singapore is the clearing house for the region's wealth which comes in the form of coconut, maize, oil, rice, rubber, spices, timber and tin, among others.

Since Singapore attained independence, its economy has boomed. In 1965 its coffers were almost empty, but less than 30 years later the government boasted a revenue surplus of US$2.5 billion. Singapore, geographically one of the smallest countries in the world, is today its 17th greatest trading nation. The severe unemployment of 1965 has been replaced by a figure of about 2 percent (it is practically impossible for unemployment to fall below this level) and an acute shortage of labour. More than 150,000 foreign workers are employed in Singapore.

A derrick on Pulau Bukom, an oil-refining island off the coast of Singapore.

Singapore suffered a temporary economic setback in the mid-1980s, but this was soon overcome, largely as a result of belt-tightening and increased productivity. Since independence in 1965, the republic has achieved annual economic growth averaging 9 percent, while real GDP has increased nearly eight times.

Singapore's major trading partners are, in terms of exports, the United States followed by Malaysia, Japan, Hong Kong and Thailand,

As many as 45,000 vessels call at the port annually with a shipping tonnage of more than 480 million gross registered tons in the early 1990s, making it the world's busiest in terms of shipping tonnage.

and, in import terms, Japan followed by Malaysia, Taiwan, Germany and China. The success of the economy is partly due to the continuing low rate of inflation (less than 2.5 percent), its free trade policy and low interest rates.

Although trade unions exist, only about 20 percent of the workforce of 1.2 million belongs to one and strikes are rare as snow. The most recent strike, the first in eight years, occurred at a US-owned oil equipment plant in 1986. Not without interest is the fact that when Lee Kuan Yew, later to become prime minister until he was succeeded by Goh Chok Tong in 1990, returned to Singapore in 1950 from his studies in England, he acted as legal adviser to several trade unions and participated in negotiations to obtain higher wages for members.

Since 1980, international risk analysis firm BERI (Business Environment Risk Intelligence) has rated the Singapore worker the world's best specifically in terms of productivity, attitude and technical skills, in a list which includes Switzerland, Taiwan, Japan, Belgium, West Germany, South Korea, the United States and the United Kingdom. Still with such a small workforce and a standard of living that, in Asia, is surpassed only by Japan and oil-rich Brunei, and that far exceeds the standard of living in such Asian giants as India and Indonesia, Singapore cannot compete in labour-intensive markets.

Transshipment

The observant visitor may wonder how a country with a population of only slightly more than 3 million and no natural resources can be the busiest seaport in the world. The answer is transshipment. Singapore remains today, as in the days of Raffles, an entrepôt port, and it is one of the few places in the world where goods can move freely in and out. To facilitate transshipment, Singapore has five free trade zones, four for seaborne cargo and one for airborne.

In 1990, more than 35 percent of Singapore's exports consisted of re-exports. Among these were natural products from the region to be shipped to Europe, the United States and Japan, in return for sophisticated equipment from these countries to be dispatched throughout the region. Barter, rather than cash payment, is not uncommon.

A significant proportion of Thai trade, and to a lesser extent Malaysian trade, is transshipped via Singapore. Thai ports are too shallow for container ships, and much of its produce (rubber, tin, maize) arrives in Singapore in small feeder ships. As for Malaysia, many companies have relocated labour-intensive industries – clothing, for example – across the causeway from Singapore, to re-export their products via Singapore for assembly and quality control.

Singapore has no social security but the Central Provident Fund (CPF), a mandatory saving scheme which requires monthly contributions from both employers and employees, gives employees some security in their old age. People can draw on their CPF to buy their own homes and pay for hospital bills. Other than such uses, and except in cases of incapacity, CPF savings may not be withdrawn until the normal retirement age of 55.

Industry Niches

"Singapore needs to focus on a few activities within each sector," argues a government spokesman, "so that there are economies of scale and a better chance for that industry to grow in depth and sophistication." The government prefers not to select economic niches, however, but "to create a favourable environment to allow niches to emerge and grow". An example of successful niching is the production of disk drives, in which Singapore already accounts for 60 percent of the world supply.

Manufacturing occupies more than 25 percent of the workforce and accounts for the same proportion of the gross domestic product. In the forefront is the electronics industry, in which some 60,000 workers, employed by 230 companies, produce microchips, printed circuit boards and the like. Next is petroleum refining and petrochemicals, then transport equipment, electrical goods, clothing, chemical products and metal and heavy engineering.

The names of the multinational companies who operate factories in Singapore read like a *Who's Who* of big business. This is partly due to the fact that there are no restrictions on the level

New skyscrapers constantly spring up all over the island – developers never seem to tire of their little game of see-who's-the-tallest-of-them-all.

of foreign ownership, no foreign exchange controls, no protectionism against overseas control of local industry. Allied to this is an impressive array of incentives to foreign investment. Different schemes exist, ranging from a venture capital scheme that allows up to 100 percent tax offset against equity investment to a "pioneer status" scheme, which encourages the introduction of new technology by reducing corporate tax by 31 percent for up to 10 years.

Most multinational companies are located in one of the 29 industrial estates managed by the Jurong Town Corporation (JTC), a government statutory board established in 1968. The JTC allocates prepared land sites with infrastructure on lease terms of 30 to 60 years. It also constructs flatted factory buildings, and develops and manages industrial estates. It provides port and bulk cargo-handling facilities at the Jurong Industrial Port, and logistic back-up to the Asia-Pacific offshore oil industry at the Jurong Marine Base.

By far the largest industrial estate is that at Jurong, in western Singapore, which occupies more than 5000 hectares. All in all, about 4000 companies, of which 70 percent are run by foreign companies, are located in the industrial estates. These companies employ almost 250,000 workers, who represent 83 percent of the manufacturing workforce.

The JTC plans to develop "business parks", which will be a hybrid of traditional industrial estates, offices and distribution centres. They will accommodate all kinds of support activities, such as research and design, light manufacturing, warehousing and distribution, marketing and office administration.

The government is aware that, in order to increase productivity and encourage niching, it must ensure an educated workforce. There are three polytechnics and a host of vocational schools, and the government is considering a scheme to make vocational training compulsory for all who leave school at an early age. Five training institutions have been established jointly with foreign governments (France, Germany, Japan) or leading international companies noted for the excellence of their training (Philips, Precision Engineering). The Singapore Science Park, next to the National University, is a focal point of research and development activities, and houses overseas centres of big-timers such as AT&T and Sony.

A Global City

Today, almost 170 years since its founding, Singapore is recognized for its growing service economy, which ranges from traditional shipping services to sophisticated computer software. This is what the government would wish, for its aim is for Singapore to become a "global city", not only in products but also in services that facilitate business.

In 1990, Singapore attracted more than 5 million visitors, who occupied more than 22,000 hotel rooms of international standard. More hotels are under construction and attempts are made to prolong the stays of visitors. The Singapore Cruise Centre, a project that includes a purpose-built international passenger terminal, will open in 1991 to handle the burgeoning interest in ocean cruises and to make Singapore the "cruise gateway" of Southeast Asia.

It will come as no surprise to learn that in the second half of the 1980s Singapore Telecoms spent US$1.8 billion on communications infrastructure. The city boasts the highest density of public payphones in Asia (in impeccable condition), and the world's first nationwide ISDN (Integrated Services Digital Network) which allows voice, data and video communications in one line.

Such excellent telecommunications assist Singapore in its aspirations to become a global financial centre – aspirations spurred by the fact that, although the financial sector contributes more than 25 percent of the gross domestic product, it employs only 10 percent of the workforce. Foreign banks with a full licence outnumber local banks by 22 to 13, while there are a further 14 banks with restricted licences. There are also 87 offshore banks and 65 merchant banks which are engaged in the Asian Dollar Market, where currencies other than the SING dollar are transacted.

An active stock exchange that, in terms of market capitalization, is second in Asia only to Tokyo (albeit a very distant second), deals in the stocks and shares of 327 companies, while the second-tier Stock Exchange of Singapore Dealing with Automated Quotations (SESDAQ) lists 14 companies. SESDAQ is linked directly with the National Association of Securities Dealers (NASD), which permits investors to diversify their portfolios with both US and European stocks. The Singapore International Monetary Exchange (SIMEX), which is linked with the Chicago Mercantile Exchange, deals in a variety of futures, including gold and oil.

The Stock Exchange of Singapore (SES) has taken a major step towards internationalization by giving foreign broking houses the right to hold trading seats. Nine of the 26 seats on the Stock Exchange have been allocated to foreign brokers who have entered into partnerships with local companies, all but one with the maximum permitted stake of 49 percent.

Another Singapore success story is the container port, the busiest in the world. It lies within a few hundred metres of Shenton Way and the heart of the business district, and its bright yellow equipment is clearly visible. The port is the focal point to the 700 shipping lines that link it with more than 80 countries. A second terminal is planned, which, when completed, will be linked by a causeway with the existing Tanjong Pagar Terminal. In addition, Singapore is the top bunkering centre in the world.

Also visible are the oil-refining facilities on some of the offshore islands, which make Singapore the world's third

It was in 1931 that Sir Cecil Clementi, the Singapore governor then, predicted "I expect to see Singapore become one of the largest and most important airports in the world." Today, the Changi Airport has been voted the "Best Airport" by the Business Traveller magazine.

largest oil-refining centre, after Rotterdam and Houston. Attempts are in progress to boost capacity and to improve the storage and distribution of the oil.

Even before Changi Airport opened its second terminal in 1990, plans were announced to lengthen the runways from 4000 to 4500 metres and to build a third terminal. A *fourth* terminal is being planned for the 21st century, by which time Changi expects to handle 36 million passengers a year.

Do You "C" What I Have Just Got?

Singapore's economic miracle has made its people rich, and like the nouveau riche all over the world, they are flaunting their wealth for all who care to see. Fridges, televisions and videos, once the hallmarks of success, have given way to the latest status symbols such as the computer, camcorder, cellular phone and other electronic gadgets. In fact, the hallmarks of Singaporean success tend to begin with "C".

• A walk down Orchard Road will reveal chic shoppers clutching the hottest fashion accessory, the **cellular phone**. These handhelds are being snapped up so fast that the national telecoms company that installs the transmitters sometimes cannot keep abreast of demand, as happened during the August 1991 election campaign. This nation must have one of the highest densities of cellular phones in the world.

• SLR cameras are quickly fading out in favour of the **camcorder** (or portable video cameras) as the choice for recording birthdays, weddings and overseas holidays. Young parents no longer carry snapshots of their babies learning to walk – now they show Video 8 or VHS-C movies.

• Today's party-talk upmanship often centres round the personal **computer**: "I've just got an IBM AT for my little Michelle to do her schoolwork." "Oh, we got rid of our old AT a year ago and our Vicky now has a Macintosh." The point is often not in using but having it. As with cellular phones, the nation probably has one of the highest densities of electronic white elephants in the world.

• The cliché used to be that the Singaporean aspires to have One Wife, Two Kids, a Three-roomed Public Housing Apartment, Four Wheels, and a Five-figure Salary. Not any more: The **condominium** has replaced public housing as the dream home. The asking price for a prime-area 1,400 sq feet pad? – Half a million cool ones.

• **Cars** make Singaporeans go crazy because theirs is the only country which has a quota on the car population, where motorists have to bid for ownership licences, and where the car is a political issue. Steep taxes make owning and maintaining a car here three times dearer than anywhere else. The car is the yuppie's dream – and his wallet hole-burner. Still, every tenth car on the road is a Mercedes Benz (prices start from US$60,000).

• Those who cannot afford snazzy wheels collect credit and **charge cards** instead. It's nice to have a card, but the really hip go for several, and preferably the "gold" ones at that. Only this way can they bank on getting a good impression everywhere. Almost every card owner pays his bills on time: The prestige and not the credit is the draw.

• Those who have cash like to cut a dash by wearing watches that talk, that is, they make statements about the owner. Ordinary people have watches but the rich have **chronometers**, the very rich have "timepieces", and the very very rich have a big drawerful of these. XO Cognac is the top drink here, Rolex the top chronometer.

• This country has scarce enough space for housing and roads, and hence precious little to spare for land-guzzling golf courses. Joining one of the few **country clubs** here is the ultimate sign that you have reached the top of the heap. Then you can drive there in your Porsche from your condominium wearing your timepiece on one hand and clutching your cellular phone in the other, and pay your bills on a credit card. Never mind that you don't play golf.

Conspicuous consumption takes a new turn in the island state with the (over)use of handphones.

A satellite image of the island city from 870 kilometres.

TG. SURAT

P. TEKONG
RESERVOIR

PULAU
TEKONG
KECHIL

P. SAJAHAT

P. SAJAHAT
KECHIL

CHANGI
BEACH PARK

RECLAIMED

CHANGI

LOYANG
INDUSTRIAL
ESTATE

SINGAPORE CHANGI
AIRPORT

LOYANG

P. SELETAR

PULAU
UBIN

P. SERANGOON
(CONEY ISLAND)

PULAU KETAM

PUNGGOL

JALAN
KAYU

KANJI ROAD

YIU CHU
KANG

SELETAR HILLS

ANG MO KIO
NEW TOWN

SERANGOON
GDN

HOUGANG
NEW TOWN

PASIR RIS

TAMPINES
ROAD

TAMPINES
NEW TOWN

BEDOK
RESERVOIR

LOYANG–CHANGI ROAD

UPPER CHANGI ROAD

PAN–ISLAND EXPRESSWAY

EAST COAST EXPRESSWAY

RECLAIMED

PAYA
LEBAR

BISHAN

TOA PAYOH ESTATE

ALAN TOA PAYOH

ST. MICHAEL'S
ESTATE

NEWTON

FARRER
PARK

ORCHARD ROAD

ESPLANADE

MARINA
CENTRE

SINGAPORE
RIVER

RAFFLES
PLACE

CLIFFORD
PIER

TANJONG PAGAR

EMPIRE DOCK

BENNETT
ESTATE

MACPHERSON

MRT LINE

BEDOK NEW TOWN

MRT LINE

SIGLAP

EAST COAST ROAD

MARINE PARADE

NATIONAL
STADIUM

EAST COAST PARKWAY

BENJAMIN
SHEARES
BRIDGE

RECLAIMED

MRT LINE

UPPER EAST COAST ROAD

NEW UPPER
CHANGI ROAD

BEDOK
VILLAGE

EAST COAST PARKWAY

SWIMMING LAGOON

KALLANG

OLD KALLANG
AIRPORT EST.

BRAH

Geography

The Republic of Singapore lies approximately 136.8 kilometres north of the equator, between latitudes 1° 09' north and 1° 29' north, and longitudes 103° 38' east and 104° 06' east. Situated at the southern tip of Peninsular Malaysia, the main island of Singapore is joined to the Malaysian state of Johor by a 1.3-kilometre causeway. Its strategic location, halfway between China and India and on shipping routes running east to west and vice versa, has largely contributed to its importance, which is greater than its size would seem to justify.

Because of its proximity to the equator, Singapore's temperature highs and lows range from 31°C (at noon) and 24°C (in the early morning mist or late at night).

Singapore consists of a main island, 573 square kilometres in area, and 58 smaller islands, about 24 of which are inhabited. The largest of these islands is Tekong Besar, while others include Brani (a tin-smelting centre) and Sentosa (now a tourist resort). Several other small islands, south of the main island, have been developed into recreation areas with sandy beaches and picnic facilities.

35

For that first acquaintance with the city,
this aerial view of the colonial part of town is as good as any.

The View from the Top

A good introduction to any city is the view from the top, and, although helicopter flights can be arranged (call National Utility Helicopters, telephone: 481 8374, but note that photography is not permitted), some may prefer to relax over a drink or a meal in one of several sky-high locations. The Compass Rose, on the 70th storey of the Westin Stamford Hotel, serves lunch, high tea (the *highest* tea in town!) and dinner. The Pinnacle, on the 60th storey of the OUB Building, serves both European and Chinese *cuisine* at lunch and dinner. Do not expect great views from the bar, however.

In the Pan Pacific Hotel at Marina Square is the Hai Tien Lo restaurant, which serves Cantonese *cuisine* with views of the port and the neighbouring Indonesian islands of the Riau archipelago. Further west is the revolving Prima restaurant, located above a grain silo, which gives excellent views of the port, Indonesia and Malaysia. The Prima serves *dian xin* and other Cantonese and Beijing dishes. Another revolving restaurant is the Top of the M, in the Mandarin Hotel. The glass-enclosed bar on the floor below the restaurant gives grand views of the Orchard Road area and beyond.

The main island is mostly undulating country with low hills, the highest being the 165-metre Bukit Timah to the northwest of the city. Mount Faber, a popular lookout point to the southwest of the city, is 117 metres high.

As might be expected in a location so close to the equator, Singapore has a warm and humid climate with very little variation in temperature between day and night, and only slight seasonal variation. The average maximum temperature during the day is 30.7 degrees centigrade, dropping to an average minimum of 23.8 degrees during the evening. There is an average of five hours of bright sunshine every day during the year.

Although November through January is generally referred to as the monsoon period, there isn't any marked difference between the seasons. The November–January northeast monsoon winds bring somewhat more rain than usual, although the showers are often sudden, heavy and brief, leaving the atmosphere refreshed. The mean annual rainfall is 236.9 centimetres, with November the cloudiest month.

A year-round summer supports the rampant growth of a tropical plant like the canna (ginger plant).

The orchid enclosure is reason enough for a visit to the Botanic Gardens,
a popular destination for both locals and visitors.

Flora & Fauna

Singapore is a concrete jungle. A garden city, but still one of the most urbanized nations in the world.

So goes the popular myth. Half true, but in fact, the tourism-promoters' slogan "Surprising Singapore" really comes true when you start to look around for raw Nature on the island. Destruction of the natural environment did start way back with the landing of the British colonials in 1819. The pace accelerated after full independence in 1965.

But there are still about 2000 hectares of wild land left, and about 11 percent of the island is still farmland.

It is hard to believe that the shy Slender Squirrel, also known as the Sundasciurus Tenuis, is a close relative of the dastardly rodent.

Singapore's is a tropical ecology and as such, still richly stocked with biodiversity. The fact that all this is available so close to a big city makes it all the more valuable.

One of the most astounding statistics in Singapore's quiverful of facts and figures is the one that says there is one tree to every four people in Singapore – that is over half a mil-

41

*Beware of the Long-tailed Macaque –
they are greedy creatures highly attracted to bright clothing.*

lion trees, of more than 100 different kinds. Not all are indigenous, however, since many have been planted under Singapore's urban greening campaigns.

Struggle For Survival

Changing habitat has of course meant changing fauna. Deep forest animals like the Mousedeer, the Pangolin and the Flying Lemur have been driven back to the remaining small patches of forest in the central north of the island – the Central Catchment forest spanning MacRitchie, Pierce, Seletar and Mandai, and that 75-hectare gem of primary rainforest, the 165-metre-high Bukit Timah Nature Reserve.

Desperate stragglers in the struggle for survival are the Pangolin or Scaly Anteater, the small Leopard Cat, the Cream-coloured Giant Squirrel and the delicate Leaf Monkey, which still roam the northern parts of the island.

The larger mammals have retreated to the offshsore islands – the Dugong or Sea Cow, still swims around Pulau Tekong, for example, and this island, to the northeast, off Changi, also hosts a healthy population of Wild Pig. Alas, Tekong is out of bounds for ordinary visitors, being a restricted military zone. However, Pulau Ubin in the same area, and St John's Island off the south coast, remain interesting hiking and nature-study locations.

And yet it is still possible to spot wild

A Singapore Beauty

Henry "Rubber" Ridley, who introduced rubber to Singapore and Malaysia, was also an orchid fancier. In 1893, Miss Agnes Joaquim, a member of Singapore's exiguous Armenian community, visited Ridley with a purple orchid hybrid that she had found growing in a bamboo stand in her garden. Ridley confirmed that this was a cross between *Vanda hookerana* and *Vanda teres*, and that it constituted a new species. It is also special because it is a natural "hybrid" produced not by artificially man-devised methods but by the passing carpenter bees.

And so evolved *Vanda Miss Joaquim*, later to become the national flower. It was thus knighted only in 1981 at an orchid "beauty contest". Its upper sepal and petals are purple with deeper coloured veins, while its lateral sepals are pale purple, almost white. The prominent lip is a deeper shade of purple, with crimson spots.

Because it perishes easily – once cut, it stays good for only three days – attempts have been made to cast it in more permanent forms. The flora forms the concrete motif designs of public housing flats at the Pasir Ris new town on the eastern part of the island. Vanda Miss Joaquim is also used in the manufacture of a range of golden brooch orchids which are popular souvenir buys. The fresh flower is strengthened by plating it with a base metal and then finished with a layer of gold. The orchid motif is also used in fabrics like batik and spun rayon, as application of an idea that the orchid motif be used to distinguish garments made in Singapore.

As for Miss Agnes Joaquim herself, she joins Henry Ridley in the Sentosa's Wax Chamber of famous personalities.

The mauve orchid has strict conditions for growth – it requires space in which to flourish and once cut, it stays fresh for 3 days only.

animals in central Singapore – the Civet Cat still visits homes off wooded Mount Faber; Long-tailed Macaques still roam residential areas around Thomson Road and the MacRitchie Reservoir, besides tourist sites on Sentosa Island; and the Plantain Squirrel abounds.

Less attractive denizens of the wild – the Python, the Cobra, the Monitor Lizard, the Scorpion and Giant Centipede among them – are also still relatively abundant. But you are unlikely to encounter them, for they are as fearful of you as you of them. Singapore's remaining wilderness areas are essentially visitor-friendly, for the larger predators, such as the tiger, were exterminated before the turn of the century.

Tree Talk

Trees, plants and flowers are easier to see, since they do not run away! Even

An unusual two-in-one shot of the Monitor Lizard, or Varanus Salvator, well camouflaged in a wooded surrounding.

Foliage of the Traveller's Palm, a Madasgascan tree of the banana family, provides much of the greenery around the island.

scarlet Flame of the Forest, the feathery fir-like Casuarina. Look out too for the venerable Malayan Banyan, a sacred fig with spectacularly draped aerial roots. Fruit trees – such as the Papaya, Banana, Coconut, Jackfruit, Mango, Rambutan – are plentiful, along with aromatic spice-bearing trees, Cloves, Nutmegs and Cinnamons.

The great hardwood trees of the rainforest are best viewed at Bukit Timah Nature Reserve. Here stand the mighty Shoreas or Serayas with their reddish bark and silvery leaf-crown.

Ferns are another of the glories of a tropical climate, and there are about 100 different ferns in Singapore. Particularly attractive are two epiphytic ferns – "epiphytic" means that although these ferns grow on a host tree, they are harmless non-parasites.

The two commonest epiphytic ferns to be spotted nestling high up established trees are the Stag's Horn and the Bird's Nest ferns – Stag's Horn ferns droop and trail, while Bird's Nest ferns curve upwards to make a nest-like basket of leaves. You will find these ferns lodging happily on old buildings too – try Chinatown in the heart of the city.

Common on verges or wasteland patches are plants sometimes dismissed as weeds, but charming for all that:

The shy touch-me-not Sensitive Plant, a pink-flowered mimosa that curls up if you touch it (the locals say it's shy!), the purplish-blossomed Singapore Rhododendron, the Lantana with its multi-flowered blooms of orange, red

the most casual observer will note the brilliant Bougainvillea plants placed by thoughtful planners along road-dividers, on pedestrian bridges, and up street-lamp posts, along with climbing vines such as the Dwarf Fig.

Trees are an official obsession. Besides the ubiquitous golden-flowered Angsana, it is now government policy to cultivate the magnificent spreading Rain Tree and a variety of handsome palms, from the ornamental red-sheathed Sealing-wax Palm and feathery Fan Palm, to the Coconut Palm and stately Royal Palm.

Other common wayside trees are the delicately-flowered Frangipani, the

The green hideaway of Bukit Timah Nature Reserve lines the slopes of Singapore's highest hill with the same name.

and yellow, the long blue spike of the Common Snakeweed and the yellow buttercup-like flowers of the shrubby Dillenia or Simpoh Air – its leaves are still used by some hawkers to wrap food items like *Tempe*, a fermented soybean

cake especially loved by the Malays.

Orchids not only grow naturally in the wilder areas, but have actually been grafted onto some trees in public places, such as Orchard Road where clusters of the Pigeon Orchid's fragile, fragrant

in the late 19th century.

One of the great colonial gardens and botanical research institutions of the world, the 131-year-old Gardens house half a million or more dried specimens in its Herbarium. Among these, amateur botanists may admire an exotic tropical oddity – the Pitcher Plant, a carnivorous plant which consumes insects falling into its trumpet shaped body (actually, adapted leaves), using a fluid laced with special digestive enzymes. These fleshy plants, known as "Monkey Pots" to the locals, come in three varieties in Singapore – a fat squat one clustered on the ground, a slim graceful one hanging from tendrils higher up, and a large florid one with handsomely curved lips. To view live specimens, just take off along the Nature Trail on Sentosa island.

Mangrove Growth

Another environment very special to the tropics is the mangrove swamp, although it must be said that the remaining 600 hectares on and around the island represent only 1 percent of the original cover.

Mangrove offers a unique seaside ecology specially adapted to salt-water and the absence of oxygen. Mangrove trees typically have developed breathing mechanisms like "pneumatophores", the periscope-like pole-roots which poke out of the swamp mud like a forest of sticks, and stilted prop-roots supporting them above the mud. Hence the alien,

white flowers may suddenly and synchronously reveal themselves in the right weather conditions.

But the Botanic Gardens still is the place to see all the plants you could ever have dreamed of, and then some more. This is where Malaya's huge rubber industry began, with the planting of a few seeds of the South American rubber tree

Rites of Passage

Singapore's bird records show a balance of profits and losses: many once-familiar birds have gone forever, alienated by extreme habitat changes, but new faces have arrived to maintain the total species count at something over 300.

For example, the handsome black-and-white Magpie Robin, with its melodious song, was once common but is now a rare find, trapped as a popular cagebird and further estranged by the "tidying-up" of modern Singapore, from grass-trimming to insecticide-spraying. It was recently deliberately re-introduced, at the Botanic Gardens (junction of Napier and Cluny roads).

One extraordinary consequence of the bird-smuggling sea routes around Singapore has been the appearance or even establishment of many non-native bird species – from Chinese Hwamei to Hornbills. Another example – the raucous colony of Australian Sulphur-crested Cockatoos on the Sentosa Island resort.

One of the largest bird populations in Singapore is actually transient, migrant. The island is an important stopover on the birds' long haul from summer breeding grounds in the Siberian north to locations like Australia in the southern hemisphere winter. This epic journey touches Singapore from about October to December every year.

For the most part, the travellers are dull-brown waders like plovers, sandpipers, curlews, whimbrels and snipes, as well as attractive rari-

ties like the endangered white Chinese Egret.

To see these birds, you need to travel out to the mudflats and swamps of the northern and eastern parts of the island, such as Kranji Dam, Mandai mangroves, Senoko and Pasir Ris park, which are also good areas to view the more spectacular herons, both Purple and Grey.

But the birds most obvious to the casual

"lunar" appearance of most mangroves.

Mangrove can be viewed mostly in the north, for example at Kranji Dam and on Pulau Ubin island, targetted for a major Outward Bound School development. Easily accessible is the patch at Mandai, across the rail line opposite the Metal Box factory in Woodlands Road, close to the Causeway link across the Straits of Johor to Peninsular Malaysia.

Clockwise from top left: Collared Scops Owl; Collared Kingfisher; Crimson Sunbird; Baya Weaver; White-throated Kingfisher; and the Great Egret. Next page: a flock of Curlew Sandpipers.

layman, on wayside trees and verges, will be the cheeky Common Myna, the flute-voiced Black-naped Oriole of golden hue, one or other of the two commonest local kingfishers – the Collared (blue body, black bill) and the White-throated (turquoise, a rich chocolate head and thick red bill) – the pretty greenish Pink-necked Pigeon and the chirruping Yellow-vented Bulbul.

Try the Singapore Botanic Gardens, Fort Canning Park and Sentosa island for some gentle, general bird-watching. If you are lucky, you may be able to add less common species like sunbirds, flowerpeckers, tailorbirds and flycatchers to your list. To observe hunting kites and hawks, such as the White-headed Brahminy Kite, and even more magnificent raptors like the White-bellied Sea Eagle, you could do no worse than stand on top of Mount Faber.

When you visit a more densely forested area like Bukit Timah Nature Reserve, it gets more difficult to see the birds and familiarity with their songs becomes more necessary to the process of identification.

Barbets and babblers will undoubtedly be heard chirping away, perhaps also the old woodpecker and even a black-and-blue Asian Fairy-bluebird. You don't need to work too hard, however, to spot a Greater Racket-tailed Drongo or two on the summit – look for a glossy black bird with two long "bird-of-paradise-like" tail streamers, and a piercing call.

Here's an insider's tip. Aficionados in Singapore's bird-watching fratenity (Tel: 449 1453 for Subharaj or 772 6098 for Dr Ho Hua Chew of the Malayan Nature Society's Bird Group) favour the Choa Chu Kang cemetry hill for some really quality bird-watching (but beware the marshes below, a military live-firing area).

It's more interesting of course to visit at low tide, but be sure to use comfortable shoes – a pair that you do not mind getting filthy and which will not be easily sucked off in the squelching mud. Bird-life is abundant, also crabs and various molluscs, as well as some snakes, please note.

All in all, a closer look at Singapore reveals that what intrepid Victorian lady traveller Isabella Bird saw there in the 1880s is not far off the truth even today:

"It is intensely tropical; there are mangrove swamps and fringes of coco-palms, and banana groves... and all kinds of strangling and parrot-blossomed trailers... vegetation rich, profuse, endless, rapid, smothering, in all shades of vivid green..."

The crowd at a National Day Parade. Elaborate march pasts and flash card displays add grandeur to the 9 August annual occasion.

Stroll along the street, board a bus or take a ride on the Mass Rapid Transit trains and you will meet with the Chinese, the Malays and the Indians, some of whom, because of their headdress can be recognized as Sikhs. All are Singaporeans, however.

You will also see Caucasians (Europeans, Americans and Australasians), Thais, Filipinos, Koreans, Sri Lankans, Indonesians and Malaysians. (The last two are indistinguishable from Singaporean Malays who form the second largest ethnic group here.)

Many of these people are tourists for, on average, about 15,000 visitors are in Singapore each day of the year. Others – Japanese and Caucasians – hold managerial positions which bring them to Singapore for several years (this group of expatriates numbers about 40,000) while many Thais, Malaysians, Koreans, Filipinos, Sri Lankans and Indians are guest workers. The government is well aware of the problems which stem from these guest workers but the Singapore workforce is simply

Singaporeans often take extraordinary risks to photograph truely unforgettable keepsakes of their wedding day.

People

53

The Malays, making up 14 percent of the total population, have always been the second largest ethnic group after the Chinese.

too small: unemployment rate is negligible. This is all a far cry from 1816 when Raffles found but a handful of Malay fishermen growing gambier and pepper on the island.

The Ethnic Pie

The population rapidly grew with the influx of Chinese, Malays and Indians until today these different groups constitute respectively 78, 14 and 7 percent of a total population of just over 3 million. The majority of them are descendants of the migrants who flocked to Singapore in the early 19th century, in search of a better life. Rounding off the figure to 100 are other ethnic groups which include Arabs and Jews, Caucasians, Eurasians and Japanese.

The multi-racial, poly-cultural aspect of Singapore gives it a fascination equalled only, some say, by Hawaii. Despite the different ethnic backgrounds that the people of Singapore come from, all of them regard themselves first and foremost as Singaporeans.

More than 40 percent of the Chinese are Hokkien while nearly 25 percent are Teochew. Cantonese constitute 17 percent, Hainanese and Hakka each make up 7 percent, and about 2 percent of the Chinese are Foochows. Today these different groups all mix freely, largely because of constant government

An Early Start

Ninety percent of Singaporeans above the age of 10 are literate, despite the fact that school, which starts formally at six years of age, is not compulsory. Kindergartens are increasingly popular before the age of six, and some mothers camp overnight during registration exercise to ensure their young a place at the best kindergarten. Playschools or child care centres (similar to crèches) give children an even earlier start by admitting those who have just turned two years. These institutions are especially popular with families with both parents working.

English is the medium of instruction in Singapore schools, although each child also learns his mother tongue – Mandarin, Malay or Tamil. All children go through three grades of primary school before streaming starts, when most children enter the "normal" stream but some are relegated to the "extended" or "monolingual" streams. Those in the extended stream take five rather than three years to complete their primary education, while those in the monolingual streams, who also take five years, study a limited curriculum that is only in their mother tongue.

Most monolingual students say goodbye to formal education after their eight years in primary school. Those in the normal and extended streams sit for the Primary School Leaving Examination, and successful candidates proceed to secondary school, where they are again streamed into either special, express or normal.

The top 10 to 20 percent of students are offered the opportunity to enrol in the Special Assistance Plan (SAP). SAP students and those in the express stream study for four years, those in the normal stream for five, before all sit for the Cambridge GCE 'O' Level Examinations. Successful candidates may then proceed to either two years at one of 14 junior colleges or three years at one of four pre-university institutes (soon to be phased out in favour of junior colleges), before they sit for the Cambridge GCE 'A' Level examinations. Successful candidates can apply for admission to the local universities of which there are two, but male students from the slower streams are probably by then of National Service age (18) and may be required to undergo their two-and-a-half year military training before they enter university.

The visitor may wonder at the large number of students in the streets, on the buses and elsewhere. The catchment of each secondary school is about 10 kilometres, rather more than the primary school catchment area.

Schoolgirls letting off steam and taking a break from the academic pressure at their school sports day.

campaigns urging all Chinese to speak one language: Mandarin.

The Malays originally came to Singapore from the Malay Peninsula and the islands of the Indonesian Archipelago, while the majority of the Indians are Tamils from the state of Tamil Nadu in southern India but there are also Gujeratis, Sindhis, Bengalis and Sikhs from the north and the Indian census term includes Pakistanis, Bangladeshis and Sri Lankans.

The Peranakans, whose men are called Babas, women Nonyas, are a small group with a culture, *cuisine* and style of traditional costume all their own. They are actually the descendants of men from the Chinese mainland and Malay native women who intermarried long ago, and they are found not only here but also in Malacca and Penang.

Eurasians, who number about 250,000, are attempting to retain their identity while remaining full-blooded Singaporeans. They have successfully lobbied for official classification as "Eurasian", rather than being categorised with all the "Others" (minorities). In colonial times two groups of Eurasians were identifiable: the fair-haired descendants of Dutch officials and their aristocratic wives from Java, and the dark-skinned offspring of Portuguese sailors and Malaccan villagers. Both groups had one thing in common: nearly all were extremely handsome. In these mixed marriages, the children almost invariably inherit the best features of both parents.

While the different peoples of Singapore live side by side, tolerant of one another's customs and affected to some extent by cross-cultural influences, they retain many of their old traditions and practices. Interestingly, many occupations traditionally held by certain races are still dominated by the same races today. Thus the Chinese are foremost in the commercial world, contributing a major share towards the wealth and prosperity of Singapore by fostering overseas trade. The Chinese migrants were almost invariably hardworking and thrifty, and many who are successful and wealthy today started with little

A Chinese Chingay participant puts her foot up. Right, Hindu Tamils scramble for the best position from which to witness a temple procession.

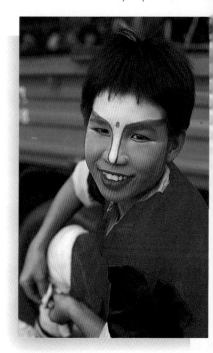

The "Kiasu" Syndrome

The universal human wish to "save one's face" has become something of a national characteristic in Singapore, on par with the British stiff-upper lip. The Singapore trait is called "kiasu". To be kiasu is to be one or all of the following: to be cautious to the point of selfishness, to be rottenly inconsiderate, to fear being left behind in the field, to be a dog in the manger. This term of disparagement originates from the Hokkien dialect and literally means "afraid of losing" or "afraid of losing out". The word is now considered part of Singlish, that is, Singapore English (also see box story page 58) and can be heard tripping off the tongues of Chinese, Malays and Indians alike: "Heh, why you so kiasu, ah!"

There are probably kiasu people in every society in every age. (The pyramid-building pharaohs and the Chinese emperors who erected the Great Wall are examples of ancient kiasuism in extremis.)

The most recent case of mass kiasu-ness was sparked off by the Gulf war, when Singaporeans panicked and bought up all the rice in the supermarkets. This despite the Government's assurance that the country has a six-month stockpile of the staple.

The quintessential instance of the kiasu syndrome on display is the habit of some people at buffet meals to take more food than they can eat, thereby wasting it. The result? Many restaurants now charge customers extra for buffet food taken but not consumed. Taking up more than one seat in a bus, not waiting for passengers to alight before embarking an MRT train, queuing up overnight to enrol one's child in a popular school, reserving tables at several restaurants because one could not decide – these are also examples of being kiasu.

Why are so many Singaporeans so kiasu? Some speculate that it is a migrant mentality bred by uncertainty about the future. The only way to survive in a shaky world, so this theory goes, is to look after one's own hide and grab as much from the world while one can. Better to be called *kiasu* than be left looking foolish...

more than the shirt on their backs.

Malays can often be found in government or the police force, while many younger Malay men work in factories, in construction, or for trading companies. Small-scale fishing, especially around the offshore islands, attracts a number of Malays.

Many Singapore Indians are enterprising traders and businessmen, dominating the textile firms and trade in consumer goods from India, Pakistan and Europe. Probably unconsciously continuing a 19th-century practice, when most public works were carried out by Indian labourers, many Indians today continue to work on government building and road-making projects.

Don't Joke, Lah!

Singaporeans speak a form of pidgin called "Singlish" which is peppered with Chinese dialect, Malay words and related grammatical structures and punctuated with bewildering abbreviations and acronyms, all strung together in a sing-song accent.

Singlish can lead to misunderstandings. Do not be offended, for instance, if a Singaporean offers to "send" or "follow" you home. He means he wants either to give you a lift home, or to accompany you home, in the politest sort of way. And when he says, "I'll horn you," he means he will sound his car-horn to alert you when he comes to "fetch" you (i.e. pick you up). "Take the PIE, then BKE, to JB" merely describes the expressway route to Johor Baru. Do not hesitate to ask what an acronym means – locals themselves sometimes need help deciphering the letters as well.

But the most noticeable feature of Singlish, the use of the Malay suffix "lah" as in "What to do, lah!" has had its primacy eroded by the Chinese equivalent, "lor" as in "Go how? – Go by bus, lor."

Sincere smiles, a characteristic of Singapore's youth.

Quite a number of them too have broken into the legal arena as lawyers.

Pakistanis and Punjabis are often found in business or the police force (as well as on the cricket pitch or the hockey field), while Sri Lankans are often attracted by the legal or medical professions, by government service or the jewellery business. Many of the Eurasians here have been successful in government, as well as in law and medicine.

The Spoken Word

English is the language of business and general administration, although the national language is Malay. Mandarin and Tamil are the other two official languages. The use of Chinese dialects is common in Chinese homes, at the hawker stalls or on the buses among the older generation minority.

Visitors to the island may notice some initial brusqueness in the persistent sales assistant, the scurrying waiter, or the man on the street stopped for direction assistance. Some locals attribute this to social shyness, others to an inadequate training of social etiquette at school but no, definitely not impoliteness. In response, the government, known to take no chances, conducts an ongoing campaign to polish

Malay boys passing time at the Orchard Road Pedestrian Mall.

up the smiles, the thank you's and the please's. Both visitors and locals are occasionally urged to put in a vote for the most friendly bus driver, the waitress with the best smile, or the most helpful sales assistant. Such contests are organized by both the government and the private sector in the service industry.

Like elsewhere in Asia, politeness is equated with saying what is thought you want to hear regardless of reality. Unless to a close friend, a local seldom admits that a new hairstyle or a new outfit is unflattering. That's being considerate for this way, so the reasoning goes, no feelings are hurt.

Visitors will find a predominant pre-

occupation with money among the locals – how much one's earnings are, how much something costs. Commonly heard is the local jingle "No money, no talk" (the Singaporean equivalent of "Money Talks").

Industriousness and achievements are virtues taught from an early age. A festivity, a new entertainment centre, a new food joint or shopping centre, or a new holiday getaway will easily draw hordes who need to take a break.

The population of Singapore is relatively young, and almost 25 percent are less than 15 years of age. This picture is about to change, however, due to the success of a government campaign

Community Centres

Throughout the island, banners announcing courses in aerobics, cookery, computing, floral arrangement and so on, can be seen on walls and fences that enclose quite modest, although often handsome, buildings. These are the 109 community centres (sometimes known as community clubs), which come under the auspices of the People's Association and are a focal point of cultural, educational, social, sporting and recreational activities within the community. In one year more than 10,000 courses attracting about 150,000 participants are offered.

Community centres are excellent places to watch children and, in the early morning, older members of the community engaged in *taichi*, or Chinese callisthenics. Almost all community centres have a kindergarten, and many have a crèche. All have a senior citizens' club, a youth group and a women's executive committee.

Much of the discipline that permeates Singapore and so impresses the visitor is generated by the community centres. And through these centres the People's Association helps people to acquire new skills, occupy their leisure creatively and preserve their cultural heritage. New courses are introduced regularly to cater to every interest. In addition, the Association owns holiday camps and sea-sport training centres, and it maintains various musical and drama groups, including a bagpipe band, Chinese, Malay and Indian orchestras.

urging young couples to have no more than two children. The "stop at two" campaign reached its target five years ahead of schedule. In fact, many couples were having only one child. A *volte-face* was announced in 1988, when the government began to encourage "three or more – if you can afford it". It is predicted that by the year 2000 the population of Singapore will reach 4 million.

The smartly turned-out clarinet members of a school band.

Islam is the religion of the local Malays. On the national level, it ranks second embracing some 15 percent of the total population.

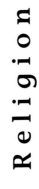

Religion

65

or statistical purposes, the Singapore government records the religious beliefs only of those above the age of 10, so the figures that follow account for only about 85 percent of the population.

A large number of Singaporeans are Taoists and/or Buddhists. The two faiths are by no means mutually exclusive, and the practice of Buddhism among Singaporeans is invariably intertwined with elements of Taoism and Confucianism. Together they claim 54 percent of the population making them the most predominant religions here.

Most Buddhists belong to the Mahayana school, while a smaller number follow the practices of the Theravada school. (In brief, adherents of the Mahayana school believe that one who attains *nirvana* has a duty to return to earth to help others attain the same state, whilst Theravada Buddhists are not so obliged.) All Buddhists and

Devout Buddhists burn joss several times a day to profess the sovereignty of the Buddha, his monkhood and his teachings.

Catholics assembling for candlelight processions to celebrate Easter.

Church Culture

Pass any church – and there are literally hundreds in Singapore – on a Sunday and observe the large number of congregants. Indeed, many churches are full, but their doors remain open so that the weekly pulpit message may reach the faithful who fail to enter.

About 12 percent of Singapore's 3 million are Christians. Of these, 40 percent are Catholics, while the born-again Christians form the remainder of the pie. They include the Anglicans, the Methodists, the Brethren and the Presbyterians. Not to be ignored are the Baptists, the Christian Nationals and the Bible Presbyterians. These groups suggest missionary activity, and large evangelical rallies are common.

More than 60 percent Christians are converts, and about 35 percent of practising Christians are professionals with a tertiary education.

Taoists are very tolerant of other religions, and it is not uncommon to see a Buddhist or a Taoist light a candle in a Christian church or place a garland on a member of the Hindu pantheon.

Rare is the Malay who is not a follower of the Islam faith (99 percent of them are), and he is joined in his beliefs by most of the Arabs and even some of the Indians. They worship at a number of mosques that exhibit a wide range of delightful architecture.

The Hindu pantheon of gods and deities on a temple.

The Feng Shui Balance

Feng shui (or geomancy) may be defined as doing the right thing in the right way at the right time, according to the advice of a geomancer. Good luck only comes when there is harmony between the two most powerful forces in geomancy – *yin* and *yang*, the positive and negative elements of Nature, and also the polarity of male and female. The ancient art of Chinese geomancy may also be explained using the *shen qi* theory. When *shen qi* (the breath of the mythical dragon which ranks top on the Chinese animal hierarchy), blowing from directions known only to those who have mastered this art, is allowed to waft through a building, its occupants will experience prosperity, peace and good fortune.

Singapore may be sophisticated and western with its microwave ovens, laptops, Megatop aircraft, test-tube baby techniques, cellular phones... But scratch the proverbial surface to find a superstitious city that consults the geomancers for a new office or a fresh home layout, for an auspicious time to open a new business or for a superior date to hold a wedding. Local examples abound.

In the early 1980s, business was poor at the Hyatt Regency Hotel in Scotts Road. The geomancer knew why – the original doors which were parallel to Scotts Road were also parallel to the hotel cashier's desk, causing wealth to "flow out". The owners were there-upon advised to "adjust" the *feng shui* of the hotel by having the main doors at an angle to Scotts Road. The owners agreed – and business has boomed since.

The rather unusual straw colour of the New Otani Hotel was chosen on the advice of a geomancer. Another geomancy guru advised the owners of the Carlton Hotel on the precise date and time at which they should open. Although the day was dry, rain poured during the opening ceremony, only to stop when it was over. This may sound unpropitious to some, but the Chinese equate the rain with money being poured onto the hotel – which has been one of the more successful ones on the island.

One of Singapore's grandest building, OUB Centre in Raffles Place, delayed its official opening by two whole years until the all auspicious date arrived – 8 August 1988 (8.8.88). The word "eight" in the Cantonese dialect sounds like "fatt" which means prosper. Chinese businessmen bid highly for car registration numbers that end with 88 which infer double prosperity, and even higher for 8888. Similarly, units on the 8th floor of a highrise invariably will be snapped up first, so also the 8th house on a row of terrace. One would have thought that only Chinese pay heed to feng shui. Not so. Even the American Club which opened on 27 May 1989 did so at precisely 3.22 pm, a date and time determined by the geomancer.

The majority of the 213,000 Indians in Singapore are Hindus, who pray at colourful temples with deities ranged above the entrance and on the walls. The not insignificant Sikh community has several places of worship, while there are other Indians who follow Mohammed or Christ. Other religious groups are the Jews, almost all Sephardic Jews from Persia, India and China (although a few are Ashkenazic). Although there are fewer than 500 Jews, there are two synagogues in Singapore. There are also Parsees (or Zoroastrians), Jains and Bahais, whose number is exiguous and none of whom has its own place of worship. Not without interest is the fact that the majority of national monuments gazetted for preservation are places of worship.

Dragon Boat races are fast becoming a fixture of
Singapore's recreational culture.

Festivals

71

The many races of Singapore mean an almost infinite number of festivals. **Christmas** has become the most significant of all, at least in commercial terms. The lights of Orchard Road and other parts of tourist Singapore are lit every evening as early as November, and they remain lit until February, when they are modified on many buildings to become Lunar New Year rather than Christmas lights.

Elaborate offerings like these are often burnt during the Hungry Ghost Festival as sacrifices to appease the gods.

The **Lunar New Year**, or Chinese New Year, occurs in late January or early February (the exact day being determined by the Chinese lunar calendar) and lasts for 15 days. The first two days are public holidays, when almost all shops and restaurants (outside the hotels), are closed and it's hard to find a taxi. To experience this festival, visit Chinatown and the banks of the Singapore River which are festooned with colour, lights and lanterns. Stalls in Chinatown selling seasonal goods like the pussy willow, mandarin oranges, special good-luck calligraphy do brisk business during the season.

Chingay, a miniature Pasadena Tournament of Roses Parade

Crowds flock to the Singapore River during the Chinese Lunar New Year to witness a blaze of colour, lights and merrymaking.

that features many colourful groups and floats, is staged towards the end of the Lunar New Year. The place is Orchard Road, the time evening, the theme Singapore's multi-cultural heritage. The different ethnic groups are represented, and invariably there are lion and dragon dances, stilt-walkers and flag-balancers. The last group balances on their foreheads heavy 12-metre-long flagpoles, which are skilfully tossed from one performer to the next. A spectacular sight worth recording on film, so don't forget your camera.

Fulfilling A Vow

At about this time, the Indian festival of **Thaipusam** takes place. Thaipusam is the feast of the Hindu god Subramaniam, son of Shiva, and it celebrates his triumph over the forces of evil. To the

Big-headed "dolls" entertain during
the annual Chingay Parade.

Here, to the accompaniment of music, penitents pass from conscious-ness to a state of religious ecstasy. And then their self-mortification begins. Some may pass a skewer (often a metre long and as thick as a man's thumb) through their cheeks. Others pass smaller skewers through their tongue or the skin on their forehead. Still others carry the *kavadi*, a semi-circular steel or wooden frame that rests on the shoulders, and which is fastened to the torso of the penitent with many long, thin hooks. The *kavadi* is heaily decorated with flow-ers and peacock feathers. (The peacock is believed to be the mode of transport of Lord Subramaniam.) Despite the evi-dence, there is never any blood, and penitents claim that they suffer no pain. Their minds, they explain, have been elevated by thoughts of Subramaniam.

The groups of penitents and their followers walk for three kilometres from

Tamils, who comprise the majority of Singapore Indians, Subramaniam sym-bolizes virtue, bravery, youth and beauty. He is also the universal dis-penser of favours, and so at Thaipusam all who wish to fulfil a vow in return for a granted favour, or to beg for a future favour, or simply to repent past sins, make their way, together with family and friends, to the Sri Srinivasa Perumal Temple in Serangoon Road.

With his body heavily skewered and bearing the metal-framed kavadi,
this penitent is ready to take part in the Thaipusam procession.

the Sri Srinivasa Perumal Temple to the Sri Thandayuthapani Temple in Tank Road, where their burden is removed, their ecstasy subsides and a coconut is hurled to the ground to signify that their vow has been fulfilled. Spectators and photography are allowed, just do not obstruct the procession.

The end of February usually sees the first of a number of year-round Chinese festivals that feature spirit mediums. They are seen at only a few temples, but the visitor will be fascinated as they witness the mediums entering into a trance. The **Birthday of the Monkey God** is celebrated with great enthusiasm because it is believed that this god, a popular Chinese mythological character, can heal the sick and even the moribund. The mediums place skewers

in their cheeks, tongue and arms, and in this respect their performance is not unlike that of the Hindu penitents during Thaipusam. During the Chinese festival, however, the mediums may also roll on knife blades or place their arms in boiling oil. They also consecrate pieces of paper with drops of their blood, and, speaking in the voice of the god who possesses them, they give advice on a variety of matters. An awesome experience for visitors can be had at the Monkey God Temple in Seng Poh Road.

The festival celebrations sometimes culminate in a walking-on-fire session, when faithful devotees are able, in some miraculous manner, to follow the medium across the glowing embers without coming to any harm. This is also the time when performances of *wayang*, or Chinese opera, can be seen.

There are no major festivals until the end of March or the beginning of April, when Chinese families observe **Qing Ming**, the equivalent of the Christian All Souls' Day, and show traditional respect for the dead. The entire family visits the cemetery and makes offerings of food and drink and even cigarettes to the dead. Joss-sticks are lit, paper money or hell notes (and more recently, even hell chequebook and hell credit cards) for use in the next world is burned, and bows of respect are made.

The best place to see Qing Ming is the Chinese Cemetery at Choa Chu Kang Road. Because of the shortage of land in Singapore, cremation rather than burial is encouraged and temples with col-

Taoist mediums going into a trance while devotees look on with reverence.

umbaria (= a building with niches for the reception of cinerary urns), such as the Kong Meng San Phor Kark See Temple in Bright Hill Drive, are very busy during Qing Ming.

Good Friday festivities (between late March and early April) can be best viewed during the candlelight service at St Joseph's Church in Victoria Street.

Holy Waters

A date that is constant, 13 April, sees **Songkran**, the first of the Buddhist festivals, which marks the celebration of the Buddhist New Year. At this time, Buddhist statues are reverently bathed in holy water, but distinctly secular manifestations have been added to what was originally a religious celebration and all who attend are likely to be drenched with holy water – or any kind of water. Songkran is best enjoyed at the Sattha Puchaniyaram Buddhist Temple in Bukit Batok West Avenue 8.

At the end of April or the beginning of May is the **Birthday of the Third Prince**, another Chinese festival that involves spirit mediums. Temple rituals can be viewed at various Chinese temples such as the one on Queen Street. Ne Zha, the Third Prince of the Lotus, is usually seen with a magical bracelet in one hand, a magical sword in the other, and wheels "of wind and fire" beneath his feet. Before his birth, his mother dreamt that a priest told her she would give birth to the son of a unicorn, and, indeed, by the time he was seven Ne Zha

was two metres tall. He accidentally killed a son of the Dragon King of the Eastern Seas and, to protect his parents from the king's anger, he surrendered to the king and allowed his own flesh to be stripped to the bones. Ne Zha's master then re-created him from lotus leaves and water-lily stalks, before teaching him martial arts.

Later in May, on the full moon of the Buddhist month of Visakha, is **Vesak Day**, the major Buddhist festival. This is the birthday of the Buddha, also the day of his Enlightenment and of his entry into *nirvana*. The best places to watch the festivities are the Sakaya Muni Buddha Gaya Temple (the Temple of 1,000 Lights) in Race Course Road and the Kong Meng San Phor Kark See Temple in Bright Hill Drive. The celebrations include *sutra* chanting, Buddhist songs by a children's choir, traditional dances and the liberation of caged birds – an act that symbolizes peace and freedom.

Love Ties

It is also at about this time that Muslims mark the festival of **Hari Raya Puasa**, which signifies the end of Ramadan, the fasting month, when all Muslims abstain from food and drink between sunrise and sunset. Hari Raya Puasa is the time to don new clothes and visit friends and relatives, renewing ties of love and brotherhood and asking forgiveness for past offences. The market at Geylang Serai is especially colourful during this fasting month when the bazaar turns into a visual delight offering traditional foods and other items for sale.

The **Dragon Boat Festival**, rather like Christmas, has lost its original meaning and is now celebrated by all. Dragon boat races are organized in Marina Bay at the end of May or the beginning of June, attracting crews from other Asian countries, Australia, Europe and the United States. The races no longer take place on the traditional fifth day of the fifth lunar month, because there is now an international dragon boat circuit competing to attract the same crews.

Thirteen-metre-long dragon boats, each with a crew of 24, thrash the water to the rhythm of a drummer who sits at the stern. The boats, which are now made of fibreglass rather than traditional wood, are painted with scales and decorated with an awesome dragon. The "eyes" of the dragon are ceremoniously dotted just before the race so that it can "see" where it is going. Until quite recently, women were not even permitted to look at the dragon's head before it was fixed to the bow of the boat, but today there are separate women's races.

The Dragon Boat Festival commemorates the suicide of the ancient Chinese poet Ch'u Yuan, who drowned himself to protest against the corruption of the king during his time. To retrieve his body before a scavenging shoal got to it, fishermen furiously paddled their boats, beating drums and throwing rice dumplings into the water to scare away and assuage the hunger of the fish.

The rice dumplings are recalled in modern-day *zong zi* – triangular cakes of glutinous rice filled with meat or bean paste and wrapped in bamboo leaves – but the tradition has been somewhat blurred by the fact that these cakes are now eaten all year round.

About six weeks after Hari Raya Puasa, there occurs another Muslim festival, **Hari Raya Haji**, which marks the conclusion of the annual pilgrimage to Mecca. Communal prayers take place at the various mosques islandwide. Goats and other animals are sacrificed to Allah, and their flesh is given to the poor, in a ceremony that commemorates Abraham's sacrifice of a ram in place of his son Ishmael. Muslims who have made the pilgrimage to Mecca wear

On a prayer mat and facing Mecca, Muslims fulfil their religious obligations.

Spirits soar during the annual National Day celebrations, when audience participation is active.

white caps and are addressed as "Haji" if male, "Hajjah" if female.

Singapore is proud of its achievements and celebrates its independence in a big way on **National Day** (9 August). It is a day of grand finery either at the National Stadium or at the Padang (check at the hotel information desk) amidst military displays, elaborate parades, community singing and music, and fireworks in the evening.

Ghostly Appetites

August-September sees the **Festival of the Hungry Ghosts**, which to the Chinese is second in importance only to the Lunar New Year. During this period, the souls of the dead are released from purgatory and wander the earth for 30 days. Temporary outdoor dining tables groan with the weight of food, to satisfy the voracious appetites of the "hungry

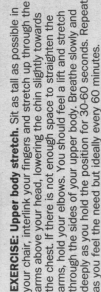

Day one

Get fit, feel fit: yoga for air travellers

By Jennai Cox
Fitness Editor

EVEN the most inactive person would not choose to sit in the same position for up to ten hours with only a narrow corridor and tiny toilet for relief. Yet this is exactly what thousands of people will be doing when boarding an aeroplane for their summer holiday.

Unless travelling first-class, the discomfort of flying is renowned and the problem is no longer a minority one.

All of a sudden the airlines, and their passengers, are beginning to think more carefully about the impact on the body of being immobile at altitude for so long.

Blood clots in the lower leg which characterise deep-vein thrombosis (DVT) are caused by inactivity and should be a concern for everyone, and not just those who have been warned they are at risk, according to yoga teacher and practitioner, Ailon Freedman. DVT kills about 2,000 people in the UK each year.

"The human body simply was not designed to sit still for long periods," he says. "When it is forced into immobility the muscles atrophy, our joints stiffen, the blood circulation weakens and our digestion becomes sluggish."

Simplified yoga moves that can be done from your seat at regular intervals can reduce the level of discomfort, Freedman says, in particular on long-haul flights.

☐ Exercise provided by Ailon Freedman, of The Lotus Exchange. See www.lotus-exchange.co.uk or call 020 7463 2234 for more information.

EXERCISE: Upper body stretch. Sit as tall as possible in your chair, interlink your fingers and stretch up through the arms above your head, lowering the chin slightly towards the chest. If there is not enough space to straighten the arms, hold your elbows. You should feel a lift and stretch through the sides of your upper body. Breathe slowly and deeply as you hold the position for 30-60 seconds. Repeat as you feel the need but ideally every 60 minutes.

Please ensure you have the consent of your GP before embarking on a new exercise regime. Do not undertake any physical activity if you are feeling unwell or recovering from an injury.

Today's fixtures

Cricket

National League
Second division
4.10, 50 overs
TRENT BRIDGE: Nottinghamshire Outlaws v Hampshire Hawks

Tour match
10.45, final day of three
ARUNDEL: South Africa v India A

SECOND XI TROPHY: Millfield School: Somerset v Glamorgan. **New Rover CC:** Yorkshire v Nottinghamshire.

Football

FRIENDLY MATCHES (7.30 unless stated): Bath v Swansea (7.15); Bideford v Swindon (7.45); Blackpool v Wrexham (7.15); Brechin v Aberdeen; Buckie Thistle v Ross County; Buxton v Macclesfield; Dulwich v Nottm Forest; Gresley v Derby; Hednesford v Walsall; Hereford v West Brom (7.45); Kidderminster v Leicester (7.45); King's Lynn v Lincoln City; Mildenhall Town v Cambridge Utd (7.45); Pennyn Ath v Sheff Utd; Threave Rovers v Airdrie (7.45).

UNDER-21 CELTIC CUP (Dublin): Men: Yesterday: Scotland 4 Wales 0; Ireland 3 France 2. **Saturday:** France 3 Wales 0; Ireland 3 Scotland 2. **Final positions:** 1, Ireland 9pts; 2, Scotland 6; 3, France 3; 4, Wales 0. **Women: Yesterday:** Scotland 2 Wales 1; Ireland 2 France 4. **Saturday:** France 3 Wales 0; Ireland 1 Scotland 3. **Final positions:** 1, Scotland 9pts; 2, France 6; 3, Ireland 3; 4, Wales 0.
MIXED INTERNATIONAL: England 1 Wales 0 (Letchworth).

TOUR MATCH: Northern United 44 BARLA Great Britain Lions 20.
NATIONAL LEAGUE: First division: Batley 16 Salford 54; Featherstone 26 Dewsbury 13; Hull Kingston Rovers 18 Rochdale 33; Oldham 31 Doncaster 20; Whitehaven 8 Leigh 20. **Second division:** Gateshead 30 Swinton 39; Keighley 20 Chorley Lynx 23; London Skolars 6 York 66; Sheffield 43 Barrow 42; Workington 18 Hunslet 22. **Third division:** Bradford DH 40 Coventry 8; Hemel 16 South London 22; Huddersfield Underbank 4 Teesside 28; Sheffield HH 18 St Albans 6; Warrington Woolston 60 Manchester 14.

TOTALRL.COM CONFERENCE: Welsh division: Bridgend Blue Bulls 84 Swansea Bulls 1; Rumney Rhinos 86 Cynon Valley Cougars 8; Torfaen Tigers 26 Aberavon Fighting Irish 22. **East division:** Cambridge Eagles 0 South Norfolk Saints 60; Essex Eels 110 Luton Vipers 12; St Ives Roosters 28 Ipswich Rhinos 52. **London/South division:** Crawley Jets 88 South London Storm A 6; Greenwich Admirals 20 Gosport & Fareham Vikings 30; Kingston Warriors 54 Hemel Stags A 12; West London Sharks 24 North London Skolars 32. **North East division:** Durham Tigers 6 Bridlington Bulls 82; Newcastle Knights 60 Sunderland City 16; Whitley Bay Barbarians 2 Gateshead Storm 86; Yorkshire Coast Tigers 6 Leeds Akademiks 6. **North Midlands division:** Crewe Wolves 74 Worksop Sharks 6; Mansfield Storm 26 Derby City 24; Nottingham Outlaws 42 Rotherham Giants 16. **North West division:** Blackpool Sea Eagles 31 Lancaster 26; Carlisle Centurions 44 Chester Wolves 10; Liverpool Buccaneers 14 Bolton le Moors 44. **South Midlands division:** Birmingham Bulldogs 64 Wolverhampton Wizards 6; Telford Raiders 24 Leicester Phoenix 0. **West division:** Bristol Sonics 4 Gloucestershire Warriors 44; Oxford Cavaliers 32 Worcestershire Saints 34; Somerset Vikings 26 Cardiff Demons 16.

NRL: Penrith 29 Newcastle 16; Canberra 28 Wests Tigers 26; New Zealand 31 Cronulla 24; St George-Illawarra 36 North Queensland 16; Brisbane 26 Melbourne 22 (aet); Parramatta 34 South Sydney 20; Sydney Roosters 50 Manly 26. **Bye:** Bulldogs.

Times Square

● The last letter of each answer is the first letter of the next. When you have completed all of the clues, arrange the letters that fall in the shaded squares into the name of a cricketing legend.

1 across: Is cricket in good shape here at the Kennington ground? (4).
1 down: Hennie, the South African who was an early pace setter in The Open at Sandwich (4).
2a: Concedes a goal, for instance (4,2).
3d: Henry and Keith, who gravitated to Goodison as Everton team-mates (6).
4d: Rod combined with a fox for the Blues (6).
5d: Winged goddess of victory who wears well on the sportsfield! (4).
6a: Eamonn, ex-Irish international who became a little haunted as Roy Keane's ghostwriter (6).
7a: They are locked in rivalry with Harvard (4).

676: Across - 1, Stewart; 2, TAG; 6, Salo; 7, Owners. Down - 1, Shunt; 3, German; 4, Tyres; 5, Nets. **Times Square name:** Ayrton Senna.

Taking care while up in the air

By Jennai Cox
Fitness Editor

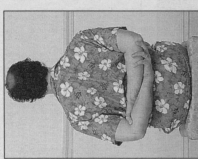

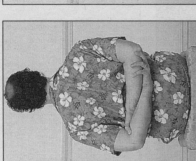

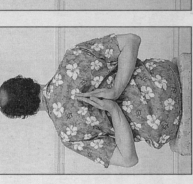

WITHOUT physical movement, blood circulation weakens, which is believed to be the reason for the increased incidence of deep vein thrombosis during air-flights, when clots form in the lower legs. Being confined to a cramped chair for any time longer than a couple of hours restricts the workings of the body, according to Ailon Freedman, who provides yoga services to those in the corporate sector.

Being stationary for long periods also makes digestion slower and constipation more likely. "Also, the air in most planes is very dehydrating and, as most travellers drink alcohol, their bodies become very dried out, making them feel stiff and tired," Freedman said.

EXERCISE: neck and shoulder release. Place hands in the prayer position behind your back. If you cannot manage this, clasp the forearms or elbows (as shown). To intensify the stretch, try to catch your left elbow or forearm with the right hand. After 30 seconds release and change to the other side. To release tension in the neck, tilt it back slightly while doing either of these stretches, while sitting near to the edge of your chair. Repeat at least every two hours

☐ *Exercise provided by Ailon Freedman, of The Lotus Exchange. See www.lotus-exchange.co.uk or call 020-7463 2234 for more information*

■ Please ensure that you have the consent of your GP before embarking on a new exercise regime and do not undertake any physical activity if you are feeling unwell or recovering from an injury

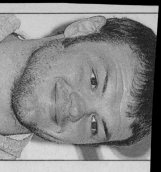

Cunningham: suspended ban

November. Sean McGuire, the St Helens chief executive, stated his support for Cunningham owing to "very significant mitigating circumstances".

"This matter, along with the career-threatening injury, has placed a great emotional burden on him," McGuire said. "Keiron has shown immense mental and physical resolve in regaining his fitness and rebuilding his career."

Wigan denials, page 32

33 RACING Kieren Fallon storms home on Princely Venture in the Scottish Derby but picks up a two-day ban for careless riding

32 GOLF Mark Roe and Jesper Parnevik pick up £8,250 each despite their disqualification for signing each other's card at the Open

31 SAILING The Australian team from the Royal Prince Alfred Yacht Club in Sydney clinched the Admiral's Cup from the Spanish

Get fit, feel fit: yoga for air travellers

Walk before you fly

By Jennai Cox
Fitness Editor

THOSE who know that they have a long flight pending should be as active as possible beforehand to reduce the effects on the body of their forthcoming confinement, Ailon Freedman, a yoga instructor, says. He suggests walking about as much as possible just before boarding, and spending the day or two before the flight engaged in fairly strenuous physical activity.

"This will help to boost the circulation and metabolism, which will slow down naturally once the body is still," Freedman says. Circumstances allowing, take two-hourly breaks from being seated to walk up and down the aisle or just move the hands and feet around. This will help to keep the body feeling supple and reduce the chances of stiffness and aches.

☐ *Exercise provided by Ailon Freedman, of The Lotus Exchange, which provides yoga and wellbeing services to business.*
See www.lotus-exchange.co.uk or call 020-7463 2234 for more information.

☐ *Send your comments to fitness@thetimes.co.uk*

Please ensure that you have the consent of your GP before embarking on a new exercise regime. Do not undertake any physical activity if you are feeling unwell or recovering from an injury

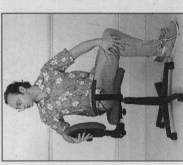

EXERCISE: Upper body twist (vital for the digestive organs and lungs). Sit up tall with the feet flat on the floor and place your left hand on your right knee and your right hand on the base of your seat behind you. Using the left arm to create leverage, lift and twist your body to the right. Hold for 15 seconds then repeat on the other side. For a more intense version of this exercise, place your right ankle across your left thigh and place your left hand on your right knee and your right hand behind you. Now lift and twist as before to open up the shoulders, chest and upper back. Hold for 15 seconds, remembering to breathe, and repeat on the other side.

Left margin fragments:

S Drowne
K Fallon 60
W Supple 47
F Norton 75
R Hughes 12
O Urbina 60
Thomas (5) 61
Martin Dwyer 69
P Dobbs 14
S Sanders 33

K Fallon [63]
ane O'Neill — M Hills
rtin Dwyer —
W Supple —
S Drowne 34
Fire, 12-1 others.

tchcott (5) 83
R Hughes [65]
M Miles (5) 74
W Supple 86
D Holland 88
K Fallon 85
N Pollard 91
cLaughlin 87

STAKES

artin Dwyer
K Fallon 86
ne (3) [93]
R Hughes 66
M Tebbutt 77
J D Smith 84
rk Flynn (7) 77
W Supple —
Zorro, 7-1 Captain

8.15 PANMURE CORPORATE FINANCE HANDICAP (£5,486: 1m 6f) (7)

1	(7)	325-63	FOURTH DIMENSION 39 (BF,D,F) A Stewart 4-10-0 ...... K Fallon	47
2	(2)	/1120-	TRAINED BYTHE BEST 214J (V,T,F) M Pipe 5-9-10 ...... D Holland	20
3	(1)	-65600	ALRIDA 14 (D,F) W Jarvis 4-9-4 ...... T Quinn	80
4	(4)	000660	BIG BERTHA 14 (G) John Berry 5-9-3 ...... G Baker	83
5	(3)	1-5041	SUDDEN FLIGHT 20 (D,F,S) R Ingram 6-8-12 ...... N Day	80
6	(5)	0-5140	SPLASH OUT AGAIN 39 (C,F,G) H Morrison 5-8-10 ...... R Hughes	73
7	(6)	0-3142	FOREVER MY LORD 7 (E,F,G,S) J R Best 5-7-12 ...... R Thomas (5)	85

7-4 Fourth Dimension, 9-2 Big Bertha, 5-1 Forever My Lord, 6-1 Trained Bythe Best, 7-1 Splash Out Again, 10-1 Sudden Flight, 12-1 Alrida.

8.45 HARRY PANMURE GORDON HANDICAP (£5,876: 5f 6yd) (14)

1	(14)	300-13	NIVERNAIS 24 (T,D,F,G) H Candy 4-9-13 ...... Dane O'Neill	75
2	(4)	254130	WHISTLER 24 (D,F,G) J Bradley 6-9-10 ...... P Fitzsimons	82
3	(3)	214103	BARRANTES 4 (D,F,G) Miss S West 6-9-10 ...... N Chalmers (5)	82
4	(11)	23-100	JAWHARI 100 (D,F,G) T Mills 9-9-10 ...... R Miles (5)	77
5	(12)	621402	FLY MORE 4 (BF,D,F,G) J Bradley 6-9-9 ...... D Holland	94
6	(13)	000133	HARD TO CATCH 17 (D,F,G) D Ivory 5-9-7 ...... C Cogan (5)	97
7	(9)	255065	ANOTHER GLIMPSE 28 (T,F,G) Miss B Sanders 5-9-3 ...... T Quinn	93
8	(6)	033434	TURIBIUS 17 (BF,D,G) T Powell 4-9-1 ...... R Hughes	88
9	(4)	004100	TABOOR 13 (D,F,G) J W Payne 5-8-10 ...... K Fallon	78
10	(2)	002531	TOMTHEVIC 9 (D,F) P Channings 5-8-9 (6ex) ...... R L Moore (3)	93
11	(10)	00-4500	LORD OF THE EAST 17 (D,F) P Howling 4-8-7 ...... D Kinsella (3)	97
12	(8)	5-0003	OUR FRED 52 (B,D,F,T) Mills 6-8-6 ...... A Clark	93
13	(12)	560004	COFFEE TIME 9 (B) D French Davis 4-8-3 ...... Martin Dwyer	92
14	(7)	005000	CARGO 13 (CD,F) H Collingridge 4-8-2 ...... J Quinn	87

9-2 Fly More, 5-1 Nivernais, 6-1 Barrantes, 7-1 Jawhari, 8-1 Our Fred, Tomthevic, 10-1 Turibius, Taboor, 12-1 Whistler, Hard to Catch, 14-1 others.

BLINKERED FIRST TIME: Catterick: 2.45 Cool Silk, Mouseman, 5.15 Rust En Vrede. **Leicester:** 7.30 Knight Onthe Tiles, Casantilla. 9.00 Zak Facta. **Lingfield Park:** 3.55 Magic Trick. 4.25 Nominate, Single Trigger. **Sandown Park:** 6.10 Seattle Express. 7.15 Due Respect. 8.15 Trained Bythe Best.

Candy 6 from 23, 26.1%; Sir M Stoute, 25 from 111, 22.5%; M Tregoning, 9 from 41, 22.0%, **Jockeys:** D Holland, 17 winners from 77 rides, 22.2%, W Supple, 8 from 37, 21.6%, R Thomas, 3 from 15, 20.0%, K Fallon, 35 from 190, 18.4%.

ANALYSIS

AMERICAN COUSIN had a tough task from a low draw when 8 3/4 ninth to Catch The Cat in a handicap at Beverley (5f, good to firm) last time, but a previous 3 1/4l fifth to Guns Blazing in a handicap at Haydock (5f, good to firm) suggests he can add to a win in a Hamilton claimer (5f 4yd, good to firm) last month. **Cark** followed a neck win from Pulse in a claimer at Newcastle (5f, good to firm) — **Shady Deal** (8lb better off) 5 1/4l seventh — with a ninth at Carlisle (5f, firm) as if to underline his unpredictability. A bigger threat may be **Eastern Trumpeter**, a respectable 3l sixth to Tomthevic in a handicap at Windsor (5f, good to firm). **Zarzu** is not easy to catch right.

5.15 WILLIE CARSON — PINKER'S POND APPRENTICE HANDICAP (£3,493: 7f) (18 runners)

1	(5)	000100	SHIFTY 21 (D,F) (Wetherby Racing Bureau 39) D Nicholls 4-9-11 ...... T O'Brien	62
2	(14)	300000	TELORI 16 (CD,F,G) (Dunnet Lads) I A Wood 5-9-11 ...... J Tucker	73
3	(10)	255000	BODFARI PRIDE 5 (D,F,G,S) (Mark Kilner) A Bailey 8-9-5 ...... Natalie Hassall	[92]
4	(2)	5-6040	HIGH POWERED 17 (Mrs J Moore) D Thompson 4-9-3 ...... D Wakenshaw	
5	(6)	000421	SHAROURA 12 (F,S) (Manor House Partnership) R Fahey 7-9-3 ...... S Archer	68
6	(15)	2000-	IROQUOIS CHIEF 215 (Mr & S Smith) C Kellett 4-8-12 ... Susannah Wileman	67
7	(16)	306025	LUCID DREAMS 11 (D) (Reds Bar Four Partnership III) M Wigham 4-8-12 .. J Jeffrey	62
8	(16)	000000	ACID TEST 7 (CD,F,S) (Fair Price Racing) M A Buckley 8-8-10 ...... D Tudhope	67
9	(17)	000006	RUST EN VREDE 6 (JV) (A Mann) D Carroll 4-8-11 ...... P Varley	67
10	(12)	000000	DUNDONALD 9 (V,D) (Stampede Racing) J Czerpak 4-8-9 ...... S Donohoe	90
11	(11)	14-006	BEAU SAUVAGE 26 (F) (K Wriglesworth) M W Easterby 5-8-9 ...... J Maher	67
12	(8)	560631	ROYAL WINDMILL 16 (P,G) (M Hammond) M D Hammond 4-8-7 ...... D Fentiman	78
13	(7)	000006	MISS CEYLON 4 (G) (Ms C Stokell) Miss A Stokell 3-8-6 ...... C Ely	91
14	(3)	000055	MY MAN FRIDAY 8 (D,F) (Mrs M Wickham) P Hiatt 7-8-5 ...... K Ghunowa	69
15	(4)	004500	SECRET CONQUEST 15 (T,CD,F,G,S) (K Nicholson) A Crook 6-8-5 D Williamson	62
16	(1)	303400	COMPTON PRINCESS 14 (SJP Racing) Mrs A Duffield 3-8-4 ... Sarah Mitchell	79
17	(13)	050045	INDIAN WARRIOR 26 (B,D,F,G) (Mr R & Mrs J Jay) J Jay 7-8-4 ...... A Rutter	79
18	(18)	065000	COLLEGE STAR 27 (J Coupland) J Coupland 5-7-12 ...... Charlotte Kerton	63

Long handicap: College Star 7-8.

BETTING: 7-2 Lucid Dreams, 4-1 Sharoura, 6-1 Royal Windmill, 7-1 Shifty, 8-1 Compton Princess, 10-1 others.

2002: TANCRED ARMS 6-9-8 Laura-Jayne Crawford (11-2) D Barker 18 ran

ANALYSIS

A big field and inexperienced apprentices make this a tough getting out stakes, but SHAROURA is entitled to go well. She made all to beat Mallia 1 1/2l in an apprentice handicap at Hamilton (6f 5yd, good to firm) last time and a favourable draw here gives her a solid chance to follow up. **Lucid Dreams** ran creditably from a wide draw when 2 1/4l fifth to Glenrock in an apprentice handicap at Chester (7f 122yd, good to firm) 11 days ago — **Bodfari Pride** (2lb better off) for being 2l away ninth — and can go well off the same handicap mark. **Royal Windmill** beat Mulkart a neck in a seller at Mussel-burgh (1m, good) last time but this is a bit more difficult.

for air travellers

e move
the air

es or heels in contact with
e floor.

"It is quite important to get
our body out of that bucket-
eat position and kneel. This
ill provide relief for a full
tomach and stretch the
nkles and thighs," he says.

☐ *Exercise provided by Ailon
Freedman of The Lotus
Exchange, which provides yoga
and wellbeing services to business. See www.lotus-exchange.
co.uk or call 020-7463 2234 for
more information.*

Tomorrow: Forward bend
posture

EXERCISE: Kneeling posture. Do not
attempt this if you have knee problems.
Remove your shoes and get into a kneeling
position in your chair. Straighten your back
and take deep breaths. Hold for as long as
possible, but no more than ten minutes or

you may get pins and needles. In this
position you can do the upper-body stretch
or upper-body twist (featured in Monday's
and yesterday's Get Fit). Take a short walk if
you can after this posture to allow the blood
to move freely through the legs.

Please ensure you have the consent of your GP before embarking on a new exercise regime.
Do not undertake any physical activity if you are feeling unwell or recovering from an injury.

Day four

TIMESONLINE
Get Fit, Feel Fit exercise
programme archive
www.timesonline.co.uk/getfit

heart, fight and character.

At least by preparing himself for this series with a run of matches for Essex, Hussain is in good shape to re-establish his own position in the side. Against a bowler of the quality of Shaun Pollock, still officially rated as the best in the world, and a frequently underestimated performer in Makhaya Ntini, whose 100 Test wickets have come at a cost of 28 and falling, England may need their batting depth. In some ways, however, little is more important than that Michael Vaughan and Marcus Trescothick should re-establish the authority of their opening partnership.

Whether they opt for a sixth batsman or a fourth fast bowler, South Africa are likely to choose Robin Peterson, their 23-year-old, left-arm orthodox spinner. In the recent match against India A at Arundel, Peterson confirmed that he is also a useful batsman and will be preferred to Paul Adams. Neil McKenzie will be first choice at five and

that suggested a split between himself and Pollock, his predecessor. "It's rubbish, absolutely rubbish," he said. Both he and Hussain know, however, that South Africa's tour will be deemed a success or a failure according to the Test results. The Twenty20 frolics in the evening sun were profitable and fun, and so were some of the one-day internationals

'I suppose I should be flattered that people keep recommending me for the Test captaincy but we've got a Test captain'

Alison Kervin meets Michael Vaughan, page 42

rated higher than Au... under the old system), b... will be the first series to... when the table is recal... at the beginning o... month. In future the... will be updated every... ensure that they refle... form of all teams. A v... England in this series... be sufficient for them t... take New Zealand i... margin would take... place. Victory by a four... above South Africa, t... Hussain will not be l... beyond today, let alo... wards the Oval in Sept...

A modest crowd of... has booked in advan... today, shorn of the... Edgbaston first-day... parties, but fewer than... tickets remain for tom... and Saturday. In a cric... if emphatically not a me... logical sense, summer... here, at least for thos... understand that a well-... series of five Test match... makes for the most abs... and satisfying form... game.

Get fit, feel fit: yoga

Keep on t... while in

By Jennai Cox
Fitness Editor

CONSTIPATION and dehy-dration are two fairly common consequences of travelling long haul by air. Physical inactivity causes food to digest more slowly and the air quality, combined with high alcohol consumption aboard some flights, can lead to a lack of water in the body.

Alion Freedman, who teaches yoga in the City, suggests changing your seat position regularly and drinking plenty of water to ease both complaints. If it is difficult to move from your chair during the flight, try to circle the wrists at 60-minute intervals or flex the feet up and down, keeping the

Papier mâché creations like this "car" are burnt as offerings to ensure the material comfort of the after-life.

ghosts". Paper "money" and other symbolic paper objects (including VCRs, mansions, clothings, computers) are burned to ensure that the ghosts have all they need. There are performances of *wayang*, or Chinese opera, for the ghosts must be entertained as well as fed!

At about the same time, Indians celebrate the 10-day festival of **Navarathri**, the Festival of Nine Nights, during which homage is paid to the supreme goddess Devi, in her three incarnations: Durga, Lakshmi and Saraswathi. The first three nights are devoted to Durga, one of the most powerful Hindu deities; the second three nights to Lakshmi, goddess of grace and wealth; and the third three nights to Saraswathi, goddess of learning. Classical Indian music and dance performances can be enjoyed nightly during the festival at the Sri Mariamman Temple in South Bridge Road, while on the tenth night a silver horse is drawn through the streets from the Sri Thandayuthapani Temple.

One of the most exciting and joyous of the Chinese festivities is the **Mooncake Festival**, usually celebrated in September. This is the time to eat mooncakes – round cakes made of bean paste and lotus seeds. Children parade with colourful and imaginative paper lanterns, often in the shape of fish or birds, and this is done with great aplomb at the

Colourful cellophane lanterns in various shapes and forms make a short appearance during the Moon Cake Festival.

Chinese Garden in Jurong.

The mooncake eaten today signifies those in which secret messages were hidden and passed among revolutionaries plotting to overthrow the tyrannical Mongol dynasty of ancient China. An alternative theory suggests that at the Mooncake Festival, the 15th night of the eighth lunar month, the moon is at its brightest. This is also the occasion of the *second* Birthday of the Monkey God. His first birthday was celebrated about eight months ago, but so important is this god in the Chinese pantheon that he enjoys two birthdays a year.

The **Pilgrimage to Kusu** takes place in October. This month-long festival attracts tens of thousands of Taoist devotees, mostly women, who voyage by ferries to the southern island of Kusu to pay their respects at the temple of Tuah Peh Kong, a god unknown in China but is regarded as the guardian of the overseas Chinese. Devotees bring offerings of food, fruit, flowers, joss-sticks and candles. Many of them also pray and place offerings in a nearby *kramat* (a Muslim shrine) on Kusu, and, in deference to the *kramat*, no devotee will include pork among her offerings. In fact, traditionally, devotees who plan to make the trip abstain from pork the day before the pilgrimage or run the risk of having their vessels capsized by the offended spirits. Many devotees today still observe that tradition. The stones and strips of cloth that adorn the trees on the island have been placed there by women who hope to be blessed with children. During the season, a special ferry service runs between Collyer Quay and Kusu.

While the Chinese and the Malays visit Kusu, the Indians walk across a pit of burning embers at the Sri Mariamman Temple in South Bridge Road. This is in honour of the goddess Devi during the festival of **Thimithi**.

More Festive Lights

Soon it is **Deepavali**, the most important festival in the Hindu calendar. Deepavali, the Festival of Lights, essen-

Prayers said on Kwan Yin's birthday are more likely to be answered.

tially a family affair, celebrates the victory of light over darkness, of good over evil, and specifically the slaying of the demon king Narakasura by Krishna. This is also the Hindu New Year. A special light-up which includes garlands and colourful arches to mark the occasion can be seen at Little India, Serangoon Road. Other public celebrations also take place at the Sri Srinivasa Perumal Temple in Serangoon Road.

At about this time, the last festival of the year to involve Chinese mediums occur. The **Festival of the Nine Emperor Gods** honours the nine sons of Tou Mu, the Goddess of the North Star. They are believed to confer good luck, wealth and long life. For nine days, the gods are paraded through the streets, to the accompaniment of lion dances, cymbals and drums. On the final night, which is also the birthday of Tou Mu, the effigies of the gods are borne to the sea and burned, and their ashes are placed in a special boat that, after a ritual, takes them to heaven…

And so it goes! If all these festivals are not enough, there is **Maulidin Nabi**, when the birthday of the prophet Mohammed is celebrated; the Indian harvest festivals of **Ponggal** and **Onam** (similar to the Catholics' thanksgiving day); the **Birthday of the Jade Emperor**; and the **Birthday of Kwan Yin**, the Goddess of Mercy. The Birthday of Kwan Yin is celebrated three times a year, mainly by women, and the celebrations are best enjoyed at the Kwan Yin Temple in Telok Blangah Drive.

The Singapore Symphony Orchestra under the baton of
resident maestro Choo Hoey at the Victoria Concert Hall.

Singapore may not be abuzz with culture, but it is by no means the cultural desert that many once claimed. Because of its modernity and glitter, and the common use of English, many visitors are apt to forget that they are in an oriental city rather than a western country. The cynic tends to forget that, because this is a multi-racial society, the target audience of any cultural activity is naturally less than the whole.

The dexterity of the puppeteers and the convoluted story-line of streetside theatre are bound to intrigue and entertain.

Take a taxi with a Chinese driver and the music on the radio is likely to be Chinese, with an Indian driver Indian music, with a Malay driver Malay music. The national goal of "One People, One Nation, One Singapore" is not seen as contradicting the insistence that racial groups must maintain their own culture.

Channel 12, one of the three TV channels here, regularly broadcasts *recherché* cultural programmes, despite the fact that the audience may be zero (at least according to the advertising industry, which considers a TV audience of fewer than 1500 to

Singapore's State of Art

In Singapore the stress on fine arts has been gaining currency largely because of the growing affluence and the rise in the standard of living.

The establishment of the Ministry of the Arts in 1990 is testimony of this recent upsurge of interest in the arts as is the growing number of students enrolling in art institutions, local participants in national and international art exhibitions, and visitors to the National Museum and Art Gallery and the Empress Place Museum. Inevitably, with the endorsement given to art by the authorities and the wider interest paid to it by society, local artists are increasingly gaining more prestige.

Despite this phenomenon, there is not a distinctive and authentic Singapore style. While this may suggest that the art scene here is as yet at a premature state of development, it is this very search for a unique style that has led to the rise of numerous artistic expressions, nearly all of which have drawn on outside influence.

Interestingly enough, because of Singapore's position on the east-west crossroads, the advancement of modern technology and expansion of communication channels, this process of assimilation is gaining intensity. As a result, the realm is becoming more cosmopolitan with both western and eastern (particularly Chinese) painting occupying an almost equal standing.

In Singapore, western painting itself is of a rich variety ranging from that of the Italian Renaissance (15th to 16th century), to the baroque artists of 17th-century Italy, the 18th-century Neoclassicists, the 19th-century French Impressionists and to the abstract and Cubist artists of the present century.

"Colour-ink" or Chinese painting, that other noteworthy style to which a substantial number of local artists subscribe, was first brought in by Chinese settlers in the 1930s. Its conventional realist style glorifying Nature and the elements through fine brushwork and black ink, has evolved into colour painting with western Impressionism and sensualism as its major influences.

Finally, given the current stature of art, the numerous styles that exist and that art galleries are mushrooming, Singapore is undoubtedly an ideal place to view or acquire a wide repertoire of works. Besides the list of art galleries and dealers that are available (refer to the *Yellow Pages*), the *Directory of Contemporary Singapore Artists* contains a comprehensive list of local artists and samples of their works. Garage sales, auctions and sales by private collectors often provide rare and original pieces at bargain prices. The National Museum and Art Gallery, the Empress Place Museum, and The Substation, the official home of the arts, are the places to see a range of art forms and artists.

A local artist capturing the traditional street scene on canvas before redevelopment changes it forever.

A Malay drama captures the pathos and joy of the Malay community.

be equivalent to zero). On Channel 12, viewers can enjoy not only Shakespeare's *Othello* but also Verdi's *Otello*.

Festival of Arts

Since 1977, the Singapore Festival of Arts has been a showcase of both international and local arts, although it must be admitted that it cannot yet begin to compete with festivals staged in Edinburgh or Spoleto. Performers in 1990 – a bumper year because it celebrated the 25th anniversary of independent Singapore – included the Alvin Ailey American Dance Theater from the United States, the China Central Ensemble of National Music from the mainland, the

Grand Kabuki from Japan, and the Ballet du Nord from France. Again, it will be noted how east and west meet in Singapore, with the United States and France occupying the same stage as China and Japan. The resulting "fringe festival" included outstanding performances from the neighbouring countries of Brunei, Indonesia, Malaysia, the Philippines and Thailand (ASEAN).

After a somewhat hesitant start, Singapore now boasts an excellent annual film festival that may one day rival that of Cannes. Many countries enter films, and the event is attended by major stars and directors.

The most firmly established performing arts company in Singapore devoted to western arts is the Singapore

With the establishment of Theatreworks, Singapore's first professional theatre was born. A rich repertoire of plays is staged the whole year round.

Symphony Orchestra, founded in 1979, which attracts a regular stream of international soloists. The orchestra presents a regular series of concerts, the repertory of which extends well beyond the works of Beethoven and Brahms. Western classical music is also played by the Singapore Youth Orchestra. The Singapore Dance Theatre, which made its debut in 1988, presents contemporary dance and attracts choreographers from Europe and the United States.

While these ensembles perform the works of the west, concerts of Chinese classical music are performed by the People's Association Chinese Orchestra and the Singapore Broadcasting Corporation Chinese Orchestra, and concerts of Indian music are performed by the People's Association Indian Orchestra and the Indian Fine Arts Society Orchestra. Local Malay dance is in the hands of the Malay Sriwana Company.

Aficionados of grand Western opera must be content with concert opera on Channel 12, but Chinese opera is almost always available, performed not only by local companies such as the Chinese Theatre Circle but also by troupes from China and Taiwan.

Dinner theatre, which some hotels present on an irregular basis, can scarcely be compared with London's Old Vic but it does give Singaporeans and visitors an opportunity to see plays by renowned contemporary playwrights and starring well-known actors. The true theatre fan need not wait for these eso-

A Taste of Singapore Culture

As a prelude to your visit to a nightspot, you may wish to attend a cultural show, with or without dinner, at the Hyatt Regency Hotel (Scotts Road), at the Cockpit Hotel (Oxley Rise) or a little more out of town, at the Singa Inn Seafood Restaurant at East Coast Parkway. At these shows, the major ethnic groups – Chinese, Malay and Indian – each demonstrates aspects of their culture. The Malay wedding may be mock, but it is still true to form. The Mandarin Hotel on Orchard Road presents a poolside cultural show that features the music and dance of not only Singapore but also Malaysia, Thailand, Indonesia and the Philippines.

The graceful Malay candle dance combines fluidity of movement with elegance.

teric occasions, however. Grassroots theatre thrives in Singapore, and productions of contemporary Western plays and plays by local writers are frequently mounted. Youth theatre is active to the extent of a Youth Theatre Festival, while Hi Theatre! ensures those who suffer from deafness are not ignored.

Visitors will observe that many of the local public places are adorned with modern sculptures. Works of local art-ists are always to be found in at least one of the art galleries. In addition, the National Museum, although small, is rich in exhibits; the Lee Kong Chian Art Museum's collection of ceramics, bronze, archaic jade and calligraphy covers 6,000 years of Chinese culture; and the Empress Place Museum exhibits outstanding treasures from China. For current seasons, refer to the "What's On" page of the daily, The Straits Times.

At the end of a long day, sip a Coke or read a comic — but do neither on the

steps of the City Hall

(the Prime Minister's office) where loitering is prohibited.

Life may be a stage to some, but opera performances and theatrical masks once a daily affair with the

today a fast disappearing tradition.

local Chinese is

City snapshots: the Elgin Bridge spanning Singapore River; it may seem

a visitor looks up to founding father Sir Stamford Raffles.

like an unending maze but it's not difficult to find your way about;

Caught in the act, amateur photographer

takes a shot at it; during after hours, these shop doors double as a convenient parking place.

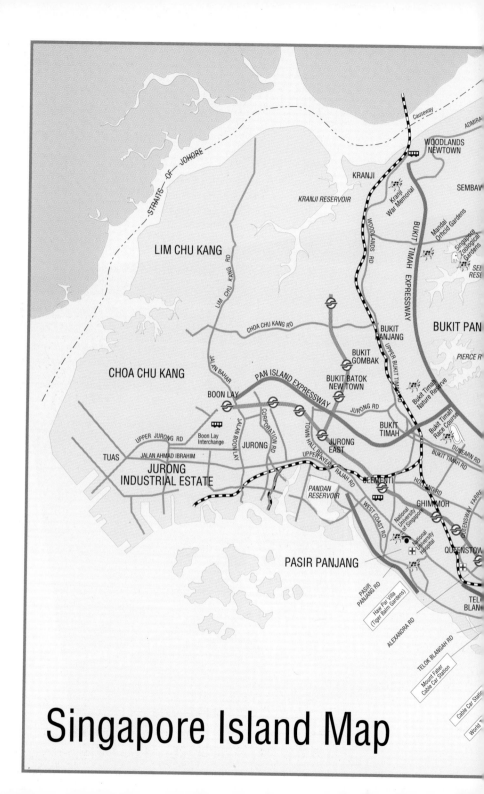

Singapore Island Map

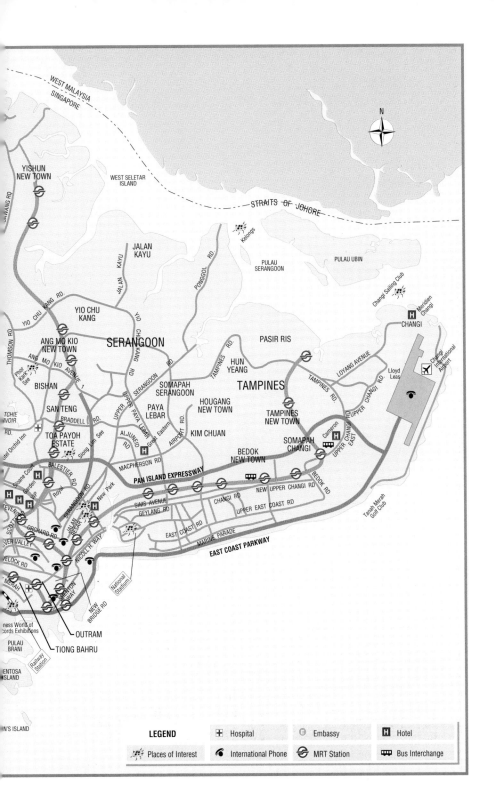

WEST MALAYSIA
SINGAPORE

N

YISHUN
NEW TOWN

WEST SELETAR
ISLAND

STRAITS OF JOHORE

Kelongs

PULAU
SERANGOON

PULAU UBIN

JALAN
KAYU

PONGGOL RD.

JALAN KAYU

YIO CHU KANG RD.

Changi Sailing Club

Meridien
Changi

H CHANGI

YIO CHU
KANG

YIO CHU KANG RD.

YIO CHU KANG RD.

PASIR RIS

TAMPINES RD.

LOYANG AVENUE

Lloyd
Leas

Changi
International
Airport

ANG MO KIO
NEW TOWN

SERANGOON

HUN
YEANG

THOMSON RD.

Phor Kark
See

ANG MO KIO AVENUE 1

SOMAPAH
SERANGOON

TAMPINES

TAMPINES RD.

UPPER CHANGI RD.

BISHAN

SERANGOON RD.

HOUGANG
NEW TOWN

TAMPINES
NEW TOWN

UPPER
EAST

SAN TENG

UPPER PAYA LEBAR

PAYA
LEBAR

BRADDELL RD.

Siong Lim See

ALJUNEID RD.

KIM CHUAN

SOMAPAH
CHANGI

Cameron

H

TCHIE
NVOIR

tel Orchid Inn

RD.

TOA PAYOH
ESTATE

Great Eastern

AIRPORT RD.

H

MACPHERSON RD.

BEDOK
NEW TOWN

BEDOK RD.

UPPER CHANGI RD

BALESTIER RD.

PAN ISLAND EXPRESSWAY

Sloane Court

Garden

H

Royn

New Park

New Park

NEW UPPER CHANGI RD

Tanah Merah
Golf Club

STEVENS

SERANGOON RD

JALAN BESAR

H

SIMS AVENUE

CHANGI RD

GEYLANG RD.

UPPER EAST COAST RD

SCOTT

ORCHARD RD.

NICOLL'N WAY

EAST COAST RD

MARINE PARADE

VER VALLEY

VELOCK RD

EAST COAST PARKWAY

MERAH

SECTION WAY

NEW BRIDGE RD

National
Stadium

ness World of
cords Exhibitions

OUTRAM

PULAU
BRANI

TIONG BAHRU

Railway
Station

ENTOSA
ISLAND

N'S ISLAND

LEGEND ✛ Hospital Ⓔ Embassy H Hotel

Places of Interest ☎ International Phone MRT Station 🚌 Bus Interchange

101

Getting around in Singapore is a breeze – if you know how. Public buses and taxis abound, the Mass Rapid Transit (MRT) system reaches the furthermost points of the island and a trishaw is suitable for sightseeing over shorter distances. Although taxis are permitted to levy various surcharges at different times of the day, they are relatively inexpensive, almost invariably air-conditioned, and rare is the occasion when the driver fails to start his meter.

Traditionally the sailing ships of the east, these Chinese junks today are used on harbour cruises and to ferry visitors from the main island to holiday resorts in the southern islands.

Within the city, where most visitors spend a good part of their time, taxis may stop to pick or drop passengers only at taxi stands, located at all hotels and shopping centres, and at various other points on major roads.

Do not be annoyed if, *en route* to an attraction on East Coast Parkway, your driver fails to stop at the destination. For stopping on this road is forbidden (as it is on all other expressways except at emergency bays thus marked

In and Out of the CBD

In an attempt to control the volume of traffic entering the city centre during peak hours, the government imposes a charge on vehicles (including taxis) entering the Central Business District (CBD), sometimes also known as the restricted zone, at certain times of the day. Singapore is fortunate that there are fewer than 30 strategic points that permit entry to the CBD. Every morning from 7.30 am to 10.15 am (except Sundays and public holidays) and afternoon from 4.30 pm to 6.30 pm (except Satur-

days, Sundays and public holidays), the words "In Operation" are illuminated on the gantries that guard these points, and policewomen take their positions here. They do not stop vehicles without a licence to enter the CBD, but they note their registration numbers and errant owners are fined.

Passengers who board a taxi without a valid CBD licence displayed on the windscreen during the hours when the licensing scheme is in operation must pay an additional $3 to purchase the CBD licence.

out for the occasional broken-down vehicle or such emergencies), so the driver must pass the destination, make a U-turn and stop at the designated spot on the return journey. Taxis will take visitors to "distant" attractions (nowhere in Singapore is *very* far), such as Jurong Bird Park or the Singapore Zoological Gardens, but it is often hard to find another taxi to take you back to the city. It may be best to hire by the hour, which is relatively expensive, and remember that no more than four adult passengers are permitted in one cab.

Trishaws can be fun, but they are not cheap. Always settle the fare *before* you start. And please don't expect the poor man to pedal long distances in Singapore's tropical heat.

Two major bus companies, the Singapore Bus Service (SBS) and the Trans-Island Bus Service (TIBS), serve the length

and breadth of Singapore. They stop at the same bus stops, and a board at most busy stops informs passengers of major roads served from the stop and the bus services plying these roads. Most services start at about 6 am, and the last bus leaves the terminal at about 11.30 pm. At peak hours, SBS and TIBS buses are joined (quite legally) by a number of freelance operators, some of whom carry the same route numbers as the "big boys", while others carry plates indicating key destinations on their routes. Almost all buses are one-man-operated. Passengers should place the exact fare in a box near the entrance, and then receive a ticket (except in the freelance-operated vehicles). Visitors may wish to purchase a one- or three-day Singapore Explorer ticket, which permits unlimited travel on any SBS or TIBS buses.

The magnificent MRT system con-

Unlike most cities in the world, the MRT stations here are clean, safe and a source of air-conditioned comfort for users.

sists of two main lines that serve 42 stations, 15 of which are underground, while one is at street level and the rest

You can take a bus to virtually any part of the island.

are elevated. The underground stations in the city centre are the showpieces of the system, complete with shops, indoor waterfalls and banks of orchids. As the train approaches the interchange stations of Raffles Place and City Hall, announcements are made in English, Chinese, Malay and Tamil (the city's four official languages). At all other stations only the names of destination stations are announced.

Sixty-six trains, each consisting of six cars and capable of carrying 1,800 passengers, operate from about 6 am to midnight. On Sundays and public holidays, the service is somewhat curtailed. Coin-change machines give the exact change required to buy a magnetically encoded ticket. Stored-value tickets, which are good for several journeys, can be bought at any ticket sales counter.

A

ORCHARD ROAD

bout 150 years ago, what is now **Orchard Road** consisted of nutmeg and pepper plantations. The thoroughfare is believed to have derived its eponymous name not from the plants it supported, however, but from its owner, Mr Orchard. Several neighbouring streets – Cuppage, Prinsep, Oxley – also bear the names of plantation owners.

The pagoda-like structure of the Dynasty Hotel adjoins a department store that offers everything under one roof.

Later, and until recently, cemeteries bordered Orchard Road, and only a few years have passed since the last one, a Jewish cemetery, was deconsecrated and the remains it protected exhumed.

Today, Orchard Road – the Fifth Avenue, the Regent Street, the Champs Elysées of Singapore – is a glittering showpiece of sun-probing skyscrapers, the vast majority of which are shopping centres built to relieve visitors of their money. Other buildings are splendid hotels which provide the visitor with accommodation and nourishment between his shopping sprees. If in town on the last Sunday of any month witness Orchard Road, between Clemenceau Avenue

and Scotts Road, being transformed into one big pedestrian mall between 5 to 10 pm when it is closed to vehicular traffic and becomes instead, the scene for some local brand of streetside merrymaking.

Shopping Mania

Non-shoppers can complete a leisurely stroll down Orchard Road in two hours: the besotted shopper may take a lifetime. The road is especially dangerous to credit-card holders. Before you begin your urban safari, you may wish to gird your loins and fill the inner man at the pavement cafes of either the Orchard Parade or Orchard hotels, which are on opposite sides of the top end of Orchard Road. These cafes are, not surprisingly, at their most vibrant in the evenings.

Immediately after the two hotels, the first of the dozen or so shopping centres is encountered. In these, the lower floors are occupied by shops while the upper floors house offices. After about 600 metres, the corner of Orchard Road and Scotts Road, which may be regarded as the Piccadilly Circus or Times Square of Singapore, is gained.

Cross Scotts Road by the underpass or, 200 metres to the left, by the overpass, and you arrive at the **Dynasty Hotel**, readily recognizable by its green-tiled pagoda-like roof, and **Tangs**. Both are under the same ownership, and the latter, a department store, may be considered the Harrods of Singapore. Drop in at the lobby of the former to view the

The floor-to-ceiling woodcarvings depicting scenes from Chinese mythology add pomp to the lobby of the Dynasty Hotel.

Peranakan Place is an entertainment-cum-conservation enterprise along
Orchard Road offering food, music and theatre on certain nights.

24 pieces of carved panels which reach up the height of the three-storey lobby. One hundred and twenty master carvers in Shanghai were engaged in the task which took two years as they used only primitive tools. The murals are based on intriguing Chinese history and legends; a booklet available from the hotel relates the 24 stories. A self-service cafe on the top floor of **Tangs** provides good views of the passing scene.

Continue down Orchard Road and, on the same side of it, arrive first at the Promenade and then the Paragon, two of the more elegant shopping centres in Singapore. A few hundred metres beyond is **Emerald Hill Road**, where a dozen shophouses in Chinese baroque style (a blend of Chinese and neoclassical styles that originated in Malacca in West Malaysia) have been restored. Observe the doors, windows, roof tiles and timber carvings, all of which have Chinese antecedents. Recurring motifs include dragons, roses, dogs, crabs, subjects which have been used not only for

Reenact a Straits-Chinese wedding within the walls of Peranakan Place.

decorative purposes but also because of their symbolic extensions – good fortune, health and longevity.

Pulsating **Peranakan Place**, which stands at the corner of Orchard Road and Emerald Hill Road, occupies half a dozen of these restored shophouses. Most are devoted to the Singaporean obsessions – shopping and eating. Baba Alley, the first part of Emerald Hill Road,

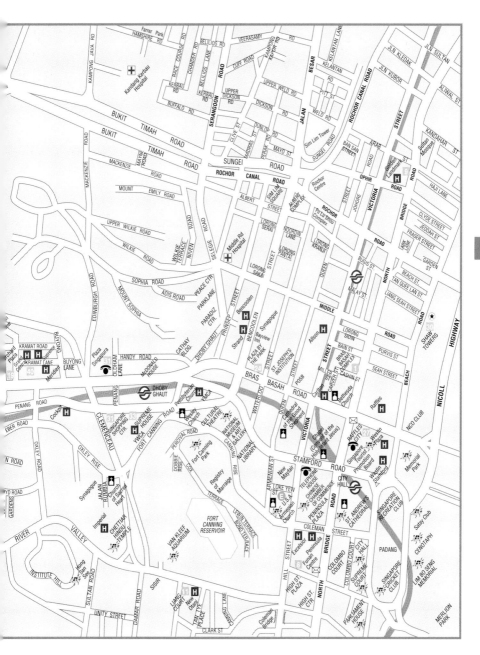

has palms and umbrella-shaded tables, and it buzzes from morning to the small hours – although the live music in the evening is more likely to be pop than Peranakan songs.

More greenery and umbrella-shaded tables fill much of the next street, **Cuppage Terrace** (a short street closed to traffic), which has restored shophouses on one side and a large shopping centre

The well-proportioned two-storey Istana building, with classical Doric and
Corinthian columns, is the official residence of the President.

on the other. The former house several somewhat upmarket restaurants, while outside the latter are sophisticated food-stalls. At the end of Cuppage Terrace is **Cuppage Centre**, with two storeys of market stalls and one of foodstalls.

Centrepoint, which stands between Emerald Hill Road and Cuppage Terrace, is probably the most successful and certainly the most popular of all the shopping centres in Orchard Road.

Clemenceau Avenue is now reached. Turn right and, after 200 metres, at the corner of Penang Road, stands the **House of Tan Yeok Nee**, a gazetted national monument now property of the Cockpit Hotel. The building is a

splendid example (and the only one extant) of an architectural style that was popular in South China a century ago. Once the headquarters of the Salvation Army, the building boasts court-yards, with delightful carvings and decorations that include keyhole gables, terracotta tiles and massive granite pillars believed to have been imported from China. Sadly, a lot of these may change depending on Cockpit Hotel's design team. At time of press, the building is scheduled for major renovations.

Return to Orchard Road and, di-agonally opposite and flanked by a stand of rare palms (the only such trees on the island), is the guarded entrance to the

Mini Manila, Little Thailand

Go to parts of Orchard Road on a Sunday and you can be forgiven for thinking you have unwittingly been transported to Manila. The accents all around you are pure Filipina. The language you overhear is Tagalog. All six storeys of Lucky Plaza, the sidewalks fronting it and Wisma Atria across the road are packed with Filipina domestic maids on their day off.

They go there for the opportunity to be with their fellow-countrywomen and to reduce the strangeness of living and working in a foreign land. The snack bars and cheap food outlets sprout *adobo* and *pangsit* for those homesick for a taste of home. The Filipino band in one of the discos in Lucky Plaza gets an early start after lunch playing for those who want some action.

Some shops like hairdressers offer Sunday specials to drum up some business. But for the Filipinas and most of the other foreign workers here like the Sri Lankans, the Indians and the Thais, the money they earn is much needed back home. So frivolous purchases are not on.

The Filipino enclave in uptown Orchard Road is just one of several where Singapore's thousands of foreign workers gather in large enough numbers to earn them tags like Mini Manila and Little Thailand.

Step into Golden Mile Complex on Beach Road on weekends and the sounds, sights and smells are Thai. The very male crowd is made up mostly of construction workers. Many of the shops sell unfamiliar products with Thai labels and even some of the shopkeepers are Thai. The food outlets have Thai specialties and Thai newspapers and magazines fill the newsstands. Cassette shops have Thai music and if all this is still not Thai enough for you, outside are the buses bound for Haadyai in Thailand.

In the heart of Little India, foreign workers from Sri Lanka and India converge at the foodstalls at Zhujiao Centre, their looks often indistinguishable from the Singapore Indian crowd. Here they meet friends and catch up on news or do a bit of shopping for home. The spicy curries and Indian specialties available here are the draw too for those wanting a taste of home food. The domestic maids often work in Chinese homes which do not dish up curries, and the construction workers don't always get the spicy food they are used to back home.

Many Malaysians work in Singapore spanning the gamut from professionals and executives down to blue-collar workers. The construction workers meet up at Rochor Centre which is conveniently near the Queen Street bus stand for Malaysia-bound buses. The centre is a good spot for last-minute purchases before they make their way home, but more useful perhaps is the presence of fellow-Malaysians who can give new arrivals tips on working conditions or pass on news from home.

And what do the locals think of these foreign invasions on weekends. "Great for business," said one shopkeeper at Golden Mile. "This place was too quiet before. Now it is almost like being in Bangkok or Haadyai."

Filipina domestic helps congregate on weekends to chit-chat in Tagalog, reminisce about home, and also to exchange notes about their employers!

Once the townhouse of a wealthy Teochew gambier and pepper merchant, the
House of Tan Yeok Nee is today part of the Cockpit Hotel.

These three buildings opposite the Dhoby Ghaut MRT Station mark the end of Orchard Road and the beginning of the city centre.

Istana, in whose grounds stands the residence of the President (home of the governor before independence). The two-storey building stands in an elevated position overlooking stately grounds that are somewhat reminiscent of the great gardens of England. The domain, once part of a nutmeg estate, whose other attractions include a golf course and a gun presented to Lord Louis Mountbatten by the Japanese after their surrender in 1945, is open to the public on New Year's Day and at Chinese New Year, Hari Raya Puasa and Deepavali. An attraction at 6 pm on the first Sunday of every month is the changing of the guard at the Istana's gates.

A little further down Orchard Road, but on the opposite side, is the pocket-handkerchief-size **Orchard Park**. If there was ever an oasis far from the madding crowd, then this is it. A Chinese restaurant on stilts serves simple meals, and, joy of joys, a water-lily pond, complete with island, bridge and stepping stones, will recharge the batteries.

From here it is only 300 metres to the bottom of Orchard Road, where the Dhoby Ghaut MRT station stands. Before you disappear underground, spare a glance on the three attractive 1920s art deco buildings across the road.

The priests of Sri Krishnan Temple gathering for their meal.

On feast days, peddlers offering religious paraphernalia set up stall around the entrance of the Kwan Yin Thong Hood Cho Temple.

A RELIGIOUS TOUR

Immediately beyond Orchard Road is **Bras Basah Road**, and on the right, halfway down, stands the ochre-coloured **Cathedral of the Good Shepherd**, with its splendid Palladian facade. The foundation stone was laid in 1843, and in 1897 the church was consecrated as a cathedral by the Bishop of Malacca. This is one of about two dozen buildings gazetted by the Preservation of Monuments Board, a government statutory board formed in 1971 to "renew old masterpieces". "We need physical reminders of our past," declares the board charter, "otherwise we will lose the sense of being part of a continuous process."

Across the road from the cathedral, at the corner of Bras Basah Road and Waterloo Street, is another gazetted building. The cream-coloured, red-tiled baroque **St Joseph's Institution**, once a school, is soon to become an art gallery.

Continue along Waterloo Street in an exploration of some of Singapore's religious buildings. Here, within a small area, are Hindu and Chinese temples, churches and a synagogue. First, on the left, and easily missed, is the **Maghain Aboth Synagogue**, the place of worship of the small Sephardic Jewish community. The simple exterior of the building belies a rich interior. This is one of two synagogues in Singapore, the other being the Chesed-El Synagogue at the top

Staying on the safe side: this Chinese lady stops to pay respect at the Sri Krishnan Temple before making her way to worship Kwan Yin next door.

of Oxley Rise, which is consecrated but not functional. The only other physical sign of this exiguous community is a Star of David that graces a 1920s building on the corner of Selegie Road and Middle Road.

Cross Middle Road into Waterloo Street and you are immediately con-

fronted by a blaze of action and colour. On the left is the **Sri Krishnan Temple**, with a frieze that consists of Hindu gods focussing on the niche above the entrance. Proof of the religious tolerance of which Singapore is rightly proud can be seen in the fact that many Chinese stop here to say a prayer before or after they visit the adjacent Chinese temple.

The **Kwan Yin Thong Hood Cho Temple** must be the busiest and most popular temple in Singapore. The exterior is colourful, but the interior is relatively small and stark. Outside, numerous women in wide-brimmed straw hats sell flowers to worshippers and fortune tellers shelter beneath large, multi-coloured umbrellas. In addition to the altars within the temple, there are usually more than half a dozen portable shrines in the street. All this is un-Singaporean, of course, and occasionally the sight of a police car sends errant soothsayers scurrying to the pavement – only to return when the coast is clear.

Cross the road and pass through a public housing estate to Queen Street, where you may see a temporary awning with shrines, joss-sticks and even a *wayang* (= Chinese opera). The occasion? One of the almost innumerable festivals that punctuate the lunar calendar, the anniversary of the nearby temple, or a funeral.

At the corner of Queen Street and Middle Road is **St Anthony's Convent School**. Many Singaporeans, regardless of their religion, believe that the best local education is found in schools staffed by Catholic brothers and sisters. The entrance to the associated **St Joseph's Church** is on Victoria Street. The church was founded by Francisco de Silva Pintoe Male, who arrived in Singapore as head of the Portuguese mission in 1826, and who on his death bequeathed all his worldly possessions, including a plot of

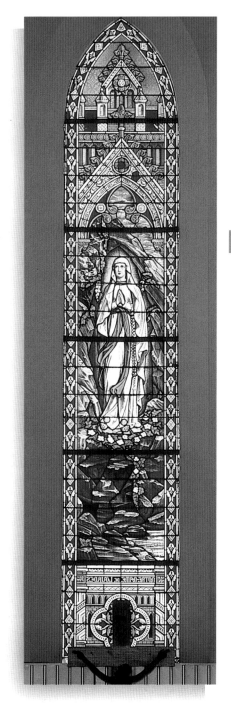

Stained-glass depicting the Virgin at the St Peter and St Paul Church.

The imposing facade of the Church of St Peter and St Paul (c. 1870).

land, to the erection of the church. These funds were augmented by a gift from the king of Portugal, and the church was named San José. The present church, the second on the site, is still run by the Portuguese mission and was for some time directed by the Bishop of Macau.

Here, in the late afternoon of Good

Friday, the faithful arrive in their thousands. Not only is the church and the surrounding courtyard jammed with worshippers, but they and their candles spill onto the balconies of neighbouring housing estates, from which vantage points they can hear the message preached from the pulpit.

From here return to Queen Street and, on the right, near Bras Basah Road, is the **Church of St Peter and St Paul** with its lovely soaring steeple.

Hark the colonial days – a cricket game at the Padang in front of the Supreme Court.

Anglican St Andrew's Cathedral, a loud Gothic statement on North Bridge Road, was built between 1856 and 1863.

CITY WALKS

123

COLONIAL HEART

Right in the centre of the colonial heart of Singapore, and occupying a pivotal position between the tourist belt and the financial district is a large, flat sward called the **Padang**. The sea lapped the southern edge of the Padang in Raffles' time, but today, as a result of reclamation, the sea is some distance away.

In the late afternoon, when the sun has lost its sting, and on Sundays, the Padang is a vast sports arena, in which cricket and hockey, soccer and rugby, tennis and lawn bowls are played.

More grisly "games" were played here in the past. On 16 February 1942, British, Australian and other Allied pris-

oners were assembled here by their Japanese victors to be informed that Singapore would henceforth be known as Syonan-to ("Light of the South"). Three years later, on 12 September 1945, a Japanese delegation led by five generals and two admirals formally surrendered to the British, and the Union Jack, hidden during the war in Changi Prison, waved once more over City Hall.

Linear, colonnaded **City Hall** (1929) is one of two neoclassical buildings bordering the northern edge of the Padang, the other being the **Supreme Court** (1939) with its patinated dome. The name City Hall is rather a misnomer as Singapore has neither a mayor nor a municipal council, and the building houses government offices.

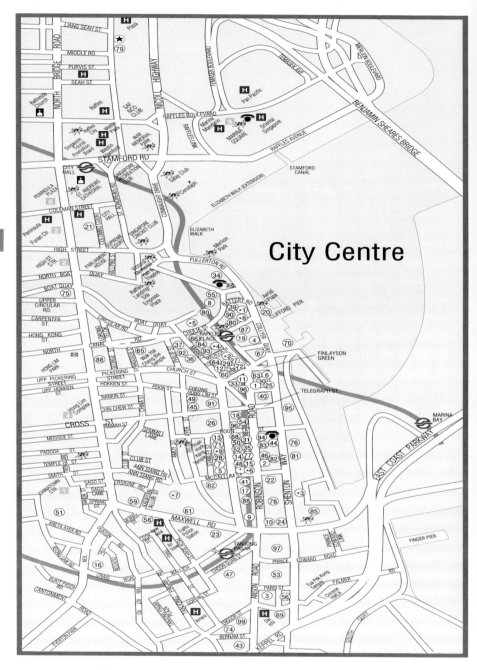

City Centre

Immediately east of City Hall, in three hectares of park, is the Anglican **St Andrew's Cathedral**, a spiky Gothic structure that seems to have been shipped, brick by brick, from the English countryside. It was built by Indian convicts transported to Singapore by the East India Company in Calcutta.

Sitting majestically on the north bank of the Singapore River
is the Empress Place Museum, named in honour of Queen Victoria.

The building was consecrated as a church in 1862, and as a cathedral in 1870. The tower and spire were added to the long nave only in 1964: It was hoped to make them even higher than they are – 64 metres from the tip of the spire to the ground – but it was decided that the weight would be too great. There are eight bells in the tower, but after they were installed it was discovered that the foundations of the cathedral would not withstand the shock of their ringing. They were therefore permanently fixed, their clappers tied, and today they are struck with hammers, producing the effect of chimes.

The present cathedral stands on the site of a predecessor designed by G D Coleman, the outstanding architect of early Singapore. The cornerstone of his church was laid in 1834, and the building consecrated in 1838. It was without a spire or a tower until Bishop Wilson of Calcutta (Singapore was part of the diocese of Calcutta until 1869) insisted that a spire be erected: "Its sacred design will be manifested and the surrounding heathen will see the honour we put upon our religion."

The original bell, presented in 1843 by Mrs Maria Revere Balestier, wife of the first American consul in Singapore and daughter of American patriot Paul Revere, is now in the National Museum. Mrs Balestier donated the bell on condition that it was struck every evening at 8 pm for five minutes.

Behind the altar of the present

Only three dollars for a ride? Ever-beckoning, boatman at Singapore River tempts the most jaded traveller.

church at the eastern end of the nave is the chapel of the Nativity, above which is the East Window. This was originally installed in 1861, destroyed during World War II and later replaced. The inscription below the window reads: "To the memory of Sir Stamford Raffles KT, the illustrious Founder of the Settlement of Singapore. This window is dedicated by the citizens AD 1861."

Culture Clubs

Retrace your steps back to the Padang where two red-tiled white buildings, both clubhouses, occupy each of its shorter sides. On the western side is the **Singa-**

pore Cricket Club (1852). Although most members today are Asians, this was not always so, and the Singapore Eurasians formed their own club in 1883. The headquarters of the Eurasian Sports Club was in the building on the eastern side of the Padang now known as the **Singapore Recreation Club**.

A cluster of handsome colonial buildings, the names of which announce that they were all built during the reign of Queen Victoria, stands in Empress Place, opposite the entrance to the Singapore Cricket Club. First, side by side and actually contiguous with each other, are the **Victoria Concert Hall** and the **Victoria Theatre**. The former, the clock tower of which showed Tokyo time during the Japanese occupation, was built almost 50 years before the latter. Minute compared to its "Big Ben" brother in London, not many locals pay attention to it nowadays although there was a time when few passed by without instinctively looking up and priming their timepieces accordingly! Perhaps if visitors were allowed into the tower, as they once were, the significance of the edifice would be greater. Apparently it was quite an experience to climb the 176 steps within the Memorial Hall to the bell tower.

Beside the Victoria Concert Hall and Theatre stands the **Empress Place Building**, erected in 1860 to house the legislative assembly and which has since served innumerable purposes. Now, after a complete restoration, it has returned to its original neoclassical glory, its beautiful facade adorned with Doric columns and rustic French windows topped by ornately decorated fanlights. It is now a museum and an exhibition centre, with shops and a restaurant, where displays of historical and cultural artifacts on loan from various parts of the world are mounted for long periods of time.

The obelisk at the centre of Empress Place reminds one of Cleopatra's Needle in London, although it is far smaller in scale. The **Dalhousie Monument** was built in 1850 to commemorate the second visit to Singapore of the governor-general of India, the Marquis of Dalhousie. Despite its historical importance as Singapore's first public monument erected when the town was only 31 years old, the Dalhousie Needle has been described by critical cynics as "a masterpiece of ugliness".

Statue Square

A few metres upriver, a poly-marble **statue of Stamford Raffles** marks the spot where the founder of Singapore is said to have landed for the first time on 30 January 1819. A well-established Chinese tradition claims, however, that this occurred not on the Singapore River but on the Rochor River, about two kilometres further east. Opponents of this theory argue that it is unlikely that Raffles would have walked from the Rochor River to the Temenggong's residence in the tropical heat.

Another statue of Raffles stands just before the Victoria Concert Hall and Theatre. Older than the one by the river, this was unveiled on Queen Victoria's Golden Jubilee Day on 27 June 1887. It was erected by the British and it has a patina of dark bronze while the one by the river was commissioned by the Singapore government, and is white.

The basic design of the fountain

National symbolic creature – the half lion, half fish Merlion stands guard at Singapore River in the company of strollers seeking quiet relaxation.

pool fronting the statue is of Italian Renaissance. When first built the area even had a raised parterre and two rows of decorative flower-vases flanking the pool. Unfortunately since the war took its toll on the colonnade and the vases in 1942, the prewar magnificence of this area has never been revived.

Parliament Lane separates the Victoria Concert Hall from **Parliament House**, the oldest government building in Singapore, which was built, but never employed, as a private residence. Another of George Coleman's creation, the House was built in 1827. The public may attend parliamentary sessions, which are arranged on an irregular basis and are televised. (Check the daily media for current details.) The handsome

elephant before the building was a gift from King Chulalongkorn of Siam, in gratitude for the hospitality that he and his entourage received during a visit in 1871. Before the black it is in now, it had been a green and prior to that, a bright red, thanks to some pranksters.

Return to the southern side of the Padang, cross Connaught Drive and enter the leafy **Esplanade Park** (also known as Queen Elizabeth Walk) – venue for a pleasant stroll. There are three monuments in this small park. The largest, the **Cenotaph**, is a memorial to the 124 Singapore men who lost their lives in World War I. The delicate cast-iron **Tan Kim Seng Fountain** honours a man who made a donation to bring a good supply of fresh water to the town.

One for the family album – in front of the Raffles Place MRT station.

And the pagoda-like **Lim Bo Seng Memorial** commemorates the eponymous World War II general who was brutally tortured and killed by the Japanese.

The largest of the war memorials soars skywards for almost 70 metres in **War Memorial Park**, beyond the eastern edge of the Padang. The Chopsticks, as this structure is fondly known, consists of four marble columns, each of which represents the civilians of one of the four cultural groups who lost their lives during the Japanese occupation. The fact that the four columns arise from a single base expresses the unity of the four groups.

Take the underpass at the southern end of the Esplanade Park to cross to the other side of the **Singapore River**, often described as Singapore's "lifeline, link and legacy". The river trade has long gone and with it the bumboats and the coolies (= labourers) who gave the river its character. Now only the godowns (= warehouses) and the old shophouses stand as silent reminders of the past. The future of the river is yet to be charted although the part of the waterway between the Cavenagh and the Read bridges has been the venue for several national celebrations.

Cross the Anderson bridge where anglers with their fishing lines is a common sight, to view at close range the **Fullerton Building**, more commonly referred to as "Gee Pee Oh" (General Post Office). Dating from 1928, the GPO is a favourite meeting place for budget-conscious travellers who come to use its international telephone facilities and run their postal errands.

On the other side of Fullerton Road in the direction of Clifford Pier is a good spot from which to admire the **Merlion**, a fanciful creature in synthetic marble eight metres high that sits in a pocket-handkerchief-size park on the western bank of the mouth of the river. The Merlion, a mythical creature that is half lion and half fish, is the symbol of Singapore. At high tide water spouts from its mouth – a spectacular sight especially during nightfall.

The MRT train that rumbles through the major underground station in **Raffles Place**, a pedestrian mall closed to traffic (about 200 metres from the GPO), can take you to your next destination.

MARINA CITY

North of War Memorial Park are the soaring silver-grey buildings of **Raffles City**, which contains two hotels, a shopping centre, offices and conference facilities. It is the work of I M Pei, the renowned China-born architect who now lives in the United States. The tallest of the four buildings in Raffles City, at 230 metres, is the **Westin Stamford**, the tallest hotel in the world. Visitors can enjoy a meal in its Compass Rose, the world's highest hotel restaurant. The interior of the shopping centre is stark and bare, and full of exposed girders and ramps. Thousands can cram into its vast atrium to enjoy a concert or an exhibition, and its elevated catwalk delights promoters of fashion shows.

Something old, something new... Against the new and modern Raffles City is the old and refurbished **Raffles Hotel**, which has undergone a major restoration programme first started in 1988. Re-opened in late 1991, it remains much as it has been for years, right down to the littlest detail: Singapore Sling, a 1915 cocktail concoction by a

Left, the Kallang River Park fronts the Marina Square complexes; top, the Singapore Sling is the best-known concoction in the island republic.

local barman, will continue to be served at the Long Bar.

The complex south of War Memorial Park, **Marina Square**, is the brainchild of John Portman, the American architect famous for his atriums, and his imprint is clearly visible as soon as you enter any of the three hotels in the complex. Not so in Marina Square Shopping Centre, an asymmetrical cruciform building that links the three hotels and claims to be the largest shopping centre in Southeast Asia.

Marina Square is in **Marina City**, a vast area that can be divided into Marina Centre, Marina South and Marina East. A few years ago, Marina City did not exist, for it consists almost entirely of land that has been reclaimed from the sea by dumping millions of tonnes of soil, fill and sand, both from Singapore and from the islands of the Indonesian archipelago of Riau.

Marina South is one of the newer leisure centres on the island and, expectedly in Singapore, the major leisure activity appears to be eating. All kinds of restaurants abound, including extensive (and rather disappointing) hawker stalls and three restaurants (open to the public) at the Marina Bay Golf and Country Club. To acquire an appetite, visit one of the two bowling alleys.

Marina Village in the vicinity

Sunbathing or is it watching the girls (?) at Marina Bay.

boasts a "Food 'N' Fun Paradise". Strollers will find something enjoyable along this linear village concept. For antique lovers, objets d' art and souvenir knick-knacks are to be found in treasure-shops. Other complements to Marina Village include a disco for the nightlife lovers and social set, an ice-skating rink, and many more food outlets.

Future plans for **Marina East** have not been finalized, but both Marina East and Marina South are rich in beaches – as is **Marina Centre**, which already contains Marina Park. Although there are no gates to the park, you know when you enter by the start of a five-metre-wide walk laid with madder brown and grey stones. Here stands a soaring abstract sculpture in stainless steel, *Joyous River*, which commemorates the successful conclusion of a 10-year plan to clean the Singapore River and the

Kallang Basin catchment area. The project began in 1977, when then Prime Minister Lee Kuan Yew exhorted: "In 10 years let us have fishing in the Singapore River and fishing in the Kallang River. It can be done." And it was...

Stop at Marina Square, half-way

The Raffles City Atrium.

between the entrance to the park and the Benjamin Sheares Bridge viaduct. Gaze across **Marina Bay**, past the eager fishermen who frequent this spot. The marriage of rural and rustic, or urban and urbane is quite dramatic. To the right is the stunning skyscraper skyline. Ahead, beyond Clifford Pier, are the tops of the yellow cranes in the container port. To the left is the Benjamin Sheares Bridge viaduct and, beyond, the ships in the eastern roads. The bay is invariably abuzz with launches, some sleek and sophisticated, others rather dilapidated.

Continue and pass beneath the Benjamin Sheares Bridge viaduct. You are now on the left bank of the Marina Channel, which is soon joined by the **Kallang Channel**. Here stands Raffles Beacon – a clock tower – a pleasant spot to seek rest in one of the gazebos that dot the park.

Proceed along the Kallang Channel for about 800 metres and pass beneath East Coast Parkway, which

roars over your head. Stretching before you for almost two kilometres is a superb beach that in parts is a whole 50 metres wide. The sand is fine and golden, and equal to that on many ASEAN beaches. The beach borders the **Kallang Basin**, and, at its western end, immediately opposite the golden sand and the palms, are functioning ship-repair yards – all that remain of 64 yards that until recently occupied the Kallang Basin.

On the opposite shore at the far end of the Kallang Basin is another beach in the lee of the **National Stadium** and the **Indoor Stadium**. The water here is clean although scarcely pellucid. Indeed the only clear water found outdoors is in swimming pools and fountains. With Singaporean ingenuity, however, it is not impossible that copper sulphate crystals soon will be tossed into the sea (as they are into pools), to make the water a sparkling blue.

A green respite in the heart of town, Fort Canning Park is well worth a visit especially in the cool early evening.

One of the last vestiges of the British is this hardy gateway
which survived the ravages of time and war.

FORT CANNING PARK

Fort Canning Park, a green lung in the heart of the city that ascends from street level to an altitude of about 35 metres, is of historical importance. It was on this hill that Raffles ordered the governor's bungalow to be built, partly because the climate was healthier than at sea level, and partly because he wanted to be buried among the rulers of old Singapura (his wish was not fulfilled). Nothing remains of the bungalow, but the site is occupied by a lookout point.

The view from the top of the hill today would have astonished and delighted Raffles, for this is the great city of which he dreamed. The concrete is al-

most impregnable, but a glimpse can be seen of the Indonesian islands and, in the foreground, dozens of merchantmen. Somewhere down there, to the right, is the Singapore River.

Before the arrival of the British, this area was known as Bukit Larang, or Forbidden Hill, and it was populated by the ghosts of past kings of ancient Singapura who were buried in its sacred grounds. Gold remains from the 14th century were unearthed here when a reservoir was under construction in 1925, and celadon fragments were found in the 1940s. Ongoing archaeological digs continue to yield exciting fort finds which included 11th-century metallic Chinese coins and porcelain fom the Yuan Dy-

Exciting finds from ongoing archaeological digs at the Park provide evidence of the island's early contact with ancient Chinese.

nasty (AD 1280-1368). These artifacts can be seen in the National Museum.

As good a place as any to enter the park, which is bounded by Hill Street, River Valley Road, Clemenceau Avenue, Fort Canning and Canning Rise, and which occupies less than 40 hectares, is through the white pseudo-Gothic arch near Canning Rise. This leads into a tree-lined walk at the foot of a sloping sward that was used to be a cemetery but now contains only a few discrete, freestanding stones.

Those less fearful than the indigenes who refused to accompany Colonel William Farquhar, the first Resident of Singapore, will ascend to the top of the hill and be able to inspect at close quar-

ters about 250 tombstones that tell something of the early colonial days. These stones were originally freestanding but are now embedded in two parallel red brick walls that mark the northern and southern boundaries of this area. Farquhar finally made the ascent accompanied by Malays from Malacca and a cannon. The cannon was loaded and fired at the summit, and the Union Jack run up a flagpole that Farquhar ordered to be erected.

Leave this area, which is about 100 metres wide, through another white pseudo-Gothic arch and stroll through a sculpture garden containing five sculptures, one from each of Singapore's ASEAN partners (Brunei, Indonesia,

The Fort Canning Centre is also home to Theatreworks,
Singapore's professional theatre company.

Malaysia, the Philippines, Thailand). A left turn here leads to the summit, where there are still vestigial remains of a fort, a children's playground (one of two in the park), a roller-skating rink and a centre of the visual and performing arts – an enchanting white building called the **Fort Canning Centre**.

Descend to the much revered *kramat* (a Muslim shrine, believed to be endowed with mystical properties) of Sultan Iskandar Shah, to which Malays still occasionally bring religious offerings. Iskandar Shah was the last ruler of ancient Singapura, and his remains are believed to be buried in this tomb, which some claim to date, despite the scant evidence, from the 14th century.

Surprisingly, there are no foodstalls in Fort Canning Park, so remember to buy a snack at the large hawker centre in Hill Street. While in Hill Street, take a look at the distinctive **Hill Street Building**, home of the National Archives, with corbelled loggias, balconies and rusticated surfaces. This building has always been regarded as bad *feng shui* (see story on page 79) by the local Chinese, who claim that they enjoyed prosperity until this structure was put up in its location, altering the topography of the area, which up to then was in the shape of the *peh toh*, the Chinese New Year fish that is a symbol of good fortune.

A number of interesting buildings surround Fort Canning Park. The Ar-

Within the quiet of Central Park, the last ruler of ancient Singapura Sultan Iskandar Shah finds his resting place.

menian Church, and the National Museum and Art Gallery will interest visitors most, while some may wish to visit the National Library, which is next to the National Museum.

The **Armenian Church**, the oldest in Singapore, was completed in 1836. It is a gem. Small but grand, simple but elegant, its exterior is one of perfect symmetry and harmony. Sadly, the effect is somewhat marred by the addition of a corrugated iron roof on four Doric columns at the western entrance. The church is a superb example of the Palladian style that Inigo Jones exploited to such good effect when English architecture returned to classicism. The caretaker of the church is not an Armenian

The Last Armenians

At the back of the Armenian Church is a smaller building, the one-time parsonage, now run as an old-folks' shelter. On sunny days, you will find an old gent of 82 with a wispy white beard outside the home, poring over his scrapbooks.

Mackertich Zacobian Martin – "Mackie" to his friends – is living history. For he is a Singaporean Armenian. Once upon a time, the Armenians, Middle-Eastern Christians, were an influential and numerically strong minority in Singapore. The most famous Armenians were surely the Sarkies brothers, the founders of Raffles Hotel. Today Singaporean Armenians number maybe a dozen at most.

Dapper Mackie is still very much the dashing bachelor he was in the Roaring Twenties, in the days of glittering fancy dress balls at the Raffles Hotel. Drop in on Mackie. He loves to talk about the old days and is an invaluable guide to the history of the Armenian Church.

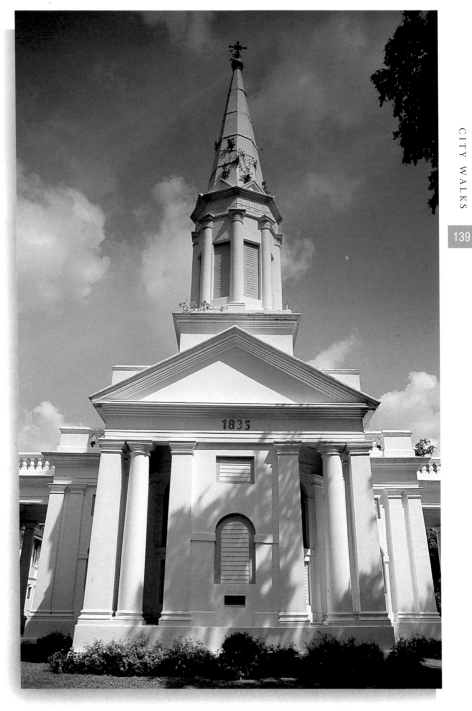

The Armenian Church stands on Hill Street as it has since 1836,
in honour of St Gregory the Illuminator (first monk of the Armenian Church).

The Silent Stone

In the National Museum sits a fragment of stone inscribed with writing that nobody can decipher. The stone's silence locks up a part of Singapore's ancient history, probably dating back to the Javanese Majapahit empire of the 14th century, which once held suzerainty over Singapore.

Weathered by time and tide, this stone once stood about three metres tall at the mouth of the Singapore River. Unfortunately, it was blown up in 1843 by a British settlement engineer when the river mouth was being widened.

The comments of the Arab-Malay scholar Munshi Abdullah bin Abdul Kadir, who witnessed this destruction, are still apposite:

"A great pity, and in my opinion, a most improper thing to do… He destroyed the rock because he did not realise its importance… As the Malays say, 'If you cannot improve a thing, at least do not destroy it.'"

This stained glass dome bespeaks the Museum's Renaissance grandeur.

but a Muslim – shades of the Holy Sepulchre in Jerusalem. Some tombstones can be found in the church yard.

The **National Museum**, which dates from 1887, was originally the Raffles Museum and Library housing an anthropological and naturalist collection started by Raffles. A major renovations programme in 1990 saw the entire building carefully restored with each glass panel, and the exterior fish-scale tiles, numbered, then removed for cleaning and repair. Today it stands as a major statement of Singapore's colonial architectural heritage.

The nation's ongoing conservation programme takes a step ahead with the re-opening of the 105-year-old National Museum after a S$5.5 million restoration.

The focal point of this handsome building today is its History of Singapore gallery, which contains 20 intricately carved dioramas in which historical scenes are re-created. Also on the first storey is the Straits Chinese gallery, which contains Peranakan clothes, ceramics and furnishings that eclectically combine Chinese, Malay and English threads. The Southeast Asian gallery is something of a misnomer for, although jammed with colourful anthropological artifacts from Borneo and Sumatra, it also houses many items from as far afield as Papua New Guinea and Japan.

The second storey contains, among other items, a stunning collection of jade (one of the largest in the world), superb ceramics, and a small number of Chinese bronzes. The museum also boasts an art gallery with a permanent collection of works by Singapore artists and temporary exhibitions by artists from the region and further afield.

Little India shopkeepers have one sales strategy:
the more you show, the more you sell.

The Indian diet is basically a macrobiotic one.

LITTLE INDIA

Cross Rochor Canal and enter Serangoon Road, and the world of **Little India**, which takes its name from the Indians who have settled here. They started to arrive from 1826 in their thousands to work in the kilns and at the constructions. It was they who, under the direction of British architects, built some of the greatest buildings in the land, such as the Istana (once the home of the Governor and now the home of the President) and St Andrew's Cathedral.

Many shop signs here are written in Tamil, but just as many are also in English. The aroma of flowers and rosewater, of pepper and cinnamon, of *betel* nuts and hot ghee, informs the visitor that he is in Little India. Beauties dressed in gorgeous *saris* and dangling dozens of golden bangles stroll past handlebar-mustachioed men in off-white *dhotis*. Muslims in small embroidered skullcaps brush past a contemplative Hindu guru, an umbrella on his arm and ash on his forehead.

Hawkers stand beside extravagantly glossy pop-art paintings of the family of Shiva – Hanuman the monkey god, Ganesh the elephant god, and the baby Krishna. In tiny cubicles, scarcely large enough to accommodate one person, garland makers string together orchids, jasmine and margosas, although, sad to say, plastic garlands are gaining favour. Also on sale are the ingredients of *betel*, a mild narcotic that results in a "bloodstained" mouth when chewed. Larger shops dazzle with their contents. Bolt after bolt of cottons and muslins, voiles and organdies, in every conceivable hue and combination of colour, stretch from floor to ceiling.

Buildings bearing the signs "Ramakrishnan Mission" and "Tamils Reformed Association" further confirm that this is Little India, but the area is by no means the exclusive domain of Indians. Immediate neighbours include a very European Methodist church (complete with belfry), a Chinese temple and the headquarters of the Peng Yong Ang Clan Association and the Nanyang Kang Clan Guild. Rudyard Kipling, who wrote that "there is neither east nor west, border nor breed, nor birth, where two strong men stand face to face though they come from the ends of the earth", would have loved it here.

At the southwestern end of **Serangoon Road**, where Little India begins, stands **Zhujiao Centre**, whose lower floors is a market and upper floors apartments. Although this market is under cover it retains much of the ambience of the outdoor market it replaced, and it has the reputation of being one of the most inexpensive markets in the city. The busy taxi rank here is occupied by pedal-power trishaws rather than diesel-power four-wheeled vehicles.

Nearby is Buffalo Road, which is immediately followed by Kerbau (actually "buffalo" in Malay) Road. These streets owe their names to the fact that they were once the centre of the cattle trade, which was dominated by Muslim Indians. Linking the upper sections of these two short roads are 28 shophouses and a bungalow that have been restored and now house traditional Indian arts and crafts and foodstuffs. The ambience may be Indian, but the hieroglyphics and decorations on the doors and window shutters of the buildings are unmistakeably Chinese.

During the 1960s, the maternity hospital here – Kandang Kerbau Hospital – boasted 65,000 births a year and claimed to be the busiest maternity hospital in the world. Since the national "Stop at Two" campaign (now *passé*), however, arrivals have dipped sharply.

Temples And Memorial Halls

Back on Serangoon Road one can scarcely fail to notice the brilliant *gopuram* (= entrance) to the **Sri Veeramakaliamman Temple**, and a couple of side streets later is Race Course Lane, where stands an unpretentious building that is

A cook's paradise – Zhujiao Centre, where ingredients for any meal can be obtained fresh. Preceding page: Ganesh the elephant god.

Despite its name, "Little India" is not all Indian.
Signboards of Chinese businesses abound.

Streetside fortune teller
awaits his next client.

of considerable import to Singapore's Indian population. The foundation stone of the **Mahatma Gandhi Memorial Hall** was laid by ex-Indian prime minister Pandit Jawarharlal Nehru.

In several side streets on the opposite side of Serangoon Road, such as Dickson Road, Upper Weld Road and Veerasamy Road, are colourful examples of Chinese shophouses. These are painted lime and lemon, mauve and purple, vivid and iridescent, and, as if to completely blind the passerby, those occupied by Chinese rather than Indians often display large, colourful paper lanterns and red banners inscribed in gold with Chinese characters. Observe in these superb examples of vernacular architecture their columns and pilasters, foliated capitals and handsome inlaid tiles decorated with floral motifs.

Back on Serangoon Road, you may stumble on one of the "birdmen" of

Every neighbourhood has at least one mama ("uncle") stall that sells candies and cigarettes, magazines and medications... you name it.

Singapore – fortune tellers who, when you reveal your date of birth, whisper it to a parrot which then selects a card bearing your fortune.

If you have ever wished to shop in India, then enter **Serangoon Plaza**, where, at first glance, you may think that non-Indians require a visa! This is the place to buy Indian audio and video tapes, while the range of perfumes and deodorants is quite staggering.

Immediately across the road from Serangoon Plaza is the solid, somewhat unimaginative, russet-coloured **Angullia Mosque**, a sombre presence among the Indian temples – each of which seems determined to outdo its neighbours in the brilliance of its statuary.

Two of these temples are soon reached.

At the **Sri Srinivasa Perumal Temple**, a gazetted national monument, those members of the Indian pantheon who cannot be accommodated in the 22-metre-high *gopuram* line the tops of the adjacent walls, which are painted with broad red and white vertical stripes. Many fewer, although much larger and more ornate, are the man-made figures that decorate the neighbouring **Sri Sivan Temple**.

Another 600 metres further, at the corner of Serangoon Road and Towner Road, we return to austerity in the large **Central Sikh Gurdwara**, the principal house of worship of the 18,000 Sikhs in Singapore. This is far more than a tem-

Flower Stalls of Serangoon Road

On a tour of Little India, you might notice small makeshift flower stalls that seem to have sprung up outside a general larger store or on a platform barely three-feet square, jutting out from a narrow recess. Framing this little shop are fragrant garlands of jasmine and roses.

But venture closer, to find the narrow shelves at the back and every available space on that platform crammed with almost all the items a Hindu would need on a visit to the temple. Besides the garlands and loose petals tied up in dried leaves, there are *betel* nuts, bananas and lemons, that are taken as offerings to the gods.

The flower shop also caters for the home altar or the prayer area, as it is called. Incense and clay oil lamps are available, and a special sootless oil can be bought here for these lamps.

Or get sandalwood in powder form; devout Hindus make a paste of this and apply it to the deities' feet. The red powder (*kumkum*), is applied to the forehead of the deities and of the worshipper. "Ittar", a perfume concentrate made of herbs and flowers comes in tiny bottles. This is used by Indians and the Chinese to anoint the bodies of the dead. Vividly coloured pictures of Hindu deities like Krishna, Shiva and Rama are arranged on neat shelves too.

Some of these flower stalls are strategically sited outside general stores that stock a much greater variety of items than the little flower stall could hold. These include framed pictures and brass figurines of deities, stainless steel trays to carry the offerings in and small plastic containers of *kumkum* and sandalwood paste.

These flower garlands form part of the shop decor before they are sold.

Hindu guardian gods at the entrance of the Sri Rama Temple.

ple, however, and is rather a community centre with accommodation, a library, a clinic, and a free kitchen where Sikh and non-Sikh, rich and poor, sit together in a *pangat* (= row).

Backtrack to the Sri Srinivasa Perumal Temple and take the side street that leads to Race Course Road (named after the race course that was once here) and the renowned **Buddhist Temple of 1,000 Lights** (Sakaya Muni Buddha Gaya), which is guarded by two stone lions – or are they tigers? The temple interior is almost entirely filled by a 17-metre-high seated Buddha. The figure is draped in gold, green and red cloth, and is surrounded by a halo of lights that are lit in the evenings or, on demand and payment, during the day. An unusual

The lights that give the temple its name form an arch around the Buddha.

feature of this temple is the fact that it is the result of the devotions of a single monk, by name Vuttisasara, whose photograph can be seen above the counter where "lucky" papers are sold.

Across the road is the **Long San See** (Dragon Mountain Temple), one of four unobtrusive Chinese temples in Race Course Road. Observe the elegant ceramic roof carvings, with dragons and chimeras in green, red and yellow, which would shame any gnome garden.

Hungry? Those in search of new experiences are in for a treat. **Komala Vilas**, in Serangoon Road, is a Singapore landmark. Here, four or five kinds of South Indian vegetarian curry are spooned into small heaps on a banana leaf, and the food eaten with the fingers. This is accompanied by a glass of tear-inducing *rasam* (pepper water) and yoghurt. The food is moderately spicy and immoderately inexpensive.

Or remain on Race Course Road, and dine at the **Banana Leaf Apollo**. Again, the food is eaten from a banana leaf, but here it is fiery and non-vegetarian. This restaurant is renowned for its fish-head curry – a large, meaty fish-head bathed in a spicy-hot gravy – a dish that is very dear to many Singaporeans and on which treatises have been written.

If you are vegetarian, however, then try **Fut Sai Kai** in Kitchener Road – a Buddhist vegetarian restaurant that features beancurd imitations of classic meat dishes so the sweet and sour pork set before you is actually beancurd!

A balancing act on the threshold of the Thian Hock Keng Temple.

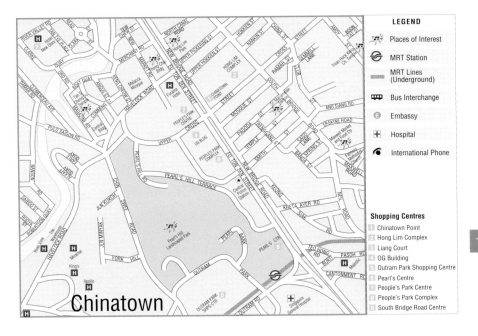

LEGEND

🐝 Places of Interest

⊖ MRT Station

▭▭▭ MRT Lines (Underground)

🚍 Bus Interchange

⊖ Embassy

➕ Hospital

📞 International Phone

Shopping Centres

1 Chinatown Point
2 Hong Lim Complex
3 Liang Court
4 OG Building
5 Outram Park Shopping Centre
6 Pearl's Centre
7 People's Park Centre
8 People's Park Complex
9 South Bridge Road Centre

Chinatown

CHINATOWN

A good place to begin an exploration of Chinatown is the **Thian Hock Keng Temple**, or Temple of Heavenly Happiness, on Telok Ayer Street, which runs parallel to Shenton Way, the financial district. Not only is this temple the premier place of worship among the local Hokkien Chinese, it is also a glorious example of rococo Chinese architecture.

The first Hokkien immigrants arrived in sailing junks not far from here. One of their first duties on arrival was to visit a joss house and give thanks for a safe passage, and so, in 1821, they established their own joss house on the site of the present Thian Hock Keng Temple. Offerings from new arrivals and successful immigrants led to a bulging kitty, and a far more ambitious building

was planned – a building that would combine the functions of both a temple and a community centre. The result was the construction, in 1840, of the temple that we see today. The main courtyard and front entrance were built with materials imported from southern China, and several Hokkien craftsmen contributed their skills to what soon became the pride of their community. The temple was lovingly restored between 1976 and 1979, and the degree of care that went into the restoration can be judged from the fact that, in a country in which massive skyscrapers rise almost in the blink of an eye, three years were required to complete the task.

The Indian snake charmers who can usually be found in the first courtyard of the temple reflect the multicultural heritage of Singapore. Another

The call to prayer from the Nagore Durgha Shrine frequented by Indian-Muslim devotees cuts through the cacophony of bustling Chinatown.

reflection of this heritage is the two buildings on either side of the temple. To the left are the twin minarets of the simple **Al-Abrar Mosque**, also known as the Koochoo Pally or Indian Mosque, built between 1850 and 1855 to replace an old mosque that had been there since 1827. When it was first built, the sea reached its front door at high tide.

To the right of the Thian Hock Keng is the **Nagore Durgha Shrine**, which somewhat resembles a fanciful wedding cake. Although it is often referred to as a mosque, it does not really deserve this designation: rather, it is a *kramat*, or place of veneration, much revered by Muslims from the Coromandel coast of South India on account of the tomb it contains of one Shabul Hamdi. The

shrine was built between 1827 and 1830.

These are not the only places of worship on Telok Ayer Street. Look upwards and observe that here, as throughout Chinatown, many homes contain small private temples. And, somewhere or other, you'll probably chance on a collection of awnings over tables, chairs and temporary altars. These signify a wedding or a funeral, or the celebration of the Buddha's birthday.

Amoy Street, the very first street in Chinatown, runs parallel to Telok Ayer Street. Several intriguing signs hang outside some of the buildings. One dangling from a building immediately opposite the back of the Thian Hock Keng Temple reads: "Kwong Thye Hin, Native Passengers, Lodging House, No.

Good-luck banners, hung in local Chinese homes, are believed to bring fortune or to banish evil.

89 Amoy Street, Licensed for 90 Lodgers." Also observe small mirrors, with their reflective surfaces turned outwards, outside some of the shutters. Supposedly, these not only repel evil spirits, but also bring home errant husbands.

A few hundred metres southeast of here on Phillip Street, in a large open courtyard in the lee of the soaring OCBC Centre, stands the **Wak Hai Cheng Bo Temple**, or Temple of the Calm Sea, built between 1852 and 1855 as a joss house for Teochew sailors and fishermen. The roof, with its superimposed figures depicting posterity and vigour, is especially attractive, as are the roof beams and their supporting brackets, carved into the shape of mythical animals and birds.

From here, proceed northwards to the junction of Church Street and China Street, and turn left into China Street, where house No. 6 (**Ban Poh Guan**) is a traditional Chinese inn. Further up China Street is Chin Chew Street, where a barber works in one of the colonnades. Beyond this, a local shrine houses a giant slumbering cobra. This street and neighbouring Nankin Street were once renowned for their tiny cubicles, some shared by several women. A few of these *Samsui* (so named after a province in China from where they come) women can still be seen in the late afternoon, sitting on stools outside their homes, talking, playing cards, drinking green tea or smoking special hand-rolled cigarettes. At one time, these women mo-

Even a dictionary will not help you with these shop signs.
A better bet is to wander inside.

nopolized the construction labour market, and 50 years ago there were more than 50,000 of them. They are sometimes known as the *hung tau kwan* (= "red headdress army"), because of their distinctive red headdress. Today, their number is exiguous.

Walk along Cross Street until you come to Club Street. The buildings here scarcely differ at all from those in other Chinatown streets, but look at the signs in Club Street and the reasons for its name become clear. Within only 100 metres are the Singapore Boxing Fellowship, the Singapore Glass Merchants and Glaziers Association and, in one building, the Nanyang Chinese Exchange Remittance Association and the Fukien Exchange Association.

Not to be overlooked is a small shop across the street. Its stock is, in monetary terms, very valuable; in terms of cultural heritage, it is priceless. It consists of sandalwood images of the Chinese pantheon, handcarved by a few men clad in vests and shorts, then colourfully painted, after which gold leaf is applied. Although there are literally hundreds of individual gods and goddesses, the carver follows no model or photograph: The details are etched in his mind.

Club Street leads on the left to Ann Siang Road, home of more clubs and associations, and on the right to Ann Siang Hill. Ann Siang Hill is scarcely longer than its name, but some occupants of its "five-foot way" (an arcade built to protect pedestrians from the sun and the rain, once common in Singapore) are quite fascinating. One creates and paints large masks of papier mâché, while another, seated before a small table, the tools of his trade before him and the evidence of it pinned to the wall beside him, is a letter writer.

The specimens are not postal letters but red scrolls on which are inscribed, in flowing Chinese characters of gold, such aphorisms as "Double Happiness" (for a wedding couple) or "May There Be No Mishaps" (to be placed on the staircase). For a trifle, the letter writer will draw one of these with a deft flourish. For rather more, he will painstakingly write a letter in Chinese, usually for an illiterate woman who still clings to the past in China or who wishes to hear from relatives in other parts of the Chinese Diaspora in Southeast Asia (known, incidentally, as *nanyang*). In addition to writing letters, these men also read out in dialect the contents of letters received.

Ann Siang Hill debouches into South Bridge Road, which cuts a broad swath through Chinatown. Many shops in this thoroughfare are pawnshops or goldsmiths, the latter protected by armed guards who are almost invariably Sikhs. Here too are solid, old-fashioned Chinese medicine halls, where, swiftly and accurately, pharmacists withdraw from wooden drawers a little of this, a dash of that, with which they concoct innumerable potions. All medicines are sold by the Chinese system of *hoon, chinh, tael* and *kati* (a *kati* is 0.6 of a kilogram). More than 1500 herbs are for sale, some grown locally, some imported from China. Not hidden in drawers but in glass bottles for all to see are other panaceas – goat horns, dried sea horses, dried frogs and lizards. And, in champagne glasses, thousands of tiny pearls: these, when ground and swallowed, magically cause wrinkles to disappear! Some of the Chinese pharmacies found in this area are now of sparkling glass and glittering chrome, but their cures are the same.

It is impossible not to notice the **Sri Mariamman Temple**, which almost faces the junction of Ann Siang Hill and South Bridge Road. Instantly recognizable are a distinctive 11-metre-high *gopuram* (= a tower that is a symbolical extension of the devotees hands raised in supplication) that stands above its entrance, and a row of life-size statues of sacred cows that sits on its walls. More than 500 Dravidian figures occupy the five levels of the *gopuram*. They depict the deeds of the goddess Mariamman, one of the nine forms of Devi, who, it is suggested, is the Hindu counterpart of the Virgin Mary in Christianity. Mariamman is credited with the power to heal smallpox and cholera. The date

Kites, lanterns and other papier mâché creations spilling from shops onto five-footways is a common sight in Chinatown.

of this building is not known, but it certainly existed as early as 1862. It was built by the same convict labourers who built St Andrew's Cathedral; they must have felt far more at home building this robust (indeed, somewhat rotund) Indian temple than building the lofty Anglican church.

It is scarcely worth putting on your shoes again, for a few steps to the east is the **Jamae Mosque**. After the flamboyance of the Mariamman, this national monument seems plain, almost to the point of austerity. It was built in about 1830 and is the mosque of the Chulias, that is, Muslims from South India.

Several streets around the Sri Mariamman Temple – Pagoda Street, Temple Street, Smith Street and, linking them,

Trengganu Street – constitute the very heart of Chinatown. Sixty years ago, this was the most densely populated area in all Asia. It is to here that tourists flock, and as a result one finds shop after shop selling bric-à-brac such as kites, lanterns, chopsticks and clogs. Traditional trades are still practised, however, and outside No. 30 Smith Street stand large, brown earthenware jars decorated with cream-coloured dragons. Chuen Cheng manufactures soya sauce. At No. 46 Temple Street you can buy "century" eggs (eggs packed in straw and mud and preserved for 100 days). And don't miss No. 37 Pagoda Street, where the sign "Bicycle Trader" has replaced the sign "Slave Trader".

These streets were once jammed with

The renovated shophouses of Tanjong Pagar against the skyscraper skyline of Shenton Way, Singapore's Wall Street.

hawkers, but few remain: in 1983, they were herded into the multi-storey Kreta Ayer Complex, the lower floors of which are devoted to a wet market and food-stalls. A few wrinkled old women appear to have escaped the net, however, and still sit outside the building selling their meagre goods. One bespectacled old soul sells nothing but tiny reddish-brown onions, while another vendor presides over a sheet of brown paper on which are arranged rows of small red and green peppers.

Dilapidated three- and four-storey shophouses in this part of town are currently under renovation, but this will scarcely be Chinatown: rather, it will result in an open-air architectural museum. This can already be seen in the

Tanjong Pagar Conservation Area (bordered by Tanjong Pagar Road and Neil Road), a little west of here, where restoration of some of the most magnificent shophouses in Singapore has been completed. Attractive three-storey shophouses painted lime-green, apple-green and russet are occupied by up-market tenants. Hawkers and foodstalls have been replaced by boutiques and offices, and the flagpole laundry once seen everywhere is now in washing machines and spin dryers. The result is a "yuppie" Chinatown.

The **Pewter Museum** on Duxton Road just next to Tanjong Pagar Road is worth a visit. Billed the world's first pewter museum, it traces the craft of pewtersmiths and features more than

Peranakan Architecture

A country with such an eclectic ethnic mix naturally produced an architectural style all its own, a mix also to be found in Peranakan culture and food. Called Straits Chinese, Palladian Chinese or appropriately Chinese Baroque, the style is best seen in the narrow shophouses and terrace houses in Chinatown, Tanjong Pagar area, Blair Road, Emerald Hill off Orchard Road, Petain Road adjoining Little India and the Joo Chiat area in the East Coast. These are older parts of the city which have not fallen under the developer's hammer.

These shophouses and their residential equivalent – the terrace houses – have highly decorated facades with Chinese, Malay and European Classical architectural details. Delicate Malay-style wooden fretwork roofs, with Chinese elements in the curved clay tiles, and in its rounded gables. Also look out for Chinese decorative tiles or gilded carvings on the doors. European details exist in the scaled down Clas-

sical columns and elegant capitals. These give the structures their stately touch while colourful wall tiles and decorative plasterwork add yet more ornamentation. Not for nothing has it been called Chinese Baroque architecture.

High ceilings, verandahs and louvred windows air and light the interiors – European architectural adaptations for the humid tropical surroundings. Road overhangs called five footways give shade from torrential tropical downpours and in the case of shophouses, added display areas. In the residential terraces, the sensible *pintu pagar* (carved and ornamented half-doors) screen residents from passers-by yet allow good ventilation in the rooms.

Prosperity at the turn of the century combined with the availability of good craftsmen to produce these lavish houses rich in the kind of craftsmanship no longer seen today. Many of the city's historic buildings were constructed during this period.

Characteristics of Peranakan architecture, left to right (top first): neat quaint rows; details on Classical columns; open air well to ensure good ventilation; ceiling-high windows.

The originals of these shophouses were narrow wooden buildings with attap roofs which combined living and working quarters. The standard floor plan was the shop floor in the front which led into the storage and living areas behind and bedrooms upstairs.

In the residential terraces, the shop front became the sitting room. Here the first sight that caught the eye of a visitor would have been the family altar. Lined along the walls on the left and right of the room would be black inlaid chairs of rosewood. In a more modern home, the more comfortable settees would be in the centre of the room.

The inner doorway would lead into the dining room where a wooden stairway connected to the bedrooms upstairs. From the dining room a doorway leads to the kitchen adjoining an open air well. This sensible feature gave good ventilation and lighting and took care of strong cooking smells.

800 crafted pieces ranging from domestic to ceremonial utensils.

The restored **Jinrikisha Station**, at the corner of Tanjong Pagar Road and Neil Road, was once the rickshaw station but is now a restaurant. Rickshaws, of which there were at one time almost 10,000, used to be the standard mode of public transport. These were replaced after World War II by the modern trishaws that now ply the streets for the tourist trade.

A glimpse of the new rather than the restored Chinatown can be had by crossing the massive pedestrian bridge that spans New Bridge Road at the top of Pagoda Street. Here is the **People's Park Complex**, the first shopping centre of its kind in Southeast Asia and the shopping centre that established the pattern of local retailing in Singapore.

Around the corner in Upper Cross Street is a Chinese coffeeshop with the splendid name of **Heng Dong Juan**. Its walls are covered with mirrors, its floor is of marble, and fans whirl overhead. The chairs are wooden rather than plastic. Ah, the good old days!

A few hundred metres further east on New Bridge Road stands the **Thong Chai Medical Institution Building**, built in the 1890s, which once served as a temple and charitable hospital in which traditional herbal medicine was dispensed. This attractive two-storey building, which with its two courtyards and much decorative carving resembles a Chinese palace, is now an antique shop that stocks some rare items.

Catching a scene like this of the Marina Square has got to be the end of the
rainbow for many visitors.

T

MALAY ENCLAVES

here are a number of Malay enclaves east of the city, and **Kampong Glam**, the most interesting and historically the most important, is closest to the city. The name is derived from *kampong*, village in Malay, and the *glam* tree, which once grew here, the bark of which was used to caulk the sailing ships that still berthed in Singapore as recently as the late 1970s. The tree also yielded medicinal oil. The names of several streets in Kampong Glam – Baghdad, Jeddah, Muscat – reflect the origins of those who settled here soon after the colony was founded, while the names of others – Haj, Arab – reveal their race and religion.

Dominating this district are the twin domes and four minarets of the **Sultan Mosque**, the largest and most sacred of the more than 80 Muslim places of worship in Singapore. The building is a remarkable mixture of Moorish and classical themes. Not obvious is the fact that the base of the dome is made of bottles. The Sultan

Semi-precious stones, buttons and simple medicines – Muslim jack-of-all-trades are everywhere in the Kampong Glam district.

Beyond The City

165

The golden domes of Sultan Mosque. If visiting, be sure
to be appropriately attired – bare legs and arms are prohibited.

Mosque, which was built between 1924 and 1928, is the youngest gazetted monument in Singapore, although a mosque has occupied the site since 1823.

A visit at midday on Friday, when the faithful gather for *jumaat* prayers, is fascinating. Skull-capped Muslim men leave their shoes at the entrance of the mosque, wash their feet before they enter and kneel on the plush red carpets that cover the marble floor inside. Inside, Koran inscriptions glisten on the high walls above the *imam* (= holy man) as he leads the congregation in prayer.

Women are segregrated in a raised section at the back of the building.

The mosque is not only a religious centre but also the focal point of the inhabitants of this neighbourhood, who like to sit and chat in its cool gardens at the end of the day. Men dressed in *sarong*

chew *betel* nut, while their wives swathed in lace veils clutch their children. The mantle of Islam hangs over this area. Prayer rugs decorate many of the countless textile stores in Arab Street, while other shops sell prayer shawls and veils, *songkok* (the traditional headdress among Muslim males), and special money belts for those intending to make the *haj* – the pilgrimage to Mecca.

The streets of Kampong Glam, especially **Arab Street**, will delight shoppers in search of the exotic. Here are incense burners and hookahs. Or you may prefer perfumes (made from a non-alcoholic base) or *agar*, the most expensive wood in the world, which comes from the forests of Burma and which burns with an incense-like fragrance. Others may be seduced by saucers embedded with glittering semi-precious stones. There are many shops with bolts of textiles – silk from China, *kain songket* (a cloth embroidered with gold thread) from Malaysia, *batik* from Indonesia – piled high to the ceiling, and lace, velvets and sequinned fabrics. Even more congested with goods are the two basket shops at the southern end of Arab Street.

At the other end of Arab Street, you may be deafened, especially at weekends, by a piercing cry: "Sixty-five dollars! Last price!" The racket is from **Thieves' Market**, which extends from Sungei Road on a stretch of the Rochor Canal to Kelantan Lane and Jalan Besar. Like many other places in Singapore, this market is not what it once was, but one can still find a wide variety of goods, from cassettes and suitcases to watches and vases. This is also a grand place if you are looking for an old clock, a rusty kettle or a ship's propeller...

As you stroll along the side of North Bridge Road opposite the Sultan Mosque, a number of men may start to wave to you. These are the "beckoners": each stands outside his Indian restaurant – the Singapore, the Victory, the Zam Zam – and tries to lure you in. Their "patter" is the restaurant menu.

East of the Sultan Mosque is Kandahar Street, where you'll find a long, low green wall with a small gate. Enter and you are in the grounds of the **Istana Kampong Glam** (= Kampong Glam Palace), which was built in 1840. The palace, a sad, two-storey yellow build-

A Hajja (= Muslim lady who has gone on a pilgrimage to Mecca).

ing with a tiled roof, was once the residence of Sultan Ali Iskander Shah, son of Sultan Hussein Mohamed Shah, who ceded Singapore to the East India Company. Today the compound houses about 20 families – only three can claim direct descent from Sultan Hussein while the others are only distantly related and have moved here during the Japanese Occupation. An 1897 court decision ruled that any family that can claim kinship with the original Sultan's family may move into the premises.

Leave the palace grounds by a large gate and enter Sultan Gate, a short street popular with scrap metal merchants. The bright yellow house on the right, with two eagles above the gatepost, once belonged to the royal family. Turn left into Pahang Street and walk past several shacks (in which artisans produce tombstones for Muslim graves), and you soon reach Jalan Sultan.

Turn right into Jalan Sultan, and after 200 metres enter Beach Road, where you'll find the **Hajja Fatimah Mosque**, the only Muslim place of worship to be named after a female benefactor. Hajja Fatimah, who built the mosque and who is buried with her daughter and son-in-law in the burial ground behind the mosque, was a Malaccan lady who married a sultan from the Celebes in Indonesia. There is a square prayer hall topped by a dome, and beside this is what seems to be a church spire with elements of European classicism. Such minarets are not unusual in Malacca, and perhaps a more unusual feature is

The Kampong Glam Istana must be the world's most humble palace complex.

the fact that the minaret actually leans. A quotation from Dr Seow Eu Jin on the occasion of a major repair programme in the 1970s gives us a little of the flavour of Singapore: "The Fatimah Mosque represents an example of virtual architectural syncretism where the classical theme is apparently used by a British architect for a Singapore mosque built by a Malaccan lady, married to a Bugis Sultan whose daughter married a scion of an Arab family from Palembang (in the Indonesian island of Sumatra), who employed Chinese architects to re-construct the main building using French contractors and Malay artisans!"

Back in Jalan Sultan, just beyond Pahang Road, are two architecturally unusual buildings that date from 1912. The parapet of the splendid **Ahamadian Press** is worthy of observation, while the **Alsagoff Arab School** has a most unusual pediment. The Alsagoffs were involved in the cultivation of lemon grass, from which citronella oil, briefly popular as an antiseptic and a treatment for rheumatism, was obtained. Continue northwards and cross North Bridge Road, and the brilliant blue and gold **Malabar Muslim Jama-ath Mosque** comes into view. Set among trees, some of them palms, one feels that this is how a mosque *should* look – a building in an oasis rather than a city. This mosque is popular with those from Malabar in India.

Two kilometres further, after you

The Jama-ath Mosque at the crossroads of North Bridge Road.

cross the Rochor Canal and the Kallang River, is **Geylang**. Geylang Road, which stretches for almost five kilometres, is the main artery of the district, from which run many small "veins", called *lorong*. Many boast splendid two- and three-storey Chinese shophouses. Observe the beautiful traditional homes on both sides of Lorong 30A, and then the disappointing more recent buildings at the southern end of the same *lorong*. Most outstanding, and well worth a visit, is the house at the corner of Lorong 19 and Lorong Bachok. Do not miss the enormous stone lions that stand outside No. 16 Lorong 31, beside a most unattractive shop (really no more than a large shed) crammed with antique Chinese furniture and porcelain.

Flags flutter, bravely or limply depending on the weather, above the clan association, pugilistic society and dragon dance headquarters, and further colour is added by the red lanterns outside the Chinese temples, two of which have caged pythons in their forecourts.

After Geylang Road, you cross Paya Lebar Road and reach **Geylang Serai**. The word *serai* (= lemon grass in Malay) points to the old farming pursuits of this area, which is still regarded as the Malay stronghold, not only because there is an overwhelming majority of Malay residents but because any Malay who visits Singapore, whether from Malaysia, Indonesia or further afield, comes here to shop and meet family and friends. The heart of the district is the market.

A bizarre convolution of tiles and carvings –
this 1929 Chinese house stands tall in Lorong 19 Geylang.

Jogging tracks along East Coast Parkway
nourish the keep-fit mentality pervading the younger generation.

The slide at the Big Splash, supposedly the largest in Southeast Asia, is not for the weak-hearted.

EAST END

The **East Coast Park** is to Singaporeans what Central Park is to New Yorkers or Hyde Park to Londoners. Singaporeans are doubly fortunate because theirs is on the ocean: Indeed, it is on land recently reclaimed from the sea.

Any time is a good time to visit the East Coast Park, but to enjoy it with the locals it's best to go on a Sunday. Then the Lims and the Lees, the Hassans and the Rashids, the Singhs and the Kaurs, the Eurasians and the expatriates can be seen in their thousands. Visit the beach and relax beneath the rhu and palm trees (Heed the notice: "Beware falling coconuts during Stormy Weath-

er"), listen to music from a strumming guitar or a cassette player, and, because this is Singapore, eat.

A snack, a fried banana, an ice cream, a soft drink, can be bought from one of the vendors who regularly cycle through the park. If you're still hungry, make for the hawker stalls at the eastern end of the park, which is about five kilometres long and 100 metres wide. And the major facilities of the park – from west to east, the Big Splash, Parkland, the Recreation Centre and the Singapore Tennis Centre – all have seafood restaurants. The restaurant at the Tennis Centre specializes in Vietnamese seafood, while that at Parkland features Thai seafood. And the **Seafood Centre**, between the Tennis Centre and the hawker stalls, boasts no fewer than eight seafood restaurants, and is the largest such complex in Singapore. A little to the west of this complex, shaded by trees, can be seen the fishing boats that assure you of the freshness of your seafood.

Swimming in the ocean, against a backdrop of cargo vessels at anchor, and beyond them islands of the Indonesian Archipelago, is popular, but those who prefer chlorine in their waves can visit the four pools of the **Big Splash**, one of which is a wave pool. The main attraction here is the giant slide, which claims to be the highest and longest in Asia. Other swimmers head for the lagoon, said to be the size of 40 Olympic swimming pools and able to accommodate 6000 bathers. Another attraction here is **Wet and Wild**, a giant twisting and turning slide.

A cycle track, which parallels the jogging path, winds through the park, and bicycles (including tandems) can be rented at fitness outlets found along the beach. Those who prefer more sophisticated activities can visit the **Singapore Tennis Centre** or the golf driving range at **Parkland**. Others may prefer the **Recreation Centre**, with its squash courts, children's rides and fast-food outlets. Board sailors will enjoy the **East Coast Sailing Centre**, where sail boards and Laser class boats can be rented, and where courses in windsurfing and sailing are available.

Near here are some 200 air-conditioned chalets, which are inevitably fully booked by Singaporeans at weekends. It may seem strange to take a vacation only 20 kilometres from your home (the furthest possible distance from the East Coast Park to any other part of Singapore), but it's clearly irresistible to take a break from living in a high-rise apartment and go for a weekend in a wooden chalet with comparative privacy, proximity to the sea, and the opportunity to enjoy an open-air barbecue.

Cross East Coast Parkway by any one of the underpasses and make your way through the high-rise housing to Marine Parade and Parkway Parade shopping centre. Parallel to Marine Parade is East Coast Road, which has plenty of good restaurants. Some roads there, such as Joo Chiat Road and Koon Seng Road, are graced by splendid examples of colourful two-storey terraced houses.

Or stay on East Coast Parkway and continue eastwards for about eight kilometres towards **Changi Village**. This village, which comes to life only at weekends and on public holidays, consists of one main street. Although it has

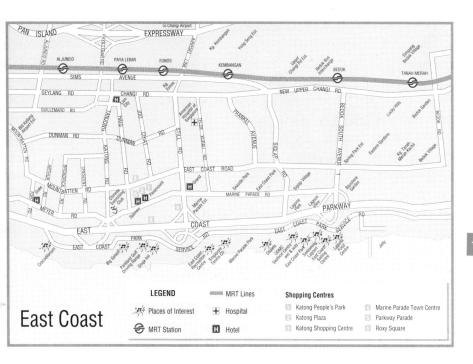

LEGEND

MRT Lines

Shopping Centres

Places of Interest · Hospital · Katong People's Park · Marine Parade Town Centre

Katong Plaza · Parkway Parade

MRT Station · Hotel · Katong Shopping Centre · Roxy Square

East Coast

---

none of the charm of an English village, it does have certain attractions. Here are the Changi Sailing Club, the nine-hole Changi Golf Club, the Meridien Changi Hotel, and other weekend accommodation in the form of holiday chalets.

Pulau Ubin

Immediately to the north of Changi Village is a small park with a seafood restaurant, and then the mouth of the Changi River. The river, which is spanned by a white pedestrian bridge, is always busy with fishing craft. On the seaward side of the bridge is a quay from which a ferry leaves on the hour between 6 am and 11 pm on a 15-minute voyage to Pulau Ubin. (Less frequent

ferries also leave here for Tanjong Pengilir in Malaysia, from where you can reach Desaru Resort – see page 283.)

A fleet of rather dilapidated taxis make a tour of **Pulau Ubin** – which is dominated by granite quarries – in less than half an hour. Fish farming from floating plastic platforms quite close to the shore and prawn farming in ponds are burgeoning industries and a new source of income for the inhabitants of Ubin. Rough, simple accommodation and delicious seafood are available, and the best spot for both is the **Pulau Ubin Seafood House**, located on a platform on stilts over the Straits of Johor at the northwestern corner of the island. Canoes and sail boards can be hired at the longhouses on the jetty.

Back at Changi, on the eastern side

East Coast Park – a good place to contemplate the meaning of life, or to just clear the mind.

of the Changi River, is the well planted **Changi Beach Park**, which is fronted by a clean, wide, sandy beach. A few hundred metres west of the Meridien Changi Hotel is Cranwell Road and a most unusual treasure.

Changi Chapel, which served Allied prisoners-of-war during World War II, contains five religious murals depicting Biblical scenes that were painted by prisoner-of-war Stanley Warren. The murals were painted over after the war, and it was only later, when the room was cleaned, that faint images were discerned. Warren was invited to return to Singapore and restore the murals, which can now be seen in all their pristine glory.

Backtrack past the Meridien Changi Hotel, and return to the city via Upper Changi Road rather than East Coast Parkway. About five kilometres from Changi Village, after you pass the remains of mangrove swamps, coconut palms, groves of papaya and untapped rubber trees, small *kampong* and fish farms, stop at **Changi Prison**. This prison held several thousand Allied prisoners-of-war during World War II. A replica of the chapel in which they prayed may be

Ferries for hire to Pulau Ubin. For the right fee, however, the boatmen at Changi jetty can be persuaded to go further.

visited, while an adjacent museum houses a collection of sketches, photographs and other memorabilia of the period. Both the chapel and the prison are included in the various World War II tours particularly popular with British and Australian visitors. (Also see page 11 and Trav' Tips at the back of book.)

Take part in Singapore life: order a cup of the local brew, mingle among the locals and listen in to the music of the birds.

The Railway Station, the only one in Singapore, is wholly owned and managed by the Malaysian government!

WEST END

A good place to start your West End tour is at the **Telok Ayer Market** (get off at the Raffles Place MRT station and walk westwards for 200 metres), a rather incongruous structure among the skyscrapers of Shenton Way, Singapore's Wall Street. The charming octagonal wrought-iron market was recently demolished and completely rebuilt, the individual components of the building having been carefully labelled and stored meanwhile. The reason for this reinforcement was the fear that the tunnelling during the construction of the Mass Rapid Transit system which ran beneath it, would cause the distintegration of this gazetted monument. The market, which, soon after Raffles landed, was the only market in the city, then stood at the water's edge: now it is some 200 metres from the sea.

This exquisite structure, which has eight longitudinal peaked roofs, from the centre of which stands a clock tower on a square pedestal, was built in Scotland by the P & W MacLellan firm, which earlier cast the iron for Cavenagh Bridge, which spans the Singapore River. Before it was closed and dismantled for the refurbishing, Telok Ayer Market boasted many excellent foodstalls. The food is now more upmarket, and there are also a number of shops and tradesmen practising traditional crafts.

Keen numismatists will want to stop at the **MAS** (Monetary Authority of

Kwan Yin, the Goddes of Mercy, finds home in the Wan Sou Shan Temple which attracts believers who seek longevity.

Singapore) **Building**, also on Shenton Way, to view the interesting collection of bank notes, local and foreign, in its Currency Gallery.

Soon after this building, Shenton Way ends and Keppel Road begins. About 400 metres along Keppel Road, on the right is the **Railway Station.** Five trains depart daily, some of which have onward connections to Thailand.

Two kilometres just after Keppel Road becomes Telok Blangah Road, you reach the **World Trade Centre**, built in this location for the convenience of exhibitions employing heavy equipment, which arrives at the adjacent wharves in containers and is transferred mechanically to the World Trade Centre exhibition halls. Here too, ocean-going cruise ships berth before an exciting voyage to the Pacific Ocean or the Indian Ocean. Back in the Centre, Asia's first **Guinness World of Records Exhibition** is on the second floor. It includes facts and features from the book of the same name. Probably of more interest to most visitors are the ferry and cable car services to the southern island of Sentosa, both of which leave from the World Trade Centre (see page 201).

Go outside again. Half a kilometre east of the World Trade Centre are two cream-coloured structures with red-tiled roofs. Nearer to the road is the **Johor Mosque**, an octagonal building with a stark interior, and just behind the mosque, on slightly elevated ground, is a royal graveyard called **Tanah Kubor**

Raja. The buildings were once part of a palace complex that stood further up the hill. The principal tomb in Tanah Kubor Raja, in which there are 32 tombs, is enshrouded in gold cloth and contains the remains of Temenggong Abdul Rahman. The Temenggong was one of the two leaders – the other was Sultan Hussein Mohamed Shah – from whom Raffles acquired Singapore for the East India Company. Lesser mortals are buried on the hillside above and below Tanah Kubor Raja.

Back on Telok Blangah Road for about two kilometres past Tanah Kubor Raja, turn into Telok Blangah Drive. Perched on a small hill in the lee of soaring public housing are two small, charming Chinese temples, both dedicated to the goddess Kwan Yin. The upper temple originally attracted only women and the lower temple only men, but this is no longer so. The temples, with hills at their backs and facing the sea, have excellent *feng shui*, which has earned them the title **Wan Sou Shan**, or Million-Year-Old Mountain. Those who worship here can expect longevity.

The upper temple, recently renovated and its statues regilded, is the more attractive of the two. It is designed on classical Buddhist lines, with a courtyard leading first to a small hall, the principal figure of which is a Maitreya Buddha. A single step leads to the main hall, in which the principal figure is Kwan Yin, the Goddess of Mercy. Before Kwan Yin is a small statue of the Monkey God, flanked on one side by the

Gods of War and Literature, on the other by the Goddess of Birth. At the back of this hall, facing Kwan Yin, is a statue of Wei Tuo, who loved Kwan Yin but was spurned by her and became her protector instead. To the left of this hall is the Goddess of Yin (the Moon Goddess), to the right the God of Yang (the Sun God). The third chamber is the hall of ancestor worship, which is dominated by a Sakayamuni Buddha. Facing this are several other deities moved here from temples in other parts of Singapore demolished in the name of modernization.

The temple is very busy on the 19th day of the 2nd, 6th, 9th and 11th lunar months, which are the occasions of Kwan Yin's birthday. You can tell the hierarchical rank of a deity in the pantheon by the number of birthdays it has.

Hilltop Songbirds

Continue along Telok Blangah Drive for another kilometre, then turn right and ascend **Telok Blangah Hill**, which, although beautifully landscaped, is seldom visited. The summit is occupied by a delightful terraced garden from which splendid views, especially of the city, can be enjoyed. Further down the hill are fitness stations, but they are ignored by the *tai chi* enthusiasts who make this their exercise ground.

Others bring songbirds to the designated bird-singing area. To train a prize-winning songbird is an obsession among some locals, and the craze is best enjoyed from 8 to 10 on a Sunday morning at a traditional-style coffeeshop on the corner of Tiong Bahru Road and Seng Poh Road only two kilometres away.

The scene there is tranquil. This is a gathering of those who take delight in bird-singing and who wish to spend time with like-minded friends. It is not a bird-singing competition. Several hundred cages hang from a trellis, while the owners (many bring two or three cages) listen to their birds, exchange ideas and occasionally move a cage so that no bird spends too long in the sun.

Sharmas and *merboks* are the Kiri Te Kanawas of the bird world. Merboks fly free in the Malaysian jungle and sell for about S\$10, but one that has been trained to opera pitch will fetch hundreds of times this sum. Potential buyers may wish to cross the road to a small shop that sells many species of birds, bird food and beautiful bamboo cages.

Next to the shop is a small Chinese temple, an ancient tree and more songbirds in bamboo cages. A hundred metres beyond the temple, a covered market gives visitors the opportunity to see how the average Singaporean does his grocery shopping. The market sells meat, fish, vegetables and flowers, and has some excellent hawker stalls.

Dominating Telok Blangah Hill is the **Alkaff Mansion**, with its distinguished twin towers, and it is not hard to picture ladies in crinoline in the arms of their beaux climbing the steps that link the gardens. This is the place for a taste of fine dining in a grand ambience.

Originally known as Mount Washington, this was the favourite of four mansions owned by the Alkaffs, a family of Arab traders who settled here and earned a considerable fortune trading in spices, sugar and coffee between Singapore, India and the Dutch East Indies (now Indonesia). The Alkaffs also owned the long gone Hotel de l'Europe, which occupied the site of today's Supreme Court and the predecessor of which, the London Hotel, predated the Raffles Hotel. And it was they who introduced the hire of horse-drawn carriages and later automobiles to Singapore.

Back on Telok Blangah Road, turn left at a busy intersection dominated by the soaring Port of Singapore Authority Building into Labrador Villa Road. After a few hundred metres, you'll reach the small but delightful **Labrador Park** and **Tanjong Berlayer Park**. Visit during the week, and you're almost certain to be alone among a splendid collection of trees and shrubs. Sit on a bench and enjoy superb views of the western anchorage and several islands. Seven of the largest petroleum companies in the world have oil refineries on five of these islands. The contrast between the urban and the rural is striking.

A steep wooden stairway (owned by British Petroleum but open to the public) leads to a beach of clean, firm sand that is covered at high tide, during which flotsam and jetsam collect here and teem with interesting marine life. Tanjong Berlayer Park has several gun emplacements, one dated 1892.

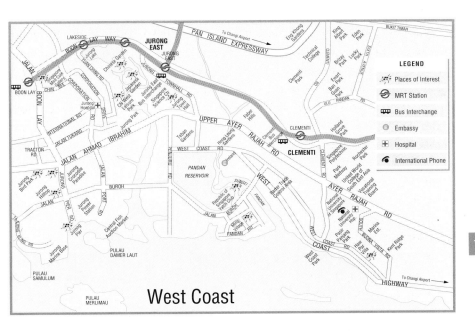

West Coast

Those with binoculars can observe the dwellings on the small island of **Seking Island**. Although its days are probably numbered, Seking is the only offshore island with a genuine residential community of 300 Malays who live in attractive *attap*-roofed houses built on stilts driven into the seabed. These homes have delightful small gardens decorated with coral. The only cottage industry on the island is the manufacture of *jokeng* – small wooden sailing craft in which the Malays love to race.

Seking Island, although in the lee of another island, Bukom Besar, where there is an oil refinery, is light years apart in other respects. Its only electricity is supplied by generators, and freshwater must be ferried from Bukom Besar. Seking has three small shops, the busiest of which is run by three brothers. You can reach Seking by chartering a *twa*

kow (= bumboat) for a couple of hours from Clifford Pier or Jardine Steps at the World Trade Centre. There is no set price for the trip, so be prepared to do some bargaining. If it is just a drop off/pick-up service, S$30 an hour is the norm.

Back on the main road, head westwards until you reach a T-junction. Take the right fork and you soon arrive at the **Haw Par Villa**, also known as the Tiger Balm Gardens. The site and the hundreds of bizarre figures it contains were donated by the Aw brothers, who made their fortune from Tiger Balm, a medicinal ointment. The figures depict characters from Chinese myths and legends. Although adult Westerners and many locals tend to dismiss the 9.5-hectare extravaganza as pure kitsch, the tableaux impress children from all over the world. Their purpose is really no different from that of frescoes painted on the

Theme park Haw Par Villa with its larger-than-life statues depicting characters from Chinese classics is sometimes known as a Confucian Disneyland.

walls of medieval European churches: if morality plays are for adults, then the Tiger Balm Gardens are for children.

Its 2000-seat open-air South China Sea amphitheatre screens daily live performances, while the second open-air theatre, the Four Seasons, dominates the highest point in the gardens and mounts daily dramatic shows. The 500-seat Spirits of the Orient theatre, in which special effects can be seen, features a multi-media presentation that reveals the richness and diversity of Chinese mythology. There is also the three-dimensional Creation of the World theatre, which presents the mythical legend of Pan Gu, the creator of the world, and Nu Wa, the creator of mankind.

No theme park is complete without rides. Board the "Wrath of the Gods" flume ride and meet a number of mythological spirits, or enjoy a more relaxed boat ride in an ancient Chinese vessel and meet Lady White Snake and

only to scare evil spirits but also to help navigate the busy waterways.

You may observe another aspect of Singapore merchant-shipping as you cross the bridge that spans the Pandan River. To the south, on the left bank, a host of green and blue sails flap on simple gaff-rigged wooden craft. These boats bring with them from Indonesia cloves and rice, returning with goods such as rice cookers and radios.

The rather inappropriately named **Ming Village**, in Pandan Road on the western side of the same bridge, is easily mistaken for just another factory. It is not, however: within its cavernous interior, skilled artisans produce beautiful Ming and Qing style pottery, which are then exquisitely painted. All are for sale.

Pick up a porcelain memento from the Ming Village.

the Eight Immortals among other legendary figures in Chinese classics, and visit the Ten Courts of Hell.

After the Tiger Balm Gardens, proceed westwards along West Coast Highway to the pleasant, immaculately landscaped **West Coast Park**, which borders the sea. Between the mainland and the island of Terumbu Retan Laut are moored a number of small craft, many of which are *tongkang*, or lighters, with "eyes" painted on their bows not

As you struggle to the top of the pagoda in the Chinese Garden, console yourself
with an ancient Chinese aphorism: "One must climb higher to see further."

JURONG

If Singapore can be said to have two cities, then Jurong, the island's industrial heart – about 15 kilometres west of Shenton Way – is the second city.

About two kilometres after you enter Jurong, a stark, white modern building appears on the right. **Jurong Town Hall** does not function as a city hall. Rather, it is occupied by the Jurong Town Corporation, which is responsible for the development and management of all industrial estates in Singapore. Twenty-four such estates, of which Jurong is by far the largest, are under its management. Jurong is essentially a factory town, with accommodation for most of the workers who staff its plants.

In 1960, Jurong was a fishing village set in a wasteland of jungle and swamp. Its economy was based on fish and fruit. Today, Jurong boasts more than 1000 factories, 70 percent of which are joint ventures. The names of multinational companies roll off the tongue in a litany to mammon. Many countries are represented by a galaxy of companies, from Asahi Techno Vision (from Japan) to Zuellig Ag (from Switzerland).

A few kilometres beyond Jurong is **Tuas**, which, although of little interest to the sightseer, explains why the Singapore economy is so robust and why it attracts so many multinational companies. When a multinational company visits any other country in the region, that country makes all kinds of promises. But when a multinational company visits Singapore, the infrastructure is already in place – roads, power, sewage, communications. The one factor that Singapore cannot assure is a supply of cheap labour.

Back in Jurong, the **Singapore Science Centre** stands about one kilometre north of the Jurong Town Hall. This was the first contemporary science museum in Asia, and it is considered one of the top 10 science centres in the world. The Science Centre houses more than 500 exhibits in five exhibition galleries. Almost all the exhibits are participatory and invite the visitor – adult or child – to push, pull, turn and pedal. Few can ignore the flight simulator, which makes you an instant pilot.

Both Omnimax and planetarium shows are screened at its Omni Theatre, in which an enormous hemisphere screen engulfs the audience. The programme, which changes from time to time, also includes NASA shuttle shows.

There are also attractions other than cerebral for the visitor to Jurong. The Jurong Town Corporation redressed Nature by damming the Jurong River and creating three small islands in the resulting lake. The most popular of the islands is the **Chinese Garden**, or Yu Hwa Yuan.

The main entrance to the Chinese Garden, which is guarded by two marble lions, leads to the 13-arch Rainbow Bridge. This is followed by a magnificent triple arch, beyond which are two courtyards – one quaint and refreshing with miniature lakes and bridges, the other delicate with the fragrance of jasmine and red pomegranate flowers.

Then comes a vast park area. Clusters of bamboo and willow, many ficus trees and lotus ponds are interspersed among pavilions and pagodas, a stone boat and a teahouse – all the ingredients of the classical Chinese garden. The stone boat, called Yao Yueh, or Moon Inviting, is especially attractive and rivals the great stone boats of China – the Fragrant Isle Boat at Soochow and the Stone Barge at Yangchow.

On the far side of the park, on a small hill, a seven-storey hexagonal pagoda reaches heavenwards. The best time to visit the Chinese Garden is on a Sunday morning, when blushing brides and their grooms arrive in all their finery to have their photographs taken for posterity against a background of classical Chinese architecture. The peak period of these occasions is during the fourth and eighth month of the lunar year, months considered especially auspicious for weddings.

Future historians may be confused when they examine photographs of a bourgeois couple against the background of the Summer Palace in Beijing, and their confusion will increase when, on closer inspection, they note that the vibrant style of the Summer Palace is muted by the placid influences of the Sung dynasty (AD 960 – 1279).

Immediately south of the Chinese Garden, on the second of the three man-made islands, is the **Japanese Garden**, or Seiwaen. Like the Chinese Garden it covers about 12 hectares, and it claims to be one of the world's largest Japanese gardens outside Japan. Therein lies its weakness: It is so large that it lacks the compelling intimacy that one expects in a Japanese garden.

The Japanese Garden is based on models of the 14th and 16th centuries, when Japanese landscape gardening was at its zenith. Facing the traditional entrance gate is a dry garden, or *kare-sansui*, with an arrangement of trees and shrubs, rocks and gravel. These symbolize the natural scenery of mountains and waterfalls, forests and streams, and are also an attempt to recall rural Jurong. Beyond the dry garden are two ponds with several islands, the home of the gods who, it is hoped, will bring eternal prosperity to Singapore.

The third of the three islands is occupied by the **CN West Leisure Park**, which has a wave pool, a water slide and other aquatic amusements, and restaurants. Most of the island is occupied by the 18-hole golf course of the Jurong Country Club.

On the western side of Jurong is its recreational pride and joy – **Jurong Bird Park**, which, occupying 20 sylvan hectares, is one of the world's largest bird parks. Once you pass through the turnstiles you are immediately greeted by excited macaws and cockatoos, and here too, perfectly at home on the equator in their air-conditioned enclosure with a private pool, is a score of penguins.

Board a tram that takes you past secretary birds from Africa, toucans from

*Savour the scenic beauty of
solitary rocks and still waters at the Japanese Garden.*

South America, red birds of paradise from Papua New Guinea, flamingoes from Chile, mynahs from Brazil – to name but a few of the 3500 birds of more than 400 species whose home is in the park. The tour is accompanied by a taped commentary. Alternatively, stroll through the grounds and press buttons on small boxes beside the cages to hear taped commentaries about the birds and their habitats. The rarest birds in the park, six pink Mauritius pigeons and a pair of breeding kiwis, are found in the nocturnal house, where night is transformed into day. Alight from the tram and visit the largest enclosed, walk-in aviary in the world, where, as you stroll through a tropical rainforest below a 30-metre-high waterfall, you'll encounter many more feathered friends.

Early risers might care to enjoy the buffet breakfast on the Songbird Terrace, where they are surrounded by melodious sharmas, thrushes and bulbuls, and where their senses are further stimulated by the Park's most psychedelic parrots which can be stroked and even given a little kiss. Then have your fortune told by a parrot that draws a card from a pack: The card is interpreted for you by the owner of the parrot.

At show time, toucans play catch, cockatoos and parrots ride miniature bicycles, fire cannons and talk. Never again will you call a friend "bird brain"! There are also thrills, when a brahminy kite swoops over tree tops from a kilo-metre away to snatch a tiny morsel of meat or when a sea eagle plucks a fish from the pond and eats it on the wing.

Facing the entrance to the Bird Park is the **Jurong Crocodile Paradise**, where visitors can board another tram to see more than 2500 crocodiles, which, most of the time, are sound asleep! Stops are made at the Underwater Viewing Gallery and the Cavern of Darkness, where the pink eyes of the crocodiles glow in the dark. Far more attractive is a pool containing dozens of fat, glistening goldfish. Not unex-pectedly, the crocs you have just seen – or at least one of their brethren – are served in the crocodalarium's Sea-food Restaurant. Enjoy thin slivers of crocodile meat sautéed with vegetables and chopped chillis, or chunks of croc meat cooked in a claypot, or in a tonic soup brewed with herbs. The Chinese believe that croco meat prevents colds and insomnia.

Tree Planting

After the visit to these nature parks, ascend the road that runs between them, which terminates at **Jurong Hill Park** and its lookout tower. Here, the Jurong Town Corporation has invited distin-guished guests to plant a tree: the first was planted by Princess Alexandra of

Britain in 1969, the last by Deng Xiao Ping of China in 1978. In 1979, the then director-general of the United Nations, Kurt Waldheim, planted the first tree in a second Garden of Fame (created when the first became crowded) outside Jurong Town Hall. While the trees are still standing, many of the dignitaries who planted them have since fallen – like the Shah of Iran (1974), Ferdinand Marcos (1976), US Vice-President Spiro Agnew (1970) and General Zia of Paki-stan (1982).

The S$70-million **Tang Dynasty Village** across the road from the Bird Park opened its doors as Asia's largest cultural and historical theme park. The development re-cre-ates Chang'An in its heyday as the capi-tal of 7th-century Tang Dynasty. The Underground Palace houses 1200 life-sized terracotta warriors in full armour. A fine replica of Emperor Tang Tai Tzong's imperial offices is found at the Imperial Palace.

After you leave the Crocodile Para-dise, turn left into Jalan Boon Lay, which after about five kilometres becomes Jalan Bahar. Another two kilometres, and on the left is the entrance to the **Nanyang Technological University**, the second university in Singapore. The beautiful, verdant campus occupies more than

The highlight of a visit to the Jurong Crocodile Paradise is showtime when men and crocodiles perform acrobatic tricks.

200 hectares. The Nanyang Technological University was originally the Nanyang University, and its origins can be seen in what was once the main administrative building, which is a rather unsuccessful marriage of Chinese and Western architecture. The language of instruction was Chinese. The campus later became the site of the Nanyang Technological Institute, but was granted full university status in 1990. The main strengths of the university are in the fields of business and engineering. Its students number almost 10,000, and, because the university is so isolated, most live on campus.

After you leave the Nanyang Technological University, continue along Jalan Bahar, which after about five kilometres crosses Choa Chu Kang Road and becomes Lim Chu Kang Road. Around this intersection are the Choa Chu Kang cemeteries – Bahai, Buddhist, Chinese, Christian, Jewish, Muslim and Parsi. These cemeteries remain, despite the government's rally for cremation in land-hungry Singapore.

Towards its northern end, Lim Chu Kang Road narrows, turns westwards and passes through a rural area with chicken farms and even a dairy farm. After a few kilometres, the road literally debouches into the Straits of Johor. Immediately offshore are several *kelong* (man-made fish traps on stilts driven into the seabed), which you can visit.

Ornate entrances is a trademark of the Siong Lim Temple.

Pigeons flock to the Siong Lim Temple grounds for their daily feed.

NORTHERN SINGAPORE

Sun Yat Sen Villa is located on Ah Hood Road, off Balestier Road, only 15 minutes from the city centre. This charming colonial house, with its shaded verandahs and pseudo-classical pillars, stands on grounds that were once a sugar plantation owned by Joseph Balestier, the first US consul to Singapore. A bronze statue of Sun Yat Sen, the leader of the Singapore branch of the Tong Meng Hui (a semi-underground body pledged to oust the corrupted Qings), stands before the house. When the Kuomintang was created after the overthrow of the Qing dynasty in China, Sun became the first provincial president of the Republic of China, and this house was the party headquarters. It contains memorabilia and examples of Sun's calligraphy.

From here, proceed to the New Town of Toa Payoh and visit the **Siong Lim Temple** which is one of the largest and most beautiful temples on the island. Building is always in progress at the Twin Groves of the Lotus Mountain Buddhist Temple (the complete Chinese name is Lin Shan Siong Lim Shan Si) but the classical structure of the Buddhist temple with three buildings and three courtyards can be readily discerned. The first hall is graced on either side by two ferocious giant Diamond Kings with blackened faces symbolizing power. The courtyard between this and the princi-

For jogging next to Nature, the tracks at MacRitchie Reservoir is a good choice.

ple prayer hall has a drum tower on the left and a bell tower on the right. Just inside the main hall, which is dedicated to Sakayamuni and on either side of which are the figures of the Eighteen Lohans, are three giant bronze incense burners. At the rear of this hall and facing the third courtyard is the much revered figure of Kwan Yin. Incidentally, if you are feeling under the weather, at the eastern side of the entrance to the temple is a clinic where indigenous medicine is practised.

Immediately to the west of this temple, and within the same compound, is a busier temple which consists of one extremely large room. It is to here that Taoists rather than Buddhists come. At weekends it is frenetically busy with racegoers searching for lucky number combinations to bet on at the weekly races. The temple is also claimed to be an auspicious place at which to decide what four-digit tickets should be purchased in the Singapore lottery.

From here, make for **MacRitchie Reservoir Park**, located near the junction of Lornie and Thomson Roads. This park, one of Singapore's leafiest, is popular with joggers, and at weekends it is often the starting point of national jogathons. Fitness stations are at strategic points, and occasionally a monkey appears to encourage the *homo sapien* in his exertions. A bridge leads to a bandstand in the reservoir, and local bands play

The Phor Kark See Complex makes a fascinating tour — unsuspecting visitors would think they have stumbled into an ancient Chinese film set.

here on Sunday afternoons.

If, as you head northwards on Upper Thomson Road, you have a yen for Chinese architecture rather than modern Western version, turn right onto Bright Hill Drive to find a vast complex of colourful classical Chinese buildings. Those who subscribe to the belief that "big is beautiful" will be delighted by the **Kong Meng San Phor Kark See Temple**. Small wonder that Chinese film-makers find Phor Kark See, as it is generally known, an ideal set: lions, dragons and phoenixes abound, ornate carvings are everywhere, and the colours are dazzling. The only problem is that the expansion of the complex never seems to end.

Some visitors may wish to bypass the older part of Phor Kark See, which consists of crematoriums, columbariums (= halls in which the ashes of the deceased are kept) and a hall of ancestor worship containing thousands of red and gold ancestral tablets, many of which bear a tiny photograph of the deceased. A large, rather unattractive turtle pond is located in this part of the complex, and dozens of stray dogs are well tended here by the monks.

The newer part of the temple, on the eastern slope of the hill, consists of the three main halls of the classical Buddhist temple, but these are separate entities and not joined by courtyards. The first hall is dedicated to Kwan Yin, the

Goddess of Mercy, who appears in a figure with many heads and limbs carved from a single 10-metre-high block of white marble. Behind this hall, across a road, is a room dedicated to Sakayamuni, and this leads, by a series of elaborate covered walkways, to an octagonal chamber of 100 Buddhas, in which all the figures are carved from ice-white marble. The main figure of the Buddha, which stands on a huge lotus composed of thousands of tiny Buddhas, is guarded by ferocious warriors with black horns. Other buildings in the complex include the Dharma Library, an old age home and quarters for the monks.

Back on Upper Thomson Road, proceed for about five kilometres and turn left onto Mandai Road. Stop for lunch at the **Ng Tion Seafood Village** on Lorong Gambas. This is a rural area, with small vegetable plots (a rare sight in Singapore, which has practically no agricultural land). The road is rough, but the distance is only about two kilometres. The seafood village consists of *attap*-roofed wooden structures on stilts at the side of two fish ponds. You can fish here, but if you fail to land a catch the restaurant will cook one according to your instructions. The menu does not list prices, so be sure to check.

Back on Mandai Road, which is lined by soaring trees and innumerable ferns, proceed westwards and, after about two kilometres, turn left onto Mandai Lake Road, which terminates at the **Singapore Zoological Gardens**. The Zoological Gardens are well named, for a fine balance has been maintained between flora and fauna. Attention has been paid to details, and trees are clearly labelled to ensure that visitors enjoy both the botany and the zoology.

The Zoological Gardens cover almost 30 hectares where the animals live in open enclosures – the one where the orangutans roam may be the most attractive. This is the world's largest social colony of such primates. Rarer than the orangutans are the leaf monkeys, with their wizened beige faces and white wrist cuffs: There are fewer than 60 of them in all the zoos in the world. Another attraction is the domain of the lions.

Visitors can practically rub noses with the polar bears (the only examples in the region), which plunge and cavort in their underwater viewing tank. In a

Polar bear in Singapore? At the Zoological Gardens – of course.

Resting in peace at the Kranji War Memorial
are soldiers who perished during World War II.

similar enclosure, visitors can watch crocodiles feed underwater or doze on the sandy banks. Next to the crocodiles are the Komodo dragons, which grow to a length of more than three metres and are the world's largest monitor lizards.

For a quick appraisal of the entire Zoological Gardens, board one of the open-sided trams for a tour accompanied by a taped commentary. Those who prefer to walk can press buttons on small boxes near the animal enclosures and listen to a taped commentary about the species and its habitats.

There is always something happening at the Zoological Gardens – feeding time for the lions, the sealion show or the polar bear show, the elephants en-

joying their bath – the list is almost endless. And then there is breakfast with the orangutans on the terrace of the same name. Not too long ago, before the Republic was awash with tourists, visitors could enjoy an intimate breakfast with Ah Meng, the matriarch of the orangutan colony here. Nowadays, the old lady puts in a token appearance only on Tuesdays and Saturdays while on other days other members of the colony act as hosts. Guests now sit at tables with their human friends – best arrive early at the Terrace or you'll find yourself occupying a table in the middle of the Terrace and surrounded on all sides by *homo sapiens* – while the orangutans sit at a separate table with a

Displays at the Mandai Garden, Singapore's largest commercial orchid garden.

mountain of fruit in front of them. At some point guests line up to be photographed with the orangutan which is on duty that morning.

After you leave the Zoological Gardens, you may wish to stop at **Mandai Orchid Garden**, four hectares of grounds on a hillside that are covered with rare and exotic orchids.

Return to Mandai Road, turn left and proceed for about five kilometres to Woodlands Road. A right turn here takes you to **Kranji War Memorial**, which honours members of the Allied forces

who sacrificed their lives during World War II. Other than a nondescript entrance, the remainder of Kranji, erected in 1946 on a hillside, is immaculate and heart-breaking. If in town on Remembrance Day (the Sunday closest to 11 November), it's worth getting up at dawn for an extraordinary sight here. Standing side by side in prayer at the Memorial are the priests of all the world's great religions, for Singapore has them all: a Parsi, a Hindu, a Jew, a Buddhist, a Roman Catholic Christian, a Protestant Christian, and so on…a rare ecumenical moment – a touching ceremony of reverence for the 24,000 war-dead. Inscriptions on the thousands of stones reveal that many of the dead had scarcely attained their majority.

Return to the city by Woodlands Road, and Upper Bukit Timah Road, and turn left onto Hindhede Road to reach the 70-hectare **Bukit Timah Nature Reserve**. The Nature Reserve, which has been in existence for more than 100 years, is the last forested frontier in Singapore. A large

map at the entrance offers a choice of four walks on well-marked paths that weave through the jungle. The terrain is hilly and attains a height of 165 metres. The best time to visit is late on a weekday afternoon. At weekends the blare of cassette players is likely to drown the shrill chorus of cicadas. Regardless of the crowd, do not brush against the trees or you may be attacked by red ants.

There are more than 100 species of trees, some of which are more than 60 metres tall. The world's oldest Serava tree (350 years) is also to be found here. An infinite variety of fungi and mosses, lichens and liverworts cover their trunks. Palms, shrubs and ferns abound, and, indeed, about 75 percent of the 100 species of ferns in Singapore are found here. The lucky visitor may also see a

lizard or a lemur, a fox or a squirrel, while a macaque monkey is sure to descend from the trees in the hope to be fed. On the ground are snakes, including the reticulated python and the oriental whipsnake.

On your return, about five kilometres from the city, you'll pass **Holland Village**. Do not expect a village green and a duck pond, however. Holland Village is a small enclave of shops and restaurants that serves an expatriate area.

And so to the **Botanic Gardens**, on the fringe of tourist Singapore, a spot popular with joggers. Newlyweds often visit on Sunday mornings, especially in the auspicious fourth and eighth months of the lunar calendar, to be photographed in their wedding finery below jade vines and orange New Guinea creepers. The Gardens have occupied this site since 1859, and their claim to fame is the *Hevea brasiliensis* – introduced here in 1876 from Brazil. Henry Ridley planted five of the rubber seedlings, and he has been known ever since as "Rubber" Ridley. The progeny of these seedlings can be seen in Palm Valley, where the double or sea coconut from the Seychelles, the largest and heaviest seed in the world, also stands. What attracts most visitors, however, are the Gardens' orchids.

A good backdrop for your Ektachrome frame –
the Sentosa Fountain Gardens is patterned after European gardens of the past.

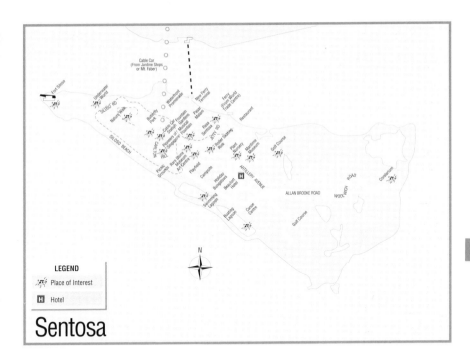

LEGEND

🕸️ Place of Interest

🅷 Hotel

Sentosa

SENTOSA AND THE ISLANDS SOUTH

For that moment of respite from city bustle, visitors head for the southern islands which come closest to the much sought-after "sun, sand and sea" holiday image. The most popular island resort is **Sentosa**. Ferries and cable cars from World Trade Centre get you there while offering fine views of the city, its harbour and the surrounding islands. You can also board the cable car from **Mount Faber**. Do not be content with the view from the cable car station, however, but walk 200 metres eastwards to

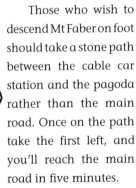

a small pagoda on a hill. Stand here, and all Singapore is yours – the glittering downtown skyline, the serried ranks of high-rise apartments to the north and the east, the bustling port and the oil refineries. Straight ahead are the islands of the Riau archipelago, the closest point of contact between Singapore and Indonesia. To the right is the tip of West Malaysia.

Those who wish to descend Mt Faber on foot should take a stone path between the cable car station and the pagoda rather than the main road. Once on the path take the first left, and you'll reach the main road in five minutes.

The Pioneers of Singapore Chamber offers an insight into the conditions under which Chinese immigrants lived when they first arrived.

Before Sentosa – the Island of Tranquillity – was developed into a holiday resort, it was known as Pulau Blakang Mati, or the Island of the Dead. This is because pirates would hide on Pulau Brani, a small nearby island, attack unsuspecting merchant ships, kill their crews and leave their bodies on Sentosa.

The dead bodies are long gone. Instead, greeting you on arrival are smooth roads bordered by a profusion of tropical flowers. Explore the island sights on foot, by bicycle, by bus, or by a rather slow monorail that stops at five stations on a six-kilometre track.

At the eastern end of the island is **Fort Siloso**, the guns of which did little to protect the island from the Japanese during World War II. They faced the sea rather than the Malay Peninsula, from

Explore the underwater wonder at the Coralarium without getting a toe wet.

Japanese on 15 February 1942. Another tableau shows the scene more than three years later when the Japanese surrendered to the Allies. The nearby **Pioneers of Singapore Chamber** recounts significant events in the evolution of Singapore, also in tableaux of wax.

Among the thousands of shells in the **Coralarium** are such treasures as the Glory of the Sea, the Cone of Bengal, the Golden Cowrie and the Rosebranch Murex, but the *pièce de résistance* is undoubtedly the Coral Cave, the highlight of which is two tanks of immaculate brain coral, in brilliantly fluorescent yellow and gold, lime and egg shell blue, mauve and purple.

Visitors to the **Underwater World** enter a curved acrylic tunnel through which they can observe and become part of a tropical marine environment. Entrance to the Underwater World is by a bridge over a pool in which there are

where the Japanese advanced, and they were fixed in position: the rest is history. The guns are part of a four-hectare maze of underground tunnels, ammunition bunkers and searchlight posts.

The consequences of the Fort Siloso fiasco can be seen in the **Surrender Chamber**, in which a tableau of wax consists of life-size and life-like figures reenacting the British surrender to the

Pedal boats at the Lagoon provide a safe form of water sports.

Lining the Valley of Spirits are totem poles flown in from different countries.

Green and Hawksbill turtles. Beyond this is another pool where visitors can handle harmless marine creatures such as starfish and hermit crabs.

On to the **Maritime Museum**, which boasts several primitive craft from local waters as well as a visual history of the development of the port of Singapore. The most unusual **Rare Stones Museum** contains more than 1000 stones with natural imprints of landscapes, famous people and animals, Chinese characters and numerals. Far more lively is the **Butterfly Park**, where more than 3000 brilliantly coloured butterflies, which represent more than 50 species, fly free. Less fortunate are the 4000 butterflies that are mounted, with scor-

The Musical Fountain cascade dances to different tunes –
a wonderful sight to behold.

pions, beetles and other insects.

Fitness enthusiasts can roller-skate at the largest rink in Southeast Asia, rent a bicycle or jog on the well-marked jogging paths. Half the enormous lagoon is reserved for bathing, half for other activities such as canoeing, windsurfing and aquabiking. The beach is attractive, especially at Fort Siloso.

In the evening, the **Musical Fountain** comes to life, with its music, coloured lights and dancing water. The Enchanted Grove of Tembusu, with

its fortune-telling genie, babbling ponds and two-metre-long clay lion, is transformed into a fairyland with nocturnal sound effects. After the Musical Fountain, eat at the Rasa Sentosa hawker foodstalls or the seafood restaurant, or shop at the *pasar malam* (= night market), which only opens at weekends.

Other Islands

Kusu, the second most popular of the southern islands, lies a few kilometres beyond Sentosa: you

Some locals believe that Kusu Island was transformed from a turtle to save two drowning sailors.

can reach it from the World Trade Centre in 25 minutes. The views of the Singapore skyline from Kusu are stunning, and they are frequently enhanced when an enormous container ship, low in the water because of its host of brightly coloured containers, glides past.

The tiny island of Kusu has two small lagoons bordered by beaches and a third crossed by a white Chinese bridge with attractive red and green gazebos in the centre and at either end. Large turtles are said to occupy this lagoon – there are certainly a couple of stone ones – and many small turtles are found in a small tank in the grounds of the **Tuah Peh Kong Temple**, which stands on the seaward side of the lagoon.

Tuah Peh Kong, the God of Prosperity, is unknown in China but very popular with overseas Chinese. This temple in his honour was built with a donation from a wealthy businessman, Chia Cheng Ho. The principal deities in this Taoist temple are Tuah Peh Kong and the ubiquitous Kwan Yin. Devotees pray to these gods for five blessings – wealth, longevity, love of virtue, tranquillity and fulfilled destiny.

From the temple, 152 steep steps, flanked by a gold-painted stair rail, lead to the summit of the island and three *kramat* (Muslim shrines).

Ten minutes from Kusu is the far larger **St John's Island**, with delightful beaches and many trees to offer protec-

A visit to Pulau Seking is like a walk into the past, when Singapore was just a fishing village on stilts.

tion from the sun. Several government and private organizations have chalets here. Visitors should note that food is not available on either Kusu or St John's.

Two ferries a day ply between the World Trade Centre and Kusu and St John's (nine a day on Sundays and public holidays), except during the Pilgrimage to Kusu, in or about October, when a vast fleet of craft leaves Clifford Pier bringing boatloads of worshippers to the island (also see page 80). On Sundays and public holidays, the ferry makes a circuit of the World Trade Centre, Kusu and St John's, then back to the World Trade Centre. Half an hour is spent at Kusu, which allows time to visit the Chinese temple but not to the *kramat*.

During the week, the ferry stops at Kusu both before and after St John's.

For more pristine beaches and less crowds, the islands further afield are better options, especially for visitors yearning for a bit of snorkelling and scuba diving. The **Sisters Islands** (twin islands, hence the name) and **Pulau Hantu** ("ghost island" – ghosts are its only inhabitants, so the local story goes) are good diving spots, while **Pulau Seking** boasts Singapore's last surviving Malay fishing village (see page 183). Take a picnic when visiting any of these islands; food is also on sale at the piers before embarkation. Hired boats or *sampan* from Jardine Steps or Clifford Pier take you to these islands daily.

A Chinese banquet – a visual and a gastronomic treat.

E

ating is the national pastime and passion. Singaporeans were foodies long before foodism became the vogue. A nation which will drive across town simply to try a new restaurant or for the best seafood is a nation of foodies. Singaporeans seem to be eating at every hour of the day – or night. A food stall somewhere on the island will be open, whatever the time and most Singaporeans know where to go for his or her favourite local dish. They even arrange meals with birds and animals. Breakfast with Singapore's highest paid model Ah Meng, the Zoological Gardens's orangutan star, is considered a high point for many visitors.

The mass production of spicy fish head curry – a hot favourite, both literally and figuratively, among the locals.

Equally, a visitor is more likely to be asked what food he has tried rather than what he has seen. Suggestions on what to do always seem to revolve around food. The business lunch is as likely to take place in a posh air-conditioned restaurant as

Food Fare

211

To many people, Indian food means curry — do you blame them?

in a more downmarket hawker centre. Smartly-dressed executives and business-men complete with briefcases tuck enthusiastically into their bowls of noodles. The business lunch is as much a culinary adventure as a business meeting and while they eat, Singaporeans will talk about food of course! The uninitiated who starts to talk business is firmly told "Eat first"!

Everyone and anyone has an opinion about food, what's good and what are the latest discoveries. Food reviewers are almost like pop stars with their own following. Every newspaper gives space to food and there is even a paper devoted solely to food.

Food ideas abound and everyone's mother, father, grandmother or aunt

has a favourite dish foodies will kill for. So the food business is big business and few restaurants or food outlets cater solely for tourists. Almost everywhere, the visitor will find locals eating alongside him. Even the posh hotel restaurants, which in other countries depend mainly on the patronage of their in-house guests, have a large percentage of local clientele. In fact there are enough restaurants, outlets and variety of food to keep any foodie eating different meals at different places for months on end without having to repeat himself.

Singaporeans eat an eclectic diet daily: an Indian-style breakfast may be followed by a steak or chops for lunch and a Chinese dinner in the evening. Or dinner could well be a combination of an Indian curry, a Chinese stir-fried vegetable, a Thai soup and a Malay dessert. For tea, there are first rate European tortes and cheesecakes at hotel coffee houses, and a variety of local fast-food, curry puffs and other local snacks to choose from.

The classic cuisines of the various ethnic groups which settled here are blended with the food ideas of the visitors from all over the world: American fast-food, European, Japanese and Korean, Thai, Vietnamese and Indonesian among others. There is even a local pizza chain. American fast-food chains stretch across the island. French and Italian food are immensely popular.

Hello, John! Roti John?

Singapore is well-known for "cross-cultural cuisine" blending elements from many great culinary cultures into a single, unique Singaporean dish – Indian fried noodles (*mee goreng*) and Chinese fish head curry are two good examples (see main story on this page).

But one of the strangest – and one of the rarest in these post-colonial days – is the streetside food-hawker's *Roti John*.

Roti in local parlance is bread, and usually one of the flat breads such as the Indian *roti paratha* or the lacey Malay *roti jala*. Roti John, however, is based on a stick of French bread and is a legacy of colonial times when all Caucasians were called "John" by the locals for convenience, since they couldn't tell one white man from another.

Roti John, simply, is a Singapore version of French toast – the bread dipped in egg with chopped onions and minced mutton, and fried crisp, with a topping of chilli-hot sambal. Delicious – try it at the older food centres, such as the one opposite the Botanic Gardens, and at the downtown Maxwell Road market.

With the close proximity of so many cuisines and the availability of a wide range of ingredients, there are unique hybrid dishes to be found nowhere else. Indian *mee goreng* is truly Indian but is found only in Singapore. It does not exist in India because *mee* or cooked wheat noodles is a Chinese ingredient. The same goes for *mee soto* which marries the delicious spicy Indonesian soup called *soto* with Chinese wheat noodles. Fish head curry has a strong claim to being a Singaporean dish. Indian curry restaurants sell this sour spicy favourite to droves of multiracial customers who would be hard put to find such a dish in India as fish head is not a prized ingredient in traditional Indian cooking.

The queen of hybrid cuisines is, of course, Straits Chinese cuisine, a mixture of Malay and Chinese resulting from the intermarriage of these two races. Pork, prohibited in traditional Muslim Malay cuisine, features in several classic Straits Chinese dishes rooted in Malay cuisine like satay babi and ayam buah keluak, the former a satay made with pork, the latter a spicy curry with pickled nuts, pork ribs and chicken. Chinese food like stewed braised pork get a special twist here as *babi pong teh* which is fragrant with spices and eaten with green chilli or *sambal belacan*, another Malay culinary favourite.

The original division of the town into different ethnic areas gave rise to areas well-known for certain kinds of food. The cuisines of the early settlers are still entrenched in these areas al-

Dim sum is a popular lunch-time treat. Served piping hot, they come in small portions – the idea is to try a little of every dish.

Of course, MacDonald's is here too.

though the ethnic groups are now spread throughout the island. The Chinese from southern China like Xiamen and Swatow were among the first to settle here. Chinatown is not the place to look for the refined cooking of the Beijing Imperial court, the fiery dishes from Sichuan and Hunan, or the sophistication of Shanghainese food. For these, go outside Chinatown into the fancy restaurants in hotels and shopping complexes. Chinatown is the stronghold for hearty southern provincial cooking.

Ellenborough Market has more than the wholesalers of Chinese dried goods. It also has good plain Teochew cooking where steaming is the principal way of cooking. Steamed fish and prawns, stir-fried vegetables and meats of various

kinds are all washed down with strong Chinese tea in tiny cups, a very Teochew touch which even the posh air-conditioned Teochew restaurants have kept.

Then there is Hokkien (or Fujian) cuisine strong on braised dishes with thick robust sauces redolent of garlic. One classic is braised pork eaten with steamed buns; others are oyster omelette, spring rolls known locally as *popiah*, and Hokkien mee both in soup and fried. The best Hokkien restaurant in town is in the Overseas Chinese Banking Corporation Building, a bank which was originally founded on the wealth and hard work of the Hokkien community, still the largest dialect group in Singapore today.

The Hainanese who were latecom-

Satay – the irresistible marinated barbecued meat served with peanut sauce –
is fast becoming an international snack.

ers settled in the Beach Road-North Bridge Road area. It was they who contributed the much-loved chicken rice to the local food fare. Even today, there are good chicken rice restaurants to be found in this area near the Raffles Hotel.

Further down the street is the old Muslim enclave in the Arab Street area. This is where traditional Indian Muslim food like *biryanis, murtabaks* and *parathas* are found. A short distance away near the beach was the original Satay Club, a collection of Malay stalls selling the little skewers of grilled meat eaten with a spicy peanut sauce. Malay satay goes down well with everyone who makes its acquaintance, and there are even Chinese hybrids using pork and seafood. The stalls were later moved to its present

location on the Esplanade where there is still a good selection of Malay food.

For southern Indian food, vegetarian or otherwise, the streets in Little India in Serangoon Road are the places to seek out the banana leaf restaurants serving a wide range of hot curries and rice and Indian bread. And much like northern Chinese cuisines, Moghul cuisine from the north arrived late on the scene – now only available in upmarket shopping complexes and hotels.

Cheap And Good

To many foodies though, hawker food has no parallel. It is certainly the cheapest. It is also the original Singapore fast-

Hawker Food

It is the original alfresco dining: tables and stools placed under the stars although most hawker centres these days are under cover. Still, there are a few around where night is the only canopy and woe betide the diner if the weather fails to cooperate. Fortunately most tropical evenings are balmy and the short tropical downpours usually come after lunch.

The backbone of hawker food is the enormous range of rice and wheat noodles. The Chinese will fix them differently from the Malays and Indians; a typical hawker centre would have a mix of ethnic offerings. Malay and Chinese satay is cheek by jowl with Indian *mee goreng* and various Chinese noodles. There may also be stalls specializing in seafood, vegetarian food, and curry and rice. Here and there steaks, chops and hot dogs may have crept in but the hot favourites, literally and figuratively, are still the spicy noodles like *ta mee* (noodles without soup), beef noodles, Hokkien fried noodles and both fish ball noodles and Hokkien mee soup.

There are also stalls specializing in desserts like ice *kacang*, ice jelly, *chendol,* sea coconut and banana fritters to end the meal plus fruits. To quench the thirst, there are fruit and sugarcane juices and soya bean milk among the usual coffee, tea and soft drinks.

Feel free to sit wherever you want. You do not have to patronize the stalls near your table unless you want to. Ordering food at a hawker centre is simplicity itself. Start by taking a good look at what your neighbours are having, decide if you would like to try that, then check out from which stall the food came. Stalls often display the names of their specialty as well as prices. These start from the usual minimum of $1.50 for most noodle dishes to much more for the costly fresh seafood items like chilli crabs or barbecued fish. The food is brought to your table and you pay when it arrives. When ordering seafood check out prices first as these fluctuate according to market rates; that way, there are no nasty surprises when the bill arrives.

Opening hours vary. Some stalls serve mostly breakfast and lunch, others lunch and dinner, and yet others dinner and supper. Some centres open from lunch time till the wee hours of the morning. One with a good mix of both tourist and local traffic and is open till very late is the Newton Hawker Centre at the start of Clemenceau Avenue. Prices here are a little higher because of the tourist traffic, but the variety is good. Also check out the Cuppage Centre near Centrepoint in Orchard Road.

There are few niceties to traditional hawker dining which are very basic. In recent years, gentrification has set in. Many hawkers have moved indoors into comfortable air-conditioned food halls in shopping complexes. Hawker food has even been adopted by the most elegant of coffee shops in the international hotels. Their offerings have a following among the locals in search of comfort. Served on beautiful china and in smart air-conditioned surroundings, the upmarket product carries a more upmarket price tag.

For a casual and economical meal, nothing beats the variety at the omnipresent hawker stalls.

When it comes to seafood, "Fresh is Best".

food: cheap food quickly prepared for the many bachelors in the migrant community working hard to support families in their home countries and without the time to cook for themselves.

Hawking food was also an easy way of making money for those with minimum capital. The one-man-kitchen on wheels was moved around by the cook. Bamboo clappers and distinctive calls announced their arrival in the neighbourhood. Today government policy has moved them into hawker centres with proper waste disposal and regular sanitary inspections but the "cheap and good" tag still holds. Nowadays modern food courts in air-conditioned complexes are a step up from stuffy hawker centres. (Also see box story on page 217.)

As befits an island, seafood is a staple in all the cuisines. Statisticians say a whopping 65 million kilos of seafood is consumed annually, some of it kept alive until just minutes before being popped into the wok (the Chinese frying pan). In certain specialty seafood restaurants, you can even pick your dinner live from a tankful of swimming fish, lobster, prawn, crayfish or crab. Seafood restaurants are found all over the island, varied and well worth a visit. The ones at the East Coast Park make the perfect ending to a day at the beach.

There are more ways to fix seafood than heaven can dream of, but surely the *pièce de résistance* for many a Singapore epicurean is chilli crab. You have to work hard to extract the tender morsels from the shell but it is worth the hard work. Much easier to do is polishing off a perfectly steamed fresh fish.

When it comes to food, "fresh is best" is the national motto. This accounts for the proliferation of wet markets, supermarkets and oddly enough, cooked food centres. If you have no time to cook your own fresh food, it makes sense to buy it freshly cooked or eat out!

For anyone interested in food and cooking, a trip to a wet market is a worthwhile experience. See what the raw ingredients of the dishes you have been enjoying look like. But be prepared for a rather damp and strong-smelling experience especially if you go towards the end of the day. Not for nothing are they called "wet markets". The drip of ice and water and regular hosing down keep the floor permanently wet.

Liveliest of these wet markets is

Cockles dipped in chilli sauce is a popular in-between-meal snack.

Zhujiao market in Little India. Open from early morning till evening, it has an incredible array of fresh produce for the varied cuisines of Singapore. The vegetable stalls brim over with all manner of edible vegetation – herbs, roots, leaves and blooms. On the fishmongers' stands lie the ocean's bounty, the shellfish still wriggling and very much alive.

The butcher will sell you only one kind of meat be it pork, beef, mutton or lamb. Islam strictures prohibit pork and all animals must be killed in a prescribed manner. To the Hindu, beef is taboo and many Chinese do not care for mutton or lamb. No wonder the butcher is a specialist, and pork, beef, mutton and poultry are sold at separate stalls.

Fruit is an unbelievable riot of colour and variety from all over the world: plums from Austrialia, apples from the United States, mandarins from China, persimmons from Japan, kiwifruit from New Zealand, pears from Europe and tropical fruit from the region (see box story on pages 220/221).

The island grows little of its food. Almost everything is imported and since the country is affluent, it can afford to go for the best and the authentic. No specialist restaurant has to make do with substitutes. The real thing can always be found for a price. Sometimes even the real McCoy is flown in to prepare authentic ethnic cuisines. These ethnic food promotions are crowd-pullers. Since ingredients are often the best, some insist that the dish tastes better here than back in the country of origin!

Tropical Treats

Apples and oranges there are aplenty in the supermarkets, but you'd be missing out on a memorable experience if you did not sample the delicious variety of tropical fruits, indigenous to this region.

Besides the supermarkets, the hawker centres are an inviting testing ground. The fruit stalls display abundant varieties of them, cut into slices and neatly arranged on blocks of ice to tempt passers-by. For as little as 50 cents a piece, you could try out several fruits in one go.

These stalls can also produce fresh fruit juices on the spot, with any concoction that catches your fancy. Have you always wondered how pears and oranges would go with watermelon? Or how bananas go with papaya and spoonfuls of milk? Well, for as little as S$2 you can try your own fruit cocktail.

Some fruits may appear a little daunting at first, especially the ones with poky bristles on the exterior, but as the locals believe, the more forbidding the outside, the sweeter and the fleshier the fruit inside.

Tropical fruits in abundance – quality, quantity and variety.

Durian

A fine example of this is the "king of fruits", the Durian. Visitors to Singapore are generally astonished by the locals' passion for this sharp spiked, thick-skinned fruit with the most unbelievable aroma. Some have likened that aroma to a jasmine bush in a cesspit.

So all-pervasive is this aroma that the fruit is banned on airlines and public transport. Yet almost all Singaporeans are hooked on this mystic fruit.

The secret lies in its delicious insides. The thick skin hides a fruit with the most incredible sweetness and creaminess. Is it any wonder, the fruit contains 12 percent sugar and 11 percent starch. Twice a year, this wondrous fruit finds its way from the trees in West Malaysia, to Singapore, sending the Singaporeans into a frenzy of buying and eating durians.

Overnight, durian stalls spring up in Chinatown and baskets of the fruit change hands after much sniffing and haggling. It's almost akin to a wine tasting session. The thick skin is cut open to reveal four of five large segments of creamy white fruit. Each segment contains two to six seeds. It is this fruit that is eaten with such gusto. Durian is also pureed and prepared as an ice cream or durian cake.

Jackfruit

Another strongly aromatic fruit, the Jackfruit, has the distinction of being the largest cultivated fruit. It can grow up to 90 cm long and weigh up to 44 kilos. The commoner varieties however, generally weigh 10 to 20 kilos.

On the outside the skin is a pale green, dotted with sharp hexagonal spines. The centre of the fruit consists of large brown seeds, each covered by golden pulp that is very sweet and

a bit rubbery. When the Jackfruit is sold in segments, the seeds are extracted from the fruit and placed on ice before being consumed.

The "Jack" is conjectured to be a Portuguese mispronunciation of the Malay word meaning round. The Malays use the leaf and root of the Jackfruit tree for several medicinal purposes and the sap is used as an effective remedy against snake bites.

Papaya

Although its origins lie in Central America, this luscious fruit has been a firm favourite in Southeast Asia since the 16th century. Inside the thin green or yellow skin, the fruit can be yellow, orange or reddish orange with a dense centre of small, glutinous black seeds. These are removed before serving. It is a very popular breakfast fruit, with a dash of fresh lime. The fruit is rich in Vitamins A and C and has laxative properties, much like prunes.

Papaya trees grow easily in this climate, but unlike most other trees, there are female and male papaya trees.

Rambutan

The fruit hangs down in clusters from the tree, and from a distance, one could almost mistake them for red flowers. On the outside, the fruit looks spiky, but the spikes are soft and can be handled easily. Rambutan derives its name from the Malay word for hair, *rambut*. The skin of the fruit is cut at the centre, to reveal the white juicy fruit which covers a large seed.

Thai folk lore tells of a young girl who chooses a man with a gruesome mask and curly hair to be her husband, because she believes that under the mask he will be handsome and good. Just like the sweet rambutan under its spiky exterior.

Mangosteen

Queen Elizabeth II was so taken with this fruit on a visit to Malaysia, that the country now sends a basket of the first fruit of the season to the Monarch every year.

It is easy to understand the Queen's preference, for this delicate fruit which is sweet yet tangy, has a pleasing aroma, and is considered the queen of fruits. The pearly white segments are enclosed in a thick, purplish covering which is as unattractive as the fruit is delectable.

Watermelon

On a hot day, nothing is more refreshing than a slice of this juicy, cooling fruit. As its name suggests, is consists mainly of water and sugar, with lots of black seeds embedded in the red flesh. The sun-dried seeds are greatly relished by the locals and can be bought in pouches from the supermarkets.

You really can shop till you drop in Singapore…
and then you can get up and shop some more!

A sk any visitor to Singapore what he or she considers one of the most exciting aspects of the city, and the reply is almost certain to be "shopping". It's not just that so many goods on sale are duty-free, or that the shops are so often modern, air-conditioned and convenient. The fantastic variety of merchandise lends a feeling of excitement to shopping here. It's as if you've stumbled upon a great treasure chest, full of goods from all over the world.

Everpresent are multi-level modern shopping complexes which boast one-stop shopping.

Lift the lid and run your fingers through a heap of jade and pearls, smoothe an antique Persian carpet, rub a length of Chinese silk, study the intricate patterns of a piece of *batik* cloth, play with the latest electronic marvel, gaze in wonder at a carved ivory figure, try a Malaysian kite, walk in a pair of sleek Italian shoes...

Because Singapore is conveniently situated at the crossroads of Asia, shopping here is a different experience: it is like being able to

Shopping

Fine cloth interwoven with gold and silver threads
is an ancient art highly valued today.

explore several countries without having to visit them. Here, certain areas are famous for specific products and often offer you a tantalizing glimpse into its multicultural heritage.

Arab Street is known for its sturdy basketware, hats, handbags and other paraphernalia made of soft rattan and wicker. It is also the ideal place to buy textiles, especially cotton batik. Tablemats, cushion covers, tablecloths, bedspreads and rugs are also to be found along the many quaint side streets and shops of Arab Street.

Serangoon Road also known as "Little India" has many similar shops which are literally crammed to the ceiling with everything under the sun. Look out especially for brass shops selling

old opium weights, ornate snuff bottles, ship lanterns and bric-à-brac. Tough Indian cottons, bright rugs and jute wall hangings painstakingly handcrafted by local Indian women can be found in the shops dotting this vicinity.

Suburban **Holland Village** has curio shops selling ornate cloisonné and enamelware, embroidered silk panels (both antique and modern) which can be framed and used as interior decor, and Straits-Chinese beaded purses and belts. Reminiscent of Singapore's past, they make perfect mementoes.

At the **Ming Village** off Pandan Road you can buy handcrafted and handpainted replicas of famous porcelain pieces of the early Chinese dynasties. Watching the craftsmen at work in the adjacent factory warehouse is half the fun. Porcelain buys are guarantee-packed for safety and can be shipped home at nominal shipping rates.

Chinatown's nooks and crannies are filled with authentic Chinese handicrafts: Chinese calligraphy, opera masks, red clogs and decorative tiles.

Truly, Singapore is like a vast emporium. Although you can buy just about anything you want, there are certain must-buy items:

Antiques

Treasures from all over Asia are available here. Chinese antiques naturally dominate the field, with lovely porcelain, carpets, snuff bottles, incense burners, carvings (in wood, jade and ivory) and furniture being the most common items.

Chinese ceramics are especially popular among collectors. Most of them on sale date from the Ming dynasty (1368-1644) or the Qing period (1644-1912), although even earlier pieces are available. Blue and white ware, and celadon are the most common, and pieces in white, soft blue or *famille rose* can also be found. Snuff bottles are popular with both collectors and visitors as mini examples of the artistry of Chinese craftsmen. The bottles are usually quite small (6 to 8 cm high), made from an astonishing variety of materials and are sometimes carved in quixotic shapes.

Less valuable, and perhaps better described as "old" rather than antique,

are dozens of interesting items to be found in the junk shops of Singapore – old Chinese silk clothing, embroidered altar cloths, jewellery, brass incense burners, silver water pipes, teapots and lacquered miniature altars.

Neighbouring Malaysia and Indonesia provide a host of interesting old items, such as carvings from Java and Bali (including small chests and other pieces of furniture, masks and puppets). *Kris*, the Malay ceremonial wavy-bladed dagger; superb tie-dyed or *ikat* textiles; silk *batik* scarves; jewellery and *gamelan* musical instruments make the range of antiques fascinating. Other Indonesian antiques are to be found – mostly brass or bronze figures, oil lamps and jewellery – but the buyer should be aware that similar modern items are available, and it is not always easy to distinguish these from the real antiques.

Batik

There is some debate as to where this ancient art originated – some say the Middle East, others China – but there is no doubt at all that the *batik* of Singapore, Malaysia and Indonesia is a must-buy for all visitors.

Batik fabric is patterned and dyed by a wax-resistant process. A design or motif is sketched onto a piece of white cloth, then outlined, either by hand or with a copper stamp (*cap*), in wax. The cloth is dipped into dye, with the waxed portions uncoloured. The wax is then re-

Singapore's reputation as a haven for duty-free electronics is world-famous.

moved after dyeing. Most Singapore *batik* involves only this process, which results in a white pattern on a coloured background, but the more complex traditional *batik* of Java may involve many different waxing and dyeing processes, giving a detailed, multi-coloured effect.

Hand-printed or *tulis batik* involves a great deal of fine detailed work, and the resulting length of material can be very expensive. Stamped *batik* is usually of very good quality, however, and a length is relatively inexpensive. Lengths of cotton or *voile batik* can be made into garments or soft furnishings, or shirts, skirts, dresses and other items.

Because *batik* is made of natural fabric, it is comfortably cool. The colours and patterns make it very distinc-

tive, a unique and practical souvenir from Singapore. Incidentally, the *batik* process is not confined to fabric for garments or soft furnishings: Small *batik* "paintings" or hangings can also be purchased. *Batik* is usually sold in *sarong* lengths (about 2.3 metres). If you see a piece that you like, ask to see the length unfolded. Often you'll find an attractive border which complements the main colour scheme of the piece.

Batik plays a unique role in Singapore: It is the base fabric for its National Dress Collection. When the idea of a national dress was mooted the first efforts that emerged were the rather unsuccessful marriage of traditional costume styles of the three major racial groups in Singapore. After much debates and deliberation, the national dress finally took shape in the form of *batik* garments made to any design with an orchid motif.

Cameras

Cameras and other photographic equipment are duty-free in Singapore, and all major brands are on sale. Price lists are available on request, and discounts, which range from 5 to 40 percent, are usually given. Be sure to bargain, to compare prices before you buy, and to ask for a warranty card.

Carpets

You can spend thousands of dollars on a superb silk Persian rug or a few dollars on a modest Indian *numdah*. You may prefer a woollen Chinese carpet, in which the design seems to have been carved into the pile, or a nomadic Turkish rug.

Carpets are duty-free in Singapore, making this one of the best places in the world to invest in a fine Persian rug. Although Persian carpets, and to a lesser extent the cheaper (but nevertheless handmade) Pakistani carpets, are well-known, don't overlook the traditional Chinese carpets. Some antiques are available, but modern reproductions of old-style Taiping carpets are made in Singapore. These are of excellent quality, and you can even have a carpet made to your own design.

Electrical Appliances

If it can be operated by electricity, you can buy it in Singapore, and at duty-free prices. Grown men and women have been known to behave like children around a Christmas tree when buying electrical appliances here. There are food processors, blenders, coffee grinders, irons, hair dryers, shavers, calculators, rice cookers, kettles... the list is endless.

When you buy an electrical appliance, be sure to check that it is of the same voltage as in your own country.

Electrical appliances are available in most shopping centres.

Fabrics

Cloth from Europe and the United States can be purchased at very reasonable prices. Most visitors take great delight in the fabrics of the east. Chinese silks, often in beautiful soft shades, are available at a fraction of the cost of silks made elsewhere. Brightly coloured rayons and brocades in traditional Chinese patterns are also available.

The exquisite colours and superb quality of Thai silks have made them much sought-after the world over. Several local shops specialize in Thai silk and cotton, both in fabric lengths and made into garments and accessories.

Apart from *batik*, the Malaysians also produce fine cloth interwoven with gold and silver thread. Quality and price vary, depending largely on the base

During sales everything must go — even at giveaway prices.

New York, Florence, Tokyo and Sydney.

All kinds of shoes, bags and fashion accessories are available here. Prices of imported fashion goods are generally on par with those in their country of origin. Most visitors are delighted to learn that locally made fashions are a fraction of the price of imported clothes, and are generally of the latest style.

One of the great attractions of Singapore is local tailoring. Clothes for both men and women can be made for surprisingly low prices, the quality is good and the service speedy. You can buy your own fabric, such as *batik*, Thai silk or Chinese brocade, and take it to the tailor, or select from the good range at his shop. Another popular item is the embroidered lengths of cotton from the Philippines, which can be made into the *barong Tagalog* shirt.

Furs

Although it may seem strange to think of furs in the tropical climate, you may want to take home the relatively inexpensive fine furs from the USSR, China and other countries on sale here.

Handicrafts

An astonishing array of Asian handicrafts is on sale in shops, department stores and Chinese emporiums. Woodcarvings (particularly from the Philippines and Indonesia), *batik*, silver, pewter, rattan and cane, oiled paper, lac-

material used. The finest *kain songket* (as this fabric is called) is made from silk. Indian *saris*, 5.5-metre lengths of glorious fabric in silk, chiffon, *voile* or nylon, are an excellent buy. So too are lengths of Filipino *jusi* or *pina* fabric.

Fashion Wear

Although some local women can still be seen in their *saris*, *sarong kebaya* and *cheongsam*, just as many look as if they have stepped out from the pages of the latest fashion magazine. Men's fashion has also improved vastly, and in the shopping centres, hotel shopping arcades and boutiques you can find top designer clothes from Paris, London,

A Chinatown shop crammed to the ceiling with quaint souvenir items.

quered goods, copper and brass ornaments, and a host of other intriguing goods are available at reasonable prices.

Jewellery

The variety that is present in every facet of Singapore is also gloriously visible in its jewellery. Buy an antique jade pendant or cheap Indian glass bangles. Bedeck yourself with a string of Japanese cultured pearls or a sophisticated Italian-designed ring. Dress up like a Malay princess in delicate filigree silver or dazzle the eye with diamonds.

Jewellery is cheaper in Singapore than in most other countries, and a high standard of workmanship is combined with an internationally acceptable taste in design. Jade is not just green; it ranges from snow white to lilac. Not forgetting, gold, freshwater and cultured pearls, rubies, diamonds, sapphires, emeralds, coral and ivory. The choice is yours.

Pewter

Pewter, an alloy of tin, copper and antimony, has graced the banquet tables of the ancient Chinese and Britons, the Romans and other races throughout the centuries. It is as popular today, with its lovely satin finish and its adaptability suitable for the most modern styles. And, because pewter is a poor conductor of heat, there's nothing better to keep beer cold than a pewter tankard.

Pewter made in Singapore and Ma-

High-quality craftsmanship and the latest in designs
give local jewellers the marketing edge.

laysia will invariably be about 30 percent cheaper than elsewhere because tin is mined in nearby Malaysia. Pewterware can be found in most department stores and in pewter boutiques; also visit the Pewter Museum (see page 159).

Reptile Skin Goods

Many years ago, after a particularly heavy downpour of rain, residents were warned to watch out for crocodiles. The reason? Crocodiles were then farmed in tanks until they are large enough to be "converted" into shoes, handbags and other items, and, on this occasion, the rain had caused the tanks – and some of the baby crocodiles – to overflow!

These days, it's the shops that overflow with high-quality skins fashioned into all kinds of accessories, available at a fraction of their cost overseas.

Silverware

Delicate filigree silver from Malaysia and Indonesia, and silverware from Italy, Germany, England and Scandinavia are good buys in Singapore.

Sound Equipment

You will hear the sound of music from shops and shopping centres all over, as locals and visitors enthusiastically try the latest radios, stereos, cassette players, compact disc players, television sets

Shopper's Tips

Before you buy the town, here are a few tips:

• **Ignore touts**. Touts, who may approach you in the streets, at the airport or even in your hotel, should be avoided at all costs, no matter how attractive their propositions. They will recommend that you buy at certain shops, and probably even arrange to take you there. But remember, this service is not free, and the price you pay for goods bought via a tout will include his commission. Touting is illegal islandwide, although only some shopping centres where touting has been more notorious, have signs to announce that. Touts are also known to use physical force to coerce people into buying their goods. Some taxi drivers moonlight as touts so watch out for that over-friendly driver who insists you do your shopping at a shop he recommends.

• **Compare Prices**. Prices may vary considerably, depending on the location of the shop, the amount of business it handles, your bargaining ability and so on. If you prefer to buy where prices are fixed, head for the major department stores. Otherwise, shop around in the shopping centres, where there will be many shops selling the same products and you do not have to walk far to obtain several quotations.

• **Examine Goods Carefully**. Check your goods thoroughly for any flaws before you buy or pay a deposit, as goods sold are normally not returnable. If you want a specific brand, ask for it by name and then check that the name is actually imprinted somewhere on the product, and not only on the packaging.

• **Warranties**. Make sure an international warranty card is included if applicable. If the shopkeeper cannot provide one, he may be selling you a parallel import, which is an item intended for the domestic market in its country of manufacture. In other words the seller has imported the item bypassing its local authorized agent. This practise is not illegal – just be sure you are prepared to do without a guarantee for your purchase. Even if you are, compare the prices for the item with and without the guarantee. If it is only marginally different, it may be better to be safe than sorry.

• **Swopped Goods**. Make sure what you paid for has not been exchanged for another product during packing.

• **STPB Sticker**. Look for the red Merlion sticker in shop windows. This is a sign that the retailer is approved by the Consumer's Association of Singapore (CASE) and the Singapore Tourist Promotion Board (STPB).

A booklet listing reputable shopkeeper members of the association is available at the information lobby of major shopping centres.

• **Credit Cards**. Major credit and charge cards are widely accepted. Some shops add a surcharge for purchases made with charge cards. Some of the main credit card companies are:-

American Express   Tel: 235 8133
Carte Blanche   Tel: 339 2922
Diners   Tel: 294 4222

• **Shipping & Insurance**. If the store is doing this for you, make sure your purchase is adequately insured.

• **Imitation Goods**. These do not come with guarantee cards and are sold by touts.

• **Receipts**. Make sure that purchases like jewellery are accompanied by receipts with details like carat, colour, clarity and the percentage of precious metals included.

• **Grievances**. Contact CASE at tel: 222 4165 or STPB at tel: 339 6622.

and video recorders. All these items are duty-free, and the best and the latest from all over the world can be found.

Be sure to buy from a reputable dealer, and compare prices before you buy. Bargaining is expected.

Watches

A duty-free bargain that few visitors can resist. The range runs from cheap children's watches, to the latest professional and elegant dress watches.

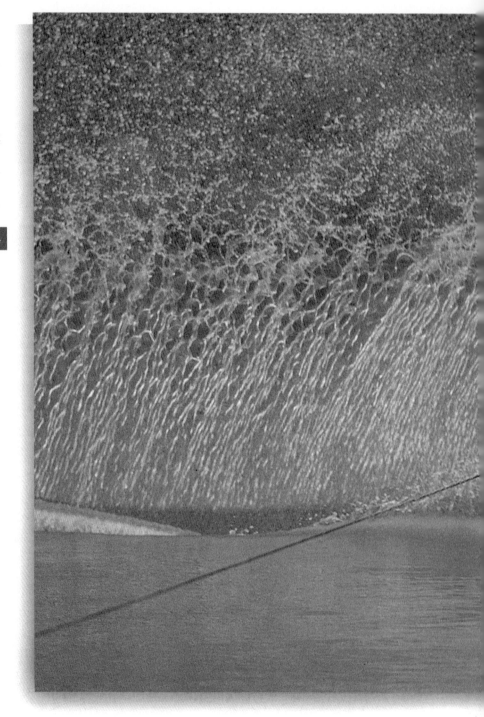

Cutting through local waters at East Coast,
waterskiing is fast gaining popularity on the island.

237

M*ens sana in corpore sano* – a healthy mind in a healthy body – may well be the aphorism uppermost in the mind of the government, which, under the aegis of the Singapore Sports Council, encourages all kinds of sporting activities. Sports for all may be its goal, but the sight of a considerable number of obese Singapore children suggests that, at least in some instances, the kitchen may have defeated the gym.

Frowned upon and discouraged by the government, scrambler cycling is considered a high-risk sports.

Sports facilities owned and managed by the Singapore Sports Council that may appeal to visitors include 67 tennis courts, 38 squash and 23 outdoor swimming complexes. Fourteen of the tennis courts and nine of the squash are located at the **National Stadium**, and another 14 of the tennis courts and the same number of the squash are located at **Farrer Park**. Another centre of racquet sports is the **Singapore Tennis Centre** in East Coast Park, which boasts 14

Bowling around the clock: 36-lane Superbowl at Marina South never closes.

floodlit plexiglass tennis courts, two squash and a pool, while the neighbouring **East Coast Recreation Centre** has 11 squash courts. Squash, incidentally, is one of the few sports in which Singapore has had some international impact, ranking among the top 10 countries in the world since the 1970s.

Only hard tennis courts are found at hotels and public sports complexes, and to play on grass the visitor will need an invitation to either the **Singapore Cricket Club** or the **Singapore Recreation Club**, both of which boast grass courts on the Padang, the large green sward before City Hall.

If your hotel pool does not satisfy you, try the **Big Splash** in East Coast Parkway, a swimming complex with a

wave pool and the longest slide in Southeast Asia. A similar complex is found in western Singapore at the **CN West Leisure Park** in Japanese Garden Road. Almost all swimming and squash complexes boast good seafood restaurants.

Although lawn bowls can be seen at the Padang on weekends, it is 10-pin bowling that entertains day and night here. There are more than a dozen bowling alleys, and the hotspots are the 36-lane **Superbowl**, which never closes, and the 32-lane **Victor's Superbowl**, open from 9am to 3 am (24 hours on weekends), both located in Marina South. The 92-lane **Kallang Bowl**, near the National Stadium, claims to be the largest bowling complex in Southeast Asia. Nearer the heart of the city is the

Ice-skating is an on-again, off-again attraction among young Singaporeans.

24-lane **Jackie's Bowl**.

Those who like to jog should visit the **Botanic Gardens**, the **MacRitchie Reservoir** or the **East Coast Park**.

There are 17 golf courses in Singapore, at 12 different locations. The best of these is the **Singapore Island Country Club**, which boasts four 18-hole courses at two different locations, whilst the exclusive **Tanah Merah Country Club**, near Changi Airport, has two 18-hole courses. At the other end of Singapore are the two 18-hole courses of the **Raffles Country Club**, and **Sentosa** also boasts two 18-hole courses.

Other clubs, each of which has a single 18-hole course, are the **Jurong Country Club**, the **Keppel Club** and the **Sembawang Club**, while nine-hole courses occupy the land of the **Changi Golf Club**, the **Seletar Country Club** and the **Warren Golf Club**. Finally, the **Tanglin Club**, in the heart of the city, has a simple seven-hole course that will attract the compulsive golfer.

Except for the Tanah Merah Country Club, visitors can play at any of these courses, especially during the week, even if unaccompanied by a member. It helps, however, if you can produce a membership card and handicap from your home club or a letter from your hotel.

The **Marina Bay Golf and Country Club** at Marina South has a three-level driving range, while other driving ranges are located at **Parkland** in East Coast Parkway and the **Admiralty House Driving Range** at Sembawang.

Although gambling is prohibited, weekly horse betting within the Turf Club is allowed.

Water Sports

Lovers of aquatic sports are well served in Singapore. Yachtsmen and women are welcome at the **Changi Sailing Club** in East Coast Parkway and the **Republic of Singapore Sailing Club** on the west coast. The former has a busy racing programme, especially from November to March, and a perusal of its notice board can often give the visitor a chance to crew in a race or obtain a berth aboard a yacht sailing to distant parts.

Most visitors to the **East Coast Sailing Centre** are board (not boat) sailors, and courses can be taken and boards hired. Scuba diving trips are organized by the **Aquanaut club**, and, although local visibility is far worse than, say, in the waters that bathe the Caribbean, a variety of fish and coral can be seen.

You can waterski at the **William Watersports Centre** at Ponggol, in northeastern Singapore; and on the waters of the Straits of Johor, which separates Singapore from West Malaysia. Canoes can be rented at the **East Coast Canoeing Centre**.

Facilities for several other sports are available, including archery, badminton, flying, horse riding, polo, ice skating and roller skating.

The more sedentary visitor, especially if he enjoys a flutter, will make for the lush grounds of the **Bukit Timah Turf Club**, the racecourse which is considered the most beautiful in Asia, and perhaps one of the finest in the world.

There are eight professional meetings a year, and each meeting is on two successive weekends. Eight or nine races are run at each meeting, and an average field is 15 mounts. In addition to local jockeys, there are riders from England and Australia. Totalizator betting is available, and the Turf Club was the first racecourse in the world to install closed-circuit video on a giant screen.

Even at weekends when there is no meeting at the Club, the screen is alive and the stands packed with punters, who can watch and bet on races at one of the other three courses that constitute the Malayan Racing Association – Ipoh, Penang and Selangor, all in Malaysia.

Sporting Events

It is appropriate that the two sporting events on the island that make the international calendar of events both involve the sea. Dragon boat races are staged in late May or early June, while the final leg of the formula one power-boat series is in December. The venue of both events is Marina Bay.

Another important event that attracts an international field (albeit mainly from Asia) is the third leg of the Asian Golf Circuit, usually held in late February or early March. A far more important golf tournament that has been staged in recent years is the qualifying tournament of the prestigious Dunhill Cup. Three-man teams from as far afield as New Zealand, Mexico and

Sweden compete in this event.

Budding Boris Beckers and Steffi Grafs from throughout the world play in international satellite tennis tournaments held some time between February and April. International marathon competitors – the best men who complete the course in about 2 hours and 20 minutes, and the best women who complete the course in about 2 hours and 45 minutes – participate in the Singapore Marathon in December.

Finally, although the seven-a-side rugby tournament (which takes place in February) cannot hope to match the similar competition in Hong Kong, it still attracts a number of first-class teams from Australia, New Zealand, Britain and Japan, as well as from all the ASEAN and some Middle East countries.

Despite city affluence, golf remains a game for the upper middle class.

A console as complicated as the pilot's – deejays play god with lights, video
cameras, music and mood.

Nightlife in Singapore is not nearly as boisterous or frenetic as in some other ASEAN cities, but this does not mean that the pavements are rolled up when the sun goes down (which, incidentally, is invariably just after 7 pm).

Disco Jingo

■   ■   ■   ■   ■   ■   ■

Scandals at the Westin Plaza offers video screens, laser lights and ear-deafening disco hits.

Singapore may well be the disco capital of the region. Singaporeans and visitors gyrate to lasers and strobes non-stop, and many hotels and other discos are frequently upgraded and redesigned to attract new patrons. Be warned, however: at discos outside hotels, those over the age of 30 will be viewed with surprise. On the other hand, despite the relative youth of most dancers, expect to see many holding handphones or have pagers strapped on their waistbelts while on the dance floor: after all, business is the name of the game here.

Before venturing out for a night of jiving, call to check the

Enjoy a Harbour Cruise

Those who enjoy the sea can board one of half a dozen craft that leave Clifford Pier between 6 pm and 7.20 pm for a harbour cruise, which comes complete with dinner and drinks. The ultimate in luxury is the 110-foot long *Singa Lady* with her six *en suite* cabins. Those who cannot bear to disembark can take the *Equator Dream*, which leaves at 10.15 pm to bob about in the waters of the harbour on a disco cruise that lasts until 1 am (2 am at weekends and on the eve of public holidays).

dress code. Every discotheque has one and some places are strict about attire. "Evening-type" outfits are *de rigueur* and most places rule out collarless tee-shirts, jeans, shorts, canvas shoes and sandals. Coat-and-tie however is rare among the locals and unnecessary.

Most durable of the hotel discos are **Chinoiserie** at the Hyatt Regency, **Xanadu** at the Shangri-la, **The Club** at the Omni Marco Polo and the **Library** at the Mandarin. The Library, which is decorated with some handsome antiquities, is far more than a disco. In addition to the dance floor, there are numerous lounges, nooks and crannies, games rooms and a theatrette. **Heartthrob** at the Meliá at Scotts has a relatively large dance floor on which old-time music fans will find joy. **Club 5** at the Plaza Hotel also concentrates on the oldies – music of "ole blue-eyes" through to the mid-70s rock is played for the jiving rock-and-roll crowd that gathers. **Scandals** at the Westin Plaza plays an eclectic range of music that includes top 40,

rock and reggae. The room is incredibly spacious and mirrored. Close by at the Pan Pacific Hotel's **Elite** discotheque you can rock on the dance floor with some of Singapore's young trendies. Perhaps more to the taste of the older crowd is the **Kasbah** at the Mandarin Hotel. The **Reading Room** at the Marina Mandarin promises a more "adventurous music policy". However, take note: the music never really varies from place to place no matter what the ads promise.

Outside the hotels, the most popular discotheques include **Rumours** in Forum Galleria and **TGIF** (= Thank God It's Friday) in Far East Plaza. During the day, TGIF is a restaurant with a bar and innumerable video screens. Those look-

Like the real thing in London, Hard Rock Cafe here is famous for its rock and roll music, burgers and shakes.

Feather boas and G-strings of Las Vegas can be enjoyed
at the Neptune Theatre Restaurant.

ing for something familiar can head for the attractive two-level **Hard Rock Café** on Cuscaden Road. The Singapore branch of this international chain opened for business in 1990, and has become a popular venue for those wanting to "chow-down" on American food and entertainment. The **Warehouse**, a conversion of two riverside godowns, or warehouses, is extremely popular with teenyboppers and features "tea dances" (actually afternoon discos) on Saturdays and Sundays. **Top Ten**, **Celebrities** and **Caesar's**, all in Orchard Towers, are rather more than discos as they feature live entertainment. Brashest of the three is Top Ten, which occupies three levels and boasts three bars.

Down at Collyer Quay is the **Neptune** theatre restaurant, which presents "tasteful" (even your grandmother will not object) topless cabaret that may be either oriental or occidental. The cuisine is Chinese and its patrons are mainly Chinese *towkays* (= rich businessmen) – the prices are a sound reflection of this. So, be prepared to spend up to three figures per person for your night out.

Those in search of female companionship may head for the **Golden Million** at the Peninsula Hotel, the **Lido Palace** at the Glass Hotel or the **Grand Palace** at Orchard Building. Rather pricey, these nightspots employ host-

Star Search

Do you ever fantasize that you sing like Tom Jones or Tina Turner? If so, visit one of the dozens of *karaoke* lounges springing up all over the island. One of the best is **Park Avenue** in Parkway Parade on Marine Parade Road, worth a visit if only for the experience. Also check out **Jiva Jive** at Holland Village. This small, friendly pub is run by two young ladies and features one of the few solely-English karaoke sessions.

Karaoke means "empty orchestra" in Japanese, and at these lounges guests are invited to take the microphone and sing a song of their choice – in English, Chinese, Malay or Japanese. Lyrics are flashed on an enormous screen. The soloist needn't worry about his less than dulcet tones as his voice is well-muffled by the background music whose pitch can be varied so that even those whose voices are atonal will sound like (well, somewhat like) Frank Sinatra or Whitney Houston. Some lounges can record your performance, if not for posterity, at least for you to take home.

Everbody is a star at the karaoke lounge where even the most demure may take to the stage and belt out the latest hits.

esses who will sit and dance with guests until the wee hours, and who, for an extra charge, can be "brought out". The earlier you arrive, the better the choice of hostesses. The cabaret is mainly oriental in decor and style and plays *cantopop* (= Cantonese pop songs). Another similar club is the **Apollo** at the Apollo Hotel on Havelock Road.

Less expensive for those in search of company is the **Red Lantern** beer garden at Collyer Quay, where the live music is simply an excuse to raise the price of the beer.

Company can also be found in the area around Desker Road and Rowell Road, on the southern side of Serangoon Road. Unknown to many tourists, this is the Reeperbahn of Singapore. The lane between the two roads can be compared to Herbertstrasse in the Reeperbahn, although here the ladies display themselves not by waiting outside the brothel but by sitting at the back of narrow, well-lit halls. It is rather tawdry, but at the same time quite fascinating. Prostitution is aggressively discouraged and government officials knit their brows at the mention of these places. Clampdowns have been known to take place but activities return to normal soon enough. The government exercises control in other ways – it maintains a register of prostitutes who are obliged to report for medical check-ups and enrol for special counselling sessions.

Similar activities take place at nearby Johore Road, close to Rochor Canal. A small gathering of men mills

Local group "Tania" performs a set at Anywhere in Tanglin Shopping Centre.

about apparently aimlessly, in a small, tree-shaded area at the rear of the buildings, while among them stroll, as elegantly as possible, "ladies" of the night – who may include transvestites or transsexuals. When an assignation is made, the couple enter the open doors at the rear of the buildings. Others sit waiting for their turns, drinking beer at rickety tables at the side of the park.

The scene in Geylang is far more decorous. Here, red lanterns decorated with Chinese characters hang outside a number of establishments in Lorong (= lane) 2, Lorong 4 and Lorong 6. Do not confuse these with similar lanterns that hang outside several Chinese temples in these *lorong* or elsewhere on the island!

The Music Goes On

Back on Orchard Road are several establishments that offer live music. Hard rock blares at **Woodstock** on the roof of Far East Plaza on Scotts Road, while **Club 392** in Orchard Towers also features raucous rock. The decibels are just as great at **Anywhere** in Tanglin Shopping Centre, where Tania, one of the most enduring bands in Singapore, continues to perform. **Brannigan's**, in the basement of the Hyatt Regency Hotel, is where young sophisticates hope to meet others of their ilk. It's large and busy and deserves its reputation as a fun pub. At 9.30 pm, the DJ is replaced by live music. The live tunes at **Ridley's**, an

Swing Singapore

If you happen to be in Singapore on the Sunday close to the 9 August National Day holiday, make your way to Orchard Road (the main shopping thoroughfare) and watch it being transformed into the city's largest open-air discotheque complete with music and mood.

The road is closed to traffic for the night, and sound systems (blaring music from enormous speakers), enthusiastic DJ's and gigantic video screens are positioned along the road. When the music starts at 7.30 pm this is "the" place to watch Singaporeans let their hair down. Though mainly for the young, some entire families (grandpa and grandaunts included) come for a family night out.

A note of caution: beware of pickpockets among the thick crowd. But rest assured these are few and far between as the Swing is conducted under the watchful eyes of uniformed duty officers from the Singapore Armed Forces. Dress appropriately; light cotton fabric is recommended to minimise the full effect of Singapore's humidity experienced amidst the sweaty bodies.

quite serious crowd which enjoys oldies. "Bebop" jazz at the **Saxophone** in Cuppage Terrace (which also boasts a small, expensive restaurant that spills onto an outside terrace) is popular with Singapore's increasing number of yuppies. Similar music can be enjoyed at the far more spacious **Somerset** bar at the Westin Plaza Hotel.

The decor at **Bibi's** theatre pub at Peranakan Place in Orchard Road depicts the interior of a *Peranakan* (= Straits-born Chinese) home. Here, you can not only listen to music but also watch innovative local revues. But be warned, many of the lines that cause the most amusement among locals will be lost on the casual visitor. Perhaps also in the realm of "theatre" is **Ginivy**, in Orchard Tow-

"Play it again Sam" – a saxophonist playing the blues at a local pub.

equally large and popular pub at the Century Park Sheraton Hotel, is more subdued until 11 pm, when one area becomes a disco. **Bill Bailey's**, in the basement of the Dynasty Hotel, is an elegant lounge rather than a bar, where groups play contemporary music.

Nostalgic melodies of the 60s fill the air at **Happy Days**, above the Orchard cinema, and similar music can be enjoyed at the **Music Room** in the Hilton Hotel between 9.30 pm and 11 pm, after which the place becomes another hotel disco. **The Cellar**, at Jack's Place in the basement of Yen San Building in Orchard Road, is often jammed with a

Good company, warm chats and cold draught beer at Hideout in the Meridien.

ers, where the Wild West goes east and country and western music fills the air.

Further from town, both revival and rock are found at **Discovery**, at the Big Splash in East Coast Parkway. And those who venture to the long popular **Europa Lounge and Restaurant** at Changi Village will be entertained with similar music in a relaxed atmosphere. Food here is inexpensive. **Europa Theatre Pub**, its branch in town, is at International Plaza on Anson Road.

A Pub Hub

Harder, but not impossible, to find is a basic pub where the decibels are kept under control, or, that *rara avis*, a pub without music. **Excalibur** in Tanglin Shopping Centre fits the bill, as does the **Mitre** in Killiney Road, where time stands still and with a little imagination you can hear the sound of air-raid sirens and see the ghostly outlines of British servicemen... From a similar era is the **Berkeley** pub at the Sloane Court Hotel in Balmoral Road.

Best of all is the pocket-size **Hideout** pub in Meridien Shopping Centre, behind the Meridien Hotel in Orchard Road. The Hideout features music and sports on a large video screen, darts and *balut* (= a dice game that originated in Asia), beer at very reasonable prices, and a warm welcome from hosts Gerard and Josephine Kleinman.

Bob's Tavern in Holland Village has a pleasant ambience and serves better-than-average "pub grub" in a rather elegant manner. Less elegant is the no-nonsense **Yard** in River Valley Road, which serves both Anchor and Tiger draught beer, and where you can play darts. Near the business district of Shenton Way, the **Wall Street** bar in the Amara Hotel serves excellent open sandwiches, features sports videos and has a small terrace outside.

By far the most elegant pub in Singapore is the **Cricketer** in the Marina Mandarin Hotel, where only the tinkling of the piano ivories disturbs the peace. Jimm's superb jazz piano is the centre of attraction at the pub of the same name in the Negara Hotel.

Almost all hotels have a piano bar or a lounge. Whenever one mentions the latter one invariably thinks of the Omni Marco Polo, where *cheongsam*-clad waitresses serve drinks to the accompaniment of music played by a Filipino orchestra.

You don't have to retire when the music stops: wind down the evening over a coffee. One of the most popular places is **El Expresso** at the Goodwood Park Hotel where a wide selection of teas and coffees greets the most discriminating of drinkers. At the **Compass Rose** in the Westin Stamford (the world's tallest hotel), you can drink in the astounding panoramic view while sipping a hot drink. Or adjourn to one of the many hotels with a 24-hour coffeeshop (eg the

Cinema Craze

Singaporeans are avid moviegoers and enjoy a wide range of English-language films from the United States and Britain, Tamil and Hindi films from India, Chinese films from Hong Kong and Taiwan. Subtitles are in one or two of the official languages: English, Chinese, Malay or Tamil.

The first show at the almost 50 cinemas usually begins at about 11 am. On Saturdays and the eves of public holidays, a midnight show is screened. Cuts are sometimes made by film distributors determined to present five or six shows a day, rather than four or five. Universally acclaimed "art" films and the films of

Dynasty, the Hyatt, the Pan Pacific, the Shangri-la or the Allson). Or try Chinese porridge at one of the restaurants that

The avante-garde has finally caught up. Movies screened at The Picturehouse often play to full house.

internationally eminent directors such as Akira Kurosawa and Satyajit Ray are screened by the Singapore Film Society. The Alliance Française and the Goethe Institute put up foreign language films. Unfortunately, many great movies last for only three or four days, while a mediocre film can run and run...

The cinema scene here has been enriched by a relatively new cinema very appropriately called **The Picturehouse**. This modern cinema with a seating capacity of 350 within its plush interior promises an exciting screenfare of foreign film festival award winners and critically acclaimed movies. Four shows are screened daily for the price of S$6 per ticket. For current seasons, look up the Cinema and the "What's On" pages of *The Straits Times*, the daily newspaper.

stays open until about 4 am, such as **Xiang Man Lou** in Bras Basah Complex and the **Chatterbox** at the Mandarin Hotel. (Refer to the Directory at the back of the book for addresses of all recommended places.)

The Marina Mandarin is not for those who suffer from vertigo.

Accommodations

Singapore has many magnificent hotels but no official grading system, so terms such as first-class and five-star are really arbitrary terms of approbation. However, many local hotels that occupy a rather low rank in Singapore would surely be considered first-class, if not deluxe, in Europe, the United States or Australia.

Sixty-eight hotels with a total of almost 25,000 rooms are gazetted (= of international standard), and there are also 76 more "basic" establishments. Atriums, cascading waterfalls, glass-bubble lifts and tumbling bougainvillea are commonplace. There is often a bar in the atrium, where entertainment is provided by a pianist, a trio or even a full orchestra.

Enjoy the impeccable service and attention at the Shangri-la, the world's second best after The Oriental in Bangkok.

Keen Competition

The Shangri-la, the Sheraton Towers and The Oriental are generally considered the top three hotels, although the Regent, with its multimillion-dollar facelift, may soon be there among

The 90-year-old tower of the Goodwood Park Hotel
was inspired by traditional Rhineland castles.

them. So too will the new "old Raffles", which consists only of suites. The ambience of the restored hotel may be of the 1920s, and visitors may be met at the airport by a vintage Rolls Royce, but the infrastructure is state-of-the-art 1990s.

With two notable exceptions, the Raffles and the Goodwood Park, all hotels were built in the last 30 years, and, indeed, about 35 percent of the gazetted hotels were built after 1984. And hotels are regularly upgraded. This does not mean mere cosmetic changes, but rather a complete renovation that may cost S$10 million or more – even if the hotel is only a few years old. As one hotel upgrades, so must its competitors.

All gazetted hotels are air-condi-tioned, and rare is the hotel that does not have international direct dial telephones and a large colour TV set in every room (in-house video is usually available at no extra charge). Most bedrooms have hair dryers, many have weighing scales, and some have trouser presses. Most hotels now have at least one non-smoking floor, and almost all have, in addition to a coffeeshop, at least one Western and one Asian restaurant. (Incidentally, smoking is forbidden in any air-conditioned restaurant, anywhere in Singapore.)

Rare is the gazetted hotel that does not have a swimming pool and more than half have business centres and gymnasiums. A word of warning: distinguish between gymnasiums and health centres; the former will be equipped with professional gymnasium equipment and may even be staffed by instructors, whereas the latter may be no more than a massage parlour.

At least a dozen major hotels stand within 300 metres of the intersection of Orchard Road and Scotts Road, the Piccadilly Circus of Singapore. Dominating the intersection is the **Dynasty**, with its pagoda-like green-tiled roof, the only hotel in Singapore to successfully marry the occident and the orient. Around the corner, in Scotts Road, are the two wings of the **Hyatt Regency**. Facing the Hyatt Regency is the **Royal Holiday Inn Crowne Plaza**, while further down Scotts Road, on the same side as the Hyatt, is the **Goodwood Park**. This low, castle-like hotel, which stands in more than five hectares of prime real estate, was originally built in 1900 as a club for German expatriates. Behind the Goodwood, sharing the same ownership and grounds, is the more modest **York**.

Back in Orchard Road, south of Scotts Road, on the same side as the Dynasty, is the **Crown Prince**, easily recognized by its external glass lifts. This hotel, which is managed by Prince Hotels of Japan, is favoured by Japanese visitors. Two hundred metres behind the Crown Prince is the **Cairnhill**, while facing the Crown Prince in Orchard Road are the soaring 40-storey towers of the **Mandarin**, which, with 1200 rooms, is the second largest hotel in Singapore. Just below the Mandarin, is the

modest **Phoenix**, and across the road, at the far end of Cuppage Terrace, the **Holiday Inn Park View**, an elegant property with well-appointed bedrooms. Shopping opportunities here are plentiful. Back on Orchard Road is the horizontal, rather than vertical, **Meridien**, whose telephone operators greet callers *"Bon jour!"*, but might be taken aback if the caller continued to speak in French.

Opposite the Meridien, and easily recognized by its unusual (can one call it Regency?) architecture is the relatively old **Cockpit**, soon to be completely renovated. Beyond this, standing in isolation on a modest hill, is the **Imperial**, popular with Indian visitors. Back on Orchard Road, but north of Scotts Road, is the evergreen and regularly upgraded **Hilton**, while at the very top of Orchard Road, facing each other and each with a pavement cafe, are the middle-range **Orchard Parade** and **Orchard** hotels. Behind the latter is the 104-room **Negara**, while between the Hilton and the Orchard Parade, on Cuscaden Road, is the 528-room **Boulevard**, which has an impressive variety of restaurants.

Continue past the Orchard Hotel up Orange Grove Road, and you soon reach the **Shangri-la**, winner of many awards. It has three wings, one of which consists entirely of suites, a small three-hole golf course and an indoor swimming pool. Across the road from here is the secluded, low-rise **Ladyhill**, which is ideal for families with children.

At the top of Orchard Road, proceed westwards up Tanglin Road for about

Alternative Accommodation

Those with large families who plan to stay in Singapore for more than a few days may wish to rent a service apartment. The best of these apartments are associated with a hotel or are immediately adjacent to a hotel, so that residents can enjoy the best of both worlds.

In the former category are **Liat Towers** (associated with the New Otani) and **Plaza Apartments** (associated with the Plaza), while in the latter is the **Ascott**, adjacent to the Dynasty and the Hyatt Regency, and **Palm Court Service Apartments**, near the Cairnhill.

A minimum stay of one week is usually required, but at times this may be extended to one month. Rates are similar to those of hotels of a comparable standard.

The Ascott service apartments offer a home away from home.

400 metres to the **Omni Marco Polo**, where, as one would expect in a hotel once the sister of the renowned Peninsula Hotel in Hong Kong, the service is impeccable. Across the road in Nassim Hill is the **ANA Hotel Singapore**, also very popular with visitors from the Land of the Rising Sun. The **Regent**, the third member of this trio, was until 1988 an Inter-Continental property. There is little doubt that it will soon be rated among the very best hotels here.

Back on Scotts Road, a few hundred metres beyond the Goodwood Park, stands a trio of disparate properties. The modest **Asia**, the **Sheraton Towers** which exudes elegance, and the **Meliá at Scotts** with its unusual ziggurat architecture, are all near the Newton MRT station and the renowned Newton Circus hawker centre.

Outside "The City"

A kilometre further from Newton Circus is the **Royal**, and north of here (which most would claim is outside the city) are three more hotels. The **Equatorial**, one of the older hotels in Singapore, has somewhat disappointing rooms but is renowned for its several splendid restaurants. The **Novotel Orchid Inn** and the **Garden**, both low-rise buildings in lush residential areas, are ideal for families. Incidentally, almost all hotels outside the Orchard Road area operate a complimentary shuttle bus service to Orchard Road and to Shenton Way, except that the shuttle bus seldom departs or

Cockpit Hotel's uniquely constructed balconies can be seen from miles away.

returns at suitable times, and it seldom stops exactly where you want.

The **New Otani**, possibly the best of the Japanese hotels, stands in River Valley Road (about 300 metres from the Imperial). Although somewhat removed from the tourist mainstream, the New Otani is part of a huge shopping complex with dozens of restaurants (mostly Japanese), and boutiques and shops.

The **YMCA**, at the bottom of Orchard Road, reflects the high standard of accommodation in Singapore: It numbers suites among its 111 rooms and there is no dormitory accommodation here. The **YWCA**, on the other hand, around the corner in Fort Canning Road, is more basic but does not have dormitory accommodation either.

Just before the YMCA, Orchard Road leads into Bras Basah Road, which continues for about one kilometre before it reaches the reclaimed land that backs the waterfront. On the left side of Bras Basah Road are the budget **Strand**, the modest **Bayview** and two large, middle-range properties, the **Allson** and the **Carlton**. Just beyond the Carlton is the "grand old lady" of Singapore hotels, the **Raffles**, the gloriously restored and expanded property that is intended for residents rather than casual visitors.

Across the road is Raffles City, a massive shopping and office complex that houses the **Westin Plaza** and the **Westin Stamford**, which together muster a total of 2051 rooms. The former, as its name suggests, is more upmarket, while the latter, with 1253 rooms, is the largest hotel in Singapore and also, incidentally, the tallest one in the world.

About a kilometre south and bathed by the waters of Marina Bay is Marina Square. The three hotels here boast a total of 1872 rooms, and they all have magnificent atriums. Most agree that **The Oriental** (a sister hotel of the Oriental in Bangkok and the Mandarin in Hong Kong) is the best of the trio, but this should not detract you from the **Marina Mandarin** (a sister hotel of the Mandarin in Orchard Road) or the soaring **Pan Pacific**, the flagship of Tokyu Hotels of Japan.

West of here are Shenton Way and the financial district, and, north of Shenton Way, Chinatown. The first hotels before Chinatown are the **Peninsula** and the **Excelsior**, twin hotels at the edge of the Padang, near Parliament House and the Supreme Court. Both are popular with Asians. Excellent shopping can be enjoyed here, and the same is true immediately west of here, at the edge of Chinatown, where the towers of the **Furama**, like the pipes of a concert organ, dominate the skyline.

From the Furama, a detour of some 400 metres leads to a clutch of five medium-size properties close to the Singapore River. The **Apollo**, the **Glass**, the **King's**, the **Miramar** and the **River View**, which share a total of about 2000 rooms, are especially popular with the Japanese. The River View is probably the best of the five, while the Glass (actually a circular glass building) has

To House a Nation

No visitor can fail to notice the vast number of high-rise apartment buildings here. The majority are government-built housing, but a few – including some of those you'll see on your way from the airport to the city – are private housing. Until recently, it was easy to distinguish between the two, due to obvious differences in quality, but these differences have now been eroded. In general, however, "flagpole" laundry is still the preserve of public housing, while it is prohibited in private housing.

Almost all public housing was built by the Housing & Development Board (HDB), a government body established in 1960 when only 9 percent of the population enjoyed low-cost public housing. Today, 86 percent of the population live in such accommodation, and 90 percent own their homes (this figure includes private housing ownership). The goal of the government is full home ownership by the end of the century. A succession of five-year housing plans has resulted in the construction of 700,000

some unusual features, including two suites with private swimming pools.

In the financial district, near the port and the World Trade Centre, which boasts the best exhibition space in Singapore, are the **Amara** and, nearer the city, the **Harbour View Dai-ichi**.

If you turn east rather than west at the bottom of Bras Basah Road, you

Left, public housing blocks – pretty as LEGO toy sets.
Above, their murals often convey a community message.

units in 30 years, and it is estimated that a new apartment "appears" every 20 minutes.

Most HDB apartments are located in New Towns, of which there are now 20. These estates, which have their own schools, markets, cinemas and places of worship, provide not only accommodation but also workplaces in the form of flatted factories that house light, non-pollutant industries. The largest New Town in terms of area is Woodlands, which occupies 1200 hectares and has 23,000 apartments. The largest in terms of population are Ang Mo Kio, Bedok and Bukit Merah, each of which is inhab-ited by almost 250,000 people.

The New Town that the visitor will find easiest to visit is Toa Payoh, which is near the city and well served by buses and Mass Rapid Transit trains. Toa Payoh, one of the first New Towns, covers an area of 400 hectares, and its population of 190,000 occupy 41,280 apartments. The best views of the New Town are from the observation tower in the Toa Payoh Park, from which you can gaze and ponder that a few years ago this was malarial swamp and market gardens with an exiguous population living in shanty towns.

reach Arab Street and Little India, an area popular not only with Malays and Indians but with all visitors to Singapore. Here are the Golden Landmark, the Plaza and the New Park. The **Golden Landmark**, with its Islamic-style architecture, is much frequented by Indian visitors. The taller part of the **Plaza** complex contains offices and apart-ments, while the seven-storey podium is occupied by the hotel. Largest of the three hotels in this area, with 525 rooms, is the **New Park**.

As you proceed eastwards, the standard of hotels tends to fall, with the exception of the **Meridien Changi**, near the airport, Changi Sailing Club and Changi Golf Club.

The land route to Malaysia is via the causeway, all 1.3 kilometres of it spanning
still waters of the Johor Straits.

Clear water and beautiful beaches – Tioman Island is the sunbather's dream.

Singapore is occasionally compared to a nut sitting in a nutcracker, the two arms of which are Malaysia and Indonesia. Why not explore these neighbouring countries? Day trips to either are perfectly possible, although an overnight stay is advisable if you want to enjoy more distant destinations and enjoy them at a leisurely pace.

MALAYSIA

Malaysia, the land of kite-flying where the sky's the limit.

Malaysia and its southernmost town of **Johor Baru**, at the northern end of the one-kilometre-long causeway that joins it to Singapore, is only 30 minutes away by bus or shared taxi. The main attractions of Johor Baru are a stroll by the **Straits of Johor**, which separates Malaysia and Singapore, the grounds of the **Istana** (= palace) and the striking **Sultan Abu Bakar Mosque**. Nightlife in Johor Baru is far more torrid than Singapore's.

More interesting is the village of **Kukup**, 80 kilometres west of Johor Baru. En route, serried ranks of rubber trees, myriad coconut trees and hectares of palm-oil trees – some of the staples of the Malaysian economy –

Beyond Singapore

The Malacca National Museum is found in this
typically Dutch house which dates from 1660.

are passed. Kukup, a former pirate refuge, is today renowned for its fish farming, its seafood restaurants poised above the Straits of Malacca, and its homes built on stilts above the water.

Alternatively, drive 40 kilometres north of Johor Baru to **Kota Tinggi**, the cool, tumbling waterfalls which are situated in a pleasant park.

Penetrate further into Malaysia by turning southeast soon after Kota Tinggi and proceeding for 55 kilometres to the beach resort of **Desaru**. Here, over a six-kilometre stretch fronted by a lovely beach, are two hotels, a number of chalets and a decent 18-hole golf course. In addition, there are floodlit tennis courts, stables with reasonable mounts, marked jungle walks, a children's playground, a discrete camping area and foodstalls, usually open only at weekends.

The beach, backed by innumerable casuarina trees and small coconut palms, is about 30 metres deep and covered with pleasant brown sand. The rocky area at its northern end is a magnet to shell collectors, and it is here that fishing is at its best. Windsurfing and waterskiing equipment can be hired, but the sea is too murky for interesting snorkelling or scuba diving.

A more interesting route to Desaru is by ferry from Changi Point in Singapore, which leaves every hour and takes 45 minutes to reach Tanjong Pengilir. The ferries are basic local craft, but rest assured that they have passed all required safety tests. Taxis meet the ferry and take about an hour to reach Desaru. Alternatively, take a taxi from Tanjong Pengilir to Renggit, about three kilometres away, and take a bus from Renggit to Desaru.

Considerably to the north of Desaru is a delightful cluster of volcanic islands, the most renowned of which is **Tioman**, which claims, with some justification, to be "one of the ten most beautiful islands in the world". The beaches on Tioman are truly magnificent, and the interior, which soars to a height of more than 1000 metres, is covered with dense jungle. Snorkelling and scuba diving are excellent, as the water is pellucid and rich in coral fish and other kinds of marine life. All types of water-sports equipment, including waterskiing boats, can be hired. A nine-hole golf course, from which there are glorious views, will please the most discerning golfer.

The island's only international-standard hotel has a swimming pool and floodlit tennis courts. A variety of more basic accommodation is also available. Daily flights leave Seletar, Singapore's second airport, to reach Tioman in only 50 minutes. Alternatively, drive to Mersing, a journey that lasts two to three hours (depending on traffic and mode of transport), from where it is a two- to three-hour boat ride to Tioman. However, the state of the tide at Mersing can delay your departure for several hours.

Closer to Mersing are the islands of **Rawa**, **Babi Besar** and **Tengah**, which will appeal to those in search of Robinson Crusoe rather than a more sophisticated life. Two other popular islands in this group but further south, and which offer similar accommodation, are **Sibu** and **Sibu Tengah**. These are reached by driving to Kota Tinggi and then, after a further 15 kilometres on the road to Mersing, swinging southeast for 25 kilometres to Tanjong Sedili. Morning and afternoon ferries make the voyage from Tanjong Sedili to the islands in two to three hours. Public transport is available to Tanjong Sedili, although several changes are involved.

On the western coast of West Malaysia, the town of **Malacca**, which overlooks the straits of the same name, is a sleepy hollow redolent with history. Situated 245 kilometres northwest of Singapore, it is reached in about four hours by express bus, which leaves Sin-

Batam island is only 20 kilometres away, that is, half an hour by ferry.

gapore on the hour for most of the day. Founded in the 15th century, Malacca boasts the oldest Chinese temple in Malaysia and several interesting historical churches and secular buildings left by the Portuguese, the Dutch and the British, who all fought for this once important trading post of which it was said "Whoever holds Malacca holds the key to the Orient." Accommodation is available in a variety of city, rural and beach hotels.

INDONESIA

Beckoning, ever beckoning, tourists and businessmen on the Singapore waterfront are the Indonesian islands of the Riau archipelago. They are readily reached. Proceed to Finger Pier, immediately south of Shenton Way, and board one of the fleet of large, high-speed, air-conditioned craft that ply between Singapore and the island of **Batam** in about 35 minutes. The trip can cost you nothing if you buy something at the duty-free shop on Batam, for even those who merely set foot on the island are allowed to return to Singapore with a bottle of liquor, a bottle of wine and three cans of beer – all duty-free. Those who forget to buy duty-free goods on Batam can buy them on their return to Singapore at the duty-free shop at Finger Pier. Incidentally, it's unnecessary to change Singapore dollars to *rupiah* on Batam, as the former are always welcome.

Despite the flocks of arrivals annually, the mysticism about Bali remains.

Batam, which is about the size of Singapore, has two attractive beach hotels, both of which boast a complete range of water-sports equipment. The island also has two good 18-hole golf courses. Seafood is excellent and inexpensive, the nightlife is exciting, although local rather than international, and a wide range of lovely *batik* products awaits your purchase.

Those who are more adventurous and have more time will board a ferry at Finger Pier bound for the more colourful and more ethnic island of **Bintan**, which is more than twice the size of Singapore, and its port and principal town of Tanjung Pinang. Tanjung Pinang is what Singapore was 30 years ago. Here, where many homes are built on stilts

above the water and the air is redolent with the aroma of *kretek* (the famous Indonesian clove-flavoured cigarettes), the trishaw is the *de rigueur* mode of transport. There is a lively night market and the seafood is glorious.

Board a *sampan*, the local water taxi, for an early morning cruise on the Snake River, which is vibrant with life. Another short boat ride leads to the delightful tiny island of **Penyengat**, once home of the sultans of Riau, whose palace and mosque you may visit. Beach lovers will make for **Trikora**, on the southern side of the island, about 40 kilometres from Tanjung Pinang. Further still, at the northern tip of the island, is the superior, but undeveloped, Pasir Panjang beach.

Sultan Abdul Samad Building in downtown Kuala Lumpur
boasts a Moorish architectural style.

FURTHER AFIELD

Longer journeys from Singapore, which require at least an overnight stay, can be made to two of the most famous tourist islands in the world – **Bali** in Indonesia and **Penang** in Malaysia. Bali, "the Morning of the World", where life is a series of elaborate rituals, is a 90-minute flight from Singapore. Its unique Balinese Hindu culture will seduce anyone, and the island boasts some good beaches and outstanding hotels.

Excellent hotels also grace Penang, "the Pearl of the Orient", which is a one-hour flight from Singapore. It is a glorious mixture of town and beach, and of Chinese, Malay and Indian cultures.

And do not miss **Kuala Lumpur** and **Jakarta**, respectively the capitals of Malaysia and Indonesia, which are even closer. Flying time to either city is about one hour, and flights are frequent, but be warned: a shuttle ticket rather than a regular ticket on the extremely busy Singapore–Kuala Lumpur service can mean hours of delay at the airport. Railway fans will make for the station in Pasir Panjang Road and board the train for a pleasant seven-hour journey to Kuala Lumpur. The same train, after a further six hours, arrives at Butterworth, immediately opposite the island of Penang. Ferries shuttle to and from across the Dindang Straits in 20 minutes. Frequent buses take seven hours to travel from Singapore to Kuala Lumpur.

Avid gamblers will make for **Gen-**ting Highlands, high in the clouds above Kuala Lumpur and easily accessible from the capital in about 40 minutes. Here, in the only casino in the region, roulette, blackjack and other Western casino games, and some Chinese games, are seen, and the tables never close. Do not expect the elegance of Cannes or Monte Carlo, but the enthusiasm is just as high, and large sums of money change hands. Genting Highlands has several hotels of varying standards and offers a host of activities – nightly revues, indoor and outdoor swimming pools, squash and tennis courts, a children's amusement park and an excellent 18-hole golf course.

The Kek Lok Si tower in Penang is Chinese at the bottom, Burmese at the top and Thai in between.

TRAVEL TIPS

AIR TRAVEL

ARRIVAL: As the hub of much East Asian international and regional air traffic, Singapore's Changi Airport is host to more than 50 scheduled passenger airlines, linking it directly to 109 cities in 53 countries. During the evening peak, an average of 20 aircraft take off and land each hour.

In spite of its hectic pace, Changi Airport (also known as the Airtropolis) remains one of the most efficient and user-friendly airports in the world. Indeed it is the world's favourite airport, having been voted "Best Airport in the World" for three years running (1988–1990) by international travel magazine *Business Traveller*.

Two passenger terminals cater for the millions who annually arrive at and depart from Singapore. Terminal 2 is the newer of the two (opened in November 1990). Expanding Changi's annual passenger handling capacity to 24 million – the highest figure in the Asia-Pacific region – terminal 2 was built to cope with Changi's fast increasing international traffic. Both terminals are connected to each other by a fast-moving, automated Skytrain with a capacity to seat 100 in fully carpeted and airconditioned comfort. And both terminals are multi-purpose buildings complete with duty-free shopping, restaurants and cafes, money changers, hotel reservation facilities, fitness gymnasium/sauna, hire car services, information counters and taxi stands. The airport also provides a baggage storage service within both the arrival and departure terminals.

Transit/transfer passengers can take advantage of complimentary city tours to Chinatown, Little India and Orchard Road. These operate twice daily at 2.30 pm and 4.30 pm from the airport. Ask for more details at the Information Counters in the Departure/Transit Lounge.

Taxis are available immediately outside the entrances to the passengers terminal buildings. Note that there is a S$3 surcharge on taxi fares from the airport. Passengers with light luggage can catch the public bus from the terminus conveniently located at the basement of the airport; service 390 (airconditioned) brings passengers downtown. Fare: S$1.20. Be sure to have exact change, though.

DEPARTURE: Departing passengers should keep enough change in local currency to pay the departure service charge when checking in: S$12 for international flights and S$5 if you are travelling to Malaysia or Brunei. Or convenient coupons can be pre-purchased at most hotels and travel agents. If you check in early enough you can enjoy some of the facilities at the Departure/Transit Lounge.

For more information and enquiries, please call the Civil Aviation Authority of Singapore at Tel: 541 2107.

BUSINESS HOURS

Most business organizations open from 9 am to 5 pm from Monday to Friday, and from 9 am to 1 pm on Saturday. Banking hours are from 10 am to 3 pm from Monday to Friday, and from 9.30 am to 11.30 am on Saturday.

The following banks, however, have extended open hours on Saturday and some of them open even on Sunday.

Chung Khiaw Bank
230 Orchard Road
Faber House #01-230
Singapore 0923
Tel: 235 0239
Banking Hours: 9.30 am – 3 pm (Sat);
11 am – 4.30 pm (Sun)

Development Bank of Singapore
Plaza Singapura #01-15
Singapore 0923

Tel: 336 2244
Banking Hours: 9.30 am – 3 pm (Sat)
United Overseas Bank
80 Marine Parade Road
Parkway Parade #01–13
Singapore 1544
Tel: 345 9811
Banking Hours: 9.30 am – 3 pm (Sat);
11 am – 4.30 pm (Sun)
OCBC (Overseas Chinese Banking Corporation)
277 Orchard Road
Specialist Centre #01-01
Singapore 0923
Tel: 737 4077
Banking Hours: 9.30 am – 3 pm (Sat);
11 am – 4 pm (Sun)

CLIMATE

As you might expect in an area so close to the equator, Singapore has a warm and humid climate with very little variation in temperature between day and night, and only slight seasonal variation. The average maximum temperature during the day is 30.7°C, dropping to an average minimum of 23.8°C during the evening. There is an average of five hours of bright sunshine every day of the year.

Although the months of December, January and February are referred to as "the monsoon season", there is really no marked difference between the seasons. The northeast monsoon winds from November to January generally bring more rain than usual. Singapore showers are often sudden, heavy and brief, easing the usual humidity. The mean annual rainfall is 236.8 mm, with November being the cloudiest month.

CLOTHING

Dressing in Singapore is normally casual. Light summer clothing, preferably of natural fabrics (synthetics are uncomfortable in high humidity), is suitable. Very few places require formal wear in the evening; visitors can telephone in advance to check. Shirts-and-ties (no coats) and evening dresses are never out of place in Singapore's glamorous nightspots, however. Most discotheques do not permit entry if you are dressed in jeans, shorts or sandals. Overall, exercise decorum in your choice of clothing especially when planning a visit to a mosque or temple.

CREDIT CARDS

Most establishments accept major credit and charge cards, although VISA seems to be the preferred card among local businesses.
American Express   235 8133
Diners   294 4222
Master   533 2888
Visa   224 9033

CRUISES

Bumboats are the traditional workhorses of the Singapore River and they remain the best way to see the river on which Singapore's history as a vital trade port began. You can enjoy a wide range of cruises, ranging from bumboat jaunts up the river to twilight junk cruises. Tides in Singapore have a 3-metre rise and fall, and a "flattering" view of the river is ensured at high tide so it's a good idea to plan your cruise then (check section 2 of the daily *Straits Times*).

• **RIVER CRUISE**
Singapore River Cruises Tel: 336 6119
Cost: S$6 adults; S$3 children
Duration: 1/2 hour
Departing: From 9 am to 6.30 pm on the hour.
Eastwind Organisation Tel: 533 3432
Cost (including refreshments): S$15 adults;
S$9.50 children
Duration: 1 hr
Departing: 10 am, noon, 2 pm, 4 pm and 6pm

• **TONGKANG CRUISE**
Eastwind Organisation Tel: 533 3432
Cost (including refreshments): S$20 adults;
S$10 children
Duration: 2-1/2 hours
Departing: 10.30 am, 3 pm & 4 pm
Twilight Cruise:
Cost (including dinner): S$36 adults;
S$18 children
Duration: 2-1/2 hours
Departing: 6 pm
Watertours Pte Ltd Tel: 533 9811
Cost: S$20 adults; S$10 children
Duration: 2-1/2 hours
Departing: 10.30 am, 3pm & 4pm
Dinner cruise:
Cost: S$33 adults;
$17 children
Duration: 2-1/2 hours
Departing: 6 pm

• HARBOUR CRUISE
Phoenix Offshore Cruises Tel: 534 1868
Morning Cruise:
Cost (including refreshments): S$28 adults;
S$15 children
Duration: 2-1/2 hours
Departing: 9.10 am
Lunch cruise (on prewar luxury cruise boat):
Cost: S$50 adults; S$35 children
Duration: 2-1/2 hours
Departing: 12.10pm
High Tea (on prewar luxury cruise boat):
Cost: S$28 adults; S$15 children
Duration: 2-1/2 hours
Departing: 3.10 pm
Dinner cruise (on prewar luxury cruise boat):
Cost: S$75 adults; S$45 children
Duration: 3-1/2 hours
Departing: 7.10 pm

Waterfront Cruises Tel: 532 4497
Cost: S$25 adults, S$15 children
Duration: 2-1/2 hours
Departing: 9.30 am & 2.30 pm
Cocktail cruise:
Cost: S$18 adults
Duration: 1-1/4 hours
Departing: 5.30 pm
Dinner cruise (on imperial chinese-style vessel):
Cost: S$65 adults; S$32 children
Duration: 2 hours
Departing: 7.30 pm

J&N Cruise Tel: 270 7100
Lunch cruise:
Cost: S$33 adults; S$20 children
Duration: 1-1/2 hours
Departing: 12.30 pm
Discovery cruise:
Cost (including high tea): S$28 adults;
S$17 children
Duration: 2 hours
Departing: 3 pm
Sunset Dinner cruise:
Cost: S$75 adults; S$45 children
Duration: 1-3/4 hours
Departing: 6 pm
Dinner cruise:
Cost: S$75 adults; S$45 children
Duration: 2 hours
Departing: 8.30 pm
Rendezvous Disco cruise:
Cost: S$30 on Friday, Saturday &
eve of holidays; S$20 other days

Duration: 3 hours
Departing: 10.30 pm

CUSTOMS REGULATIONS

All incoming travellers of at least 18 years old, and who arrive from any country except Malaysia are granted the following duty-free imports for personal consumption – 1 litre of spirits, 1 litre of wine, and 1 litre of beer, stout, ale or porter. As part of a nationwide campaign to discourage smoking, visitors are liable to a S$17 duty on each carton of cigarettes brought in.

Prohibited items include controlled drugs; cigarette lighters in the shape of a pistol or revolver; toy coins and toy currency notes; reproductions of copyright publications, video tapes or discs, records or cassettes; endangered species of wildlife and their by-products; obscene articles and publications; and seditious and treasonable materials.

Import of controlled or restricted items will only be allowed if there is an accompanying import permit or authorization from the relevant authority. These include animals, birds and their by-products; arms, explosives, bullet-proof clothing and weapons; toy guns, pistols, revolvers; pre-recorded cartridges, cassettes, films, video tapes and discs; medicines, pharmaceuticals and poisons; and telecommunication and radio communication equipment.

Travellers carrying medicines that may only be obtained by prescription under Singapore law, especially sleeping pills, depressants, stimulants, etc, must produce an accompanying prescription from his or her physician.

There is no export duty. Export permits are required for arms, ammunition, explosives, animals, gold, platinum, precious stones and jewellery (except reasonable personal effects), poisons and drugs. Any goods in excess of reasonable personal effects are to be declared at exit points and an "Outward Declaration" prepared, if necessary. If you need further information, contact:
Head, Terminal Section
Airports Branch
Customs & Excise Department
Singapore Changi Airport
Singapore 9181
Tel: 545 9495 or
The Customs Officer
Singapore Changi Airport
Tel: 541 2572

DISABLED TRAVELLERS

For the benefit of physically disabled visitors, the Singapore Council of Social Service publishes *Access Singapore*, a guide to easily accessible attractions – a comprehensive booklet which can be obtained from:

Singapore Tourist Promotion Board (STPB)
Information Centre
250 North Bridge Road
Raffles City Tower
Singapore 0617
Tel: 339 6622
Singapore Council of Social Service
SCSS Building
11 Penang Lane
Singapore 0923
Tel: 336 1544

ELECTRICITY

The voltage is 220 – 240 volts AC, 50 cycles. Most hotels have transformers to reduce the voltage to 110–120 volts, 60 cycles, if necessary.

LOCAL CUSTOMS

Because Singapore is a multi-racial society, tolerance of the customs of others is widespread and the visitor is unlikely to unwittingly cause offence. There are a few points that the visitor should remember, however.

Always remove your shoes before you enter a mosque or an Indian temple. For reasons of cleanliness, many Singaporeans leave their shoes outside the doors of their homes. This charming habit harks back to the days when Singaporeans lived mostly in *kampung* (villages), in huts surrounded by beaten-earth clearings. Shoes were taken off in order to avoid tracking mud and dust into the clean home. Today if you are invited into a Singaporean home, look to see whether shoes are worn. If not, slip out of yours too – you will find it more comfortable too!

When giving something to or receiving something from a Malay or Indian Muslim, it is considered courteous to use the right hand. The left hand should never be used to eat, because it is reserved for toilet functions and therefore considered unclean by Muslims.

Unlike most other Asian countries, Singapore follows the concept of "first come, first served". Whether you want a taxi, a postage stamp or assistance at an information counter, be sure to join the queue.

LOCAL LAWS

In Singapore rules are not made to be broken. The government takes a serious view even on the littlest offences for which it imposes a fine – for this reason, perhaps, Singapore has been nick-named a "fine city"!

DRUG ABUSE: The penalties for drug abuse in Singapore are severe. Under the Misuse of Drugs Act, it is an offence to traffic in, manufacture, import, export, cultivate, possess or consume any form of controlled drug in Singapore.

Any person who traffics in morphine in excess of 30 grams or heroin in excess of 15 grams faces the death penalty. Any person who traffics in narcotics in excess of 10 kg of cannabis, 6 kg of opium, 20 grams of morphine or 10 grams of heroin faces up to 30 years in prison and 15 strokes of the *rotan* (= cane). Any person who possesses or consumes in excess of 10 kg of cannabis faces a maximum of 10 years in prison and/or a fine of S$20,000.

Any person who traffics in a controlled drug faces 10 years in prison and 5 strokes of the *rotan*. Any person who possesses or consumes a controlled drug faces a maximum of 10 years in prison and/or a fine of S$20,000.

JAYWALKING: Pedestrians who cross a road within 50 metres of a pedestrian crossing, an overhead pedestrian bridge or an underpass risk a S$50 fine. Always cross at traffic lights if there is no special pedestrian route close by.

LITTERING: Great efforts are made to keep Singapore clean, and littering of any kind is subject to a maximum of S$1000 fine.

SMOKING: Smoking in enclosed public places – public buses, lifts, cinemas, theatres, government offices, restaurants (only outdoor restaurants such as poolside and pavement cafes are exempted from this ban) and shopping centres – is against the law and the offender is subject to a S$500 fine.

GAMBLING: Apart from charity draws, the Toto and the Singapore Sweep lotteries, and horse-racing bets placed through the Bukit Timah Turf Club, other forms of gambling are illegal.

FLUSHING OF TOILETS: In order to promote a hygienic environment, anyone caught not flushing public toilets after use will be fined S$150.

ROAD HOGGING: Motorists who are caught "hogging" the road (i.e. straying indiscriminately from lane to lane) will be subjected to a S$50 fine and given four demerit points. The accumulation of 24 points over two years results in the driver being suspended from driving for a year.

SPITTING: Spitting on the road or on any public thoroughfare may cost the offender a fine of S$500.

MEDICAL ASSISTANCE

Gone are the days when a visitor was likely to be grounded by some exotic tropical disease. Anti-mosquito campaigns have all but eliminated malaria and typhus (now so rare that an outbreak causes headlines). In fact, Singapore is without a doubt one of the healthiest cities in Asia.

Standards of medical and dental care are very high. All major hotels have a house doctor on 24-hour call. General practitioners, specialists and dental surgeons are listed in the Yellow Pages of the Singapore Phone Book. Pharmaceuticals are available from numerous outlets including supermarkets, department stores, hotels and shopping centres. Most of these outlets have a pharmacist on duty from 9 am to 6 pm.

For ambulance dial 995.

MONEY MATTERS

The unit of currency is the Singapore dollar (100 cents = S$1). Coins are available in denominations of 1¢, 5¢, 10¢, 20¢, 50¢ and $1. Notes come in denominations of S$1, S$2, S$5, S$10, S$20, S$50, S$100, S$500, S$1,000 and S$10,000. Rates of exchange for currency and travellers' cheques vary slightly from one place to another; generally money changers offer the best rate. Be sure to only approach changers who have prominent signage "Licensed Money Changer" outside their shops. They are to be found in most shopping centres. Visitors are cautioned against changing money through anyone not licensed.

Apart from money changers, money can be changed in banks and hotels. The exchange rates offered in hotels tend to be slightly poorer than that offered by banks. You can buy or sell most major foreign currencies in Singapore. There is no limit on the amount of local or foreign currency, travellers' cheques or letters of credit that you may bring in or carry out of Singapore.

Some banks charge a commission for cashing travellers' cheques. Be sure to have your passport with you.

NEWSPAPER AND MAGAZINES

Daily newspapers in Mandarin, Malay, Tamil and English are published locally. The English-language *Straits Times* and *Business Times* appear in the morning, the tabloid *New Paper* in the afternoon, and the *Sunday Times* every Sunday. American, Australian, British, French and German newspapers are readily available at major hotel newsstands and leading bookshops. International weekly news magazines published in several languages and many general interest magazines are also widely on sale.

POSTAL SERVICES

Most hotels provide postal services at the front desk. In addition, post offices are open from 8.30 am to 5 pm from Monday to Friday and to 1 pm on Saturday. Some open for longer hours:

Orchard Point Post Office
160 Orchard Road
Orchard Point #B1-16
Tel: 732 7899
Opens from 8 am to 8 pm daily except on Sunday and public holidays.

Several even offer 24-hour service:
Changi Airport
Passenger Terminal 2
Tel: 542 7899
Comcentre Post Office
31 Exeter Road
Tel: 733 7899
General Post Office (GPO)
Fullerton Building
Tel: 533 8899

Not all counters at these 24-hour offices, however, remain open around the clock. Most only offer basic postal services like mail registration, letter and parcel posting – it is advisable to call and check.

Direct inquiries on any postal matter to Tel: 165 every day except public holidays.

Some of the postal rates are as follows:–
Aerogrammes:
35 cents: All parts of the world
Airmail Postcard Rates:
30 cents: All parts of the world
Letters (under 10 grams):
30 cents: Malaysia & Brunei

35 cents: Australia, Bangladesh, Burma, China, Hong Kong, India, Indonesia, Japan, Kampuchea, Korea, Laos, Macao, Maldives, Nepal, New Zealand, Pakistan, Philippines, Sri Lanka, Taiwan, Thailand, Vietnam and the Pacific (except Hawaii)

75 cents: Africa, America (including Hawaii), Europe, and the Middle East

Postpac:

This carton provides a neat and convenient way of posting a wide range of parcels. Available from any post office, the cartons (excluding postal) are priced between S$1.40 and S$3.20 depending on the size.

RADIO AND TELEVISION

There are daily radio services in English and Chinese from 6 am to midnight (2 am on Friday, Saturday and the eve of public holidays); in Malay from 4.45 am to midnight; and in Tamil from 5 am to 9 pm. FM stereo services are from 6 am to midnight in all languages except Tamil, which is broadcast only at selected times. Reception of the British Broadcasting Corporation World Service (88.9 mhz) is excellent as there is a transmitter in Singapore.

Television programmes in English, Chinese, Malay and Tamil can be viewed daily over Singapore Broadcasting Corporation (SBC) channels 5, 8 and 12. Most TV sets also receive RTM1, RTM2 and TV3 from Malaysia.

Many hotel television sets are linked to the Teletext System, which relays information from 7 am to midnight on entertainment, sports, finance, aircraft arrivals and departures, special events and so on. Television programmes are listed in the daily newspapers.

RAIL TRAVEL

The railway station in Keppel Road and all rail services from Singapore are owned and maintained by Malayan Railways. Give yourself an hour for purchasing tickets and custom formalities before departure.

Services from Singapore run to the Malaysian capital, Kuala Lumpur; to Butterworth, near Penang; to Haadyai, in southern Thailand; and, in cooperation with the State Railway of Thailand, to the Thai capital, Bangkok. Services to several other Malaysian cities are also available.

Trains to Johor depart daily at 10 am, 11.20 am, 12.30 pm, 4 pm and 6 pm. Return journeys leave Johor at 2.10 pm, 3 pm and 7.15 pm. There are two daily airconditioned express service – one for Butterworth via Kuala Lumpur (KL) at 7.45 am and the second, direct to KL at 2.45 pm.

In addition, a mail train, with airconditioned passenger facilities, departs at 10 pm to KL daily.

Riding in the train is comfortable except for the primitive toilet facilities.

For schedules, routes and fares, contact the Singapore Railway Station at Tel: 222 5165.

SHOPPING

Shopping – a totally Singaporean pastime that can prove equally satisfying to the visitor. And why not? Shops in Singapore are open seven days a week from 10 am to 9 pm and run the whole gamut from huge airconditioned electronic emporiums and shopping centres that stretch for miles to tiny market stalls and rustic shophouses selling local handicrafts. For more information, refer to Shopping article on page 225.

Direct any complaints on your purchases to:
Singapore Tourist Promotion Board (STPB)
Raffles City Tower #36–04
250 North Bridge Road
Singapore 0617
Tel: 339 6622
The Consumers' Association of Singapore (CASE)
Trade Union House Annexe
Shenton Way
Singapore 0106
Tel: 222 2411, 222 2412

TELECOMMUNICATIONS

The efficiency of the Singapore telephone service is the envy of many other countries.

Local calls made from subscriber telephones are now free. However, the telecommunication authorities will be implementing a charge-by-minute system with effect from November 1991. Local calls made from public coinaphones is 10 cents for every three minutes.

The Telecoms cardphone service is a convenient way to make international direct dial calls to more than 170 countries. Cardphones are on sale at all post offices – stored-value begins from S$2. Also available are Home Country Direct Telephones, which allow the operator in your home country to connect the call, and charge it either collect or to your telephone credit card.

Cables, faxes, telegrams and telexes can be sent from most hotels and post offices, or from the Comcentre Building. See under Postal Services.

TIME

Singapore is eight hours ahead of Greenwich Mean Time. Time differences between Singapore and some other major cities are as follows:

City	Hours
Amsterdam	– 7
Athens	– 6
Auckland	+ 4
Bahrain	– 5
Bangkok	– 1
Bombay	– 2-1/2
Brussels	– 7
Cairo	– 6
Chicago	– 14
Colombo	– 2-1/2
Darwin	+ 1-1/2
Frankfurt	– 7
Geneva	– 7
Helsinki	– 6
Hong Kong	0
Honolulu	– 18
Jakarta	– 1
Karachi	– 3
Kuala Lumpur	0
Lisbon	– 8
London	– 8
Los Angeles	– 16
Madrid	– 7
Manila	0
Montreal	– 13
Moscow	– 5
Nairobi	– 5
New Delhi	– 2-1/2
New York	– 13
Osaka	+ 1
Oslo	– 7
Paris	– 7
Rio de Janeiro	– 11
Rome	– 7
Seoul	+ 1
Stockholm	– 7
Sydney	+ 3
Taipei	0
Tel Aviv	– 6
Tokyo	+ 1
Vancouver	– 16
Vienna	– 7
Zurich	– 7

TIPPING

The government campaigns actively against the practice of tipping, which is prohibited at the airport and discouraged in hotels and restaurants that have a 10 percent service charge. Use your discretion: if the service is outstanding, you may feel that a tip is appropriate.

TOUR PACKAGES

Hotel tour desks will provide information on the wide range of tours available.

Tourist guides can be contacted through the Registered Tourist Guides Association at Tel: 338 3441 or 338 3443. All registered guides carry official identification.

Even if your visit is only a short stopover between flights, it is possible to take in some of Singapore's sights before departure. Free sight-seeing tours, organized by the Singapore Tourist Promotion Board (STPB), are available to transit passengers. Call at the tour desk in the Changi Airport transit lounge.

The following are some of the more popular tours available (take note that prices should be double checked for currentness upon arrival).

Franco Asian Travel	Tel: 293 8282
Holiday Tours	Tel: 738 2622
Malaysia and Singapore Travelcentre	
	Tel: 737 8877
RMG Tours	Tel: 337 3377
Siakson Coach Tours	Tel: 336 0288
Singapore Sightseeing	Tel: 473 6900
Tour East	Tel: 235 5703

BIRD PARK TOUR: Several tour operators offer special bird park tours to Jurong. The Bird Park Express service coach, also called the Road Runner, departs from major hotels twice a day. Check at the front desk of your hotel.
Cost: S$25 adults; S$12 children.

CITY TOUR: This half-day tour gives you a good introduction to the city which abounds in character and contrasting cultures. Tour itineraries from different operators vary, but most offer a drive through the busy shopping district of Orchard Road and a chance to see the "Wall Street" of Singapore – Shenton Way.

All operators include a visit to Chinatown as part of this tour, and some also include Little India. A spellbinding view of the city from Mt Faber and the tranquillity of the Botanic Gardens complete the tour.

Cost: S$25 adults; S$13 children.

CRUISES: See under Cruises (page 278).

EAST COAST TOUR: This tour provides a lively mixture of urban and rural with plenty to see and do. Packages invariably include the Changi Prison Museum and the Changi Chapel, relics dating from World War II.
Cost: S$19 adults; S$10 children.

HERITAGE TRAIL: A fascinating 6- to 8-hour tour to discover some of Singapore's cultural enclaves. Chinatown, Arab Street and Little India are packed with charming sights and sounds that make up the multicultural mix of people.
Cost: S$32 adults; S$16 children.

HISTORICAL TOUR: Interesting tours retrace the footsteps of founding father Stamford Raffles, explore the old warehouses from the deck of a bumboat along Singapore River, visit the 150-year-old Thian Hock Keng Temple in Chinatown and admire the splendid colonial architecture in the city's heart.
Some tours also include the grandly restored Empress Place Museum, a former government building, more than a century old, which features exhibitions of rare Chinese archaeological and artistic artefacts.
Cost: S$32 adults; S$16 children.

HORSE RACING TOUR: Experience all the thrills of house racing at its very best.
The tour takes you to the beautifully landscaped surroundings at the Bukit Timah Turf Club where you will be welcomed with a buffet lunch and during which you have full access to the members' stand.
A complimentary racing guide will assist you in choosing your winners for a day of non-stop action.
Cost (includes lunch): S$68 adults.

HOUSING DEVELOPMENT BOARD (HDB) ESTATE TOUR: This tour provides an insight into the lifestyle of Singaporeans by visiting a local housing estate. Within these estates the multicultural heritage still flourishes – many are built around older temples and mosques. Each estate includes a community centre and numerous shopping facilities. The tour offers the chance to sample the colourful and fascinating local lifestyle; visit a medicine centre to see Chinese herbal cures and a community centre where classes (from cooking to dance, to photography) are conducted at subsidized rates for the young and old.
Cost: S$29 adults; S$12 children.

NIGHT TOUR: Sample the best of Singapore's hawker food or seafood, take in a cultural show, and round off the evening with a friendly drink in a local pub.
Cost: S$39 adults; S$29 children.

ROUND ISLAND TOUR: An award winning tour which begins with a visit to a wholesale fruit and vegetable market before visiting Ming Village, where porcelain masterpieces are made. The tour then explores the landscaping artistry of the Chinese and Japanese Gardens before visiting rural Singapore's fast disappearing *kampung* (villages) and farms.
Lunch is followed by a visit to a Singaporean home in a modern housing estate before touring the Kong Meng San Phor Kark See Temple complex. Finally off to Changi Point for a bumboat ride to see kelongs, fish farms and traps along the Straits of Johor. The tour ends with a visit to a crocodile farm.
Cost: S$60 adults.

SENTOSA ISLAND TOUR: A fun island dedicated to enjoyment, nature and history, Sentosa is well worth a visit. Travel across the busy waterway by ferry or experience a breathtaking bird's eye view from atop a cable car before arriving at the island.
Cost: S$36 adults; S$18 children.

ZOO TOUR: The airconditioned Zoo Express serves major hotels. Enroute to the zoo, the bus passes rubber plantations and rural villages – ideal for visitors who appreciate countryside beauty. At the zoo, have breakfast or high tea with an orangutan. Then explore this exceptional zoo where natural barriers replace bars, giving visitors the opportunity to see animals in the most natural environment possible.
The zoo has many endangered species and features several particularly exotic specimens, including the muscular komodo dragons.
A daily animal show, featuring chimps, reptiles and elephants, is extremely popular with both young and old.
Cost (excluding meals with orangutan): S$27 adults; S$13.50 children.

SPECIAL INTEREST TOUR: A selection of special interest tours enables the visitor to explore Singapore in-depth. A minimum of 10 persons is required, except for the half-day Battlefield Tour.

Operators conducting these tours can often tailor packages to suit the majority of the group members. Call for details at:

Franco Asian Travel   Tel: 293 8282
Malaysia & Singapore Travelcentre
                         Tel: 737 8877
Singapore Sightseeing   Tel: 473 6900

Battlefield Tour: This tour enables the visitor to re-live Singapore's experience during World War II. Options include two half-day tours or the more in-depth four- or five-day packages. The short tours include visits to the significant battle sites and end with a visit to the memorials built by the prisoners during the war years.

For further enquiries about tour prices and accommodations call:

Malaysia and Singapore Travel Centre
                         Tel: 737 8877
Singapore Sightseeing   Tel: 473 6900

Culinary Heritage Tour: A tour befitting Singapore's reputation as a culinary city. Through sightseeing and museum visits, it explores the heritage of the different types of cuisines available locally.

The best part of any food tour is the sampling of different dishes. This tour provides an endless feast from breakfast to dinner, and quite literally, the hands-on experience of eating Indian curry out of a banana leaf with your fingers!

Golf Tour: This tour provides 6 glorious days of teeing off at some of Singapore's luxurious courses.

TOURIST INFORMATION

Tourist hotlines, free publications and maps – there is never a lack of visitor's information in Singapore. Upon arrival at the airport, help yourself to the various free brochures and maps found on racks at strategic points of the terminal buildings. There are shopping guides to eating guides, tour package information, fold-out maps and hotel pamphlets, weeklies and monthlies highlighting current events… you name it.

These materials can also be picked up downtown. The Singapore Tourist Promotion Board operates two information centres at:
Raffles City Tower #01-19

Tel: 330 0431, 330 0432
Opens daily from 8.30 am to 6 pm
Scotts Shopping Centre #02-02
Tel: 738 3778, 738 3779
Opens daily from 9.30 am to 9.30 pm

Most hotels stock up on these too for the convenience of their guests. Larger shopping centres particularly those along Orchard Road also provide a good supply of information brochures; check at the main lobbies.

TRANSPORTATION

BUSES: Buses in Singapore are regular and inexpensive, and you can board a bus to almost any tourist attraction in Singapore.

As a general rule, buses carry the same route number on both onward and outward journeys. If you alight on one street to visit an attraction, the bus stop for your return journey will be opposite that first stop. If it's a one-way street, the return bus stop will be on the next parallel street. You'll need the correct fare for your journey as drivers do not give change on one-man-operated buses. The maximum fare for non-airconditioned services is 90 cents while that for airconditioned services is S$1.20. The comprehensive *Singapore Bus Guide* (90 cents) is for sale at most bookshops.

For convenience, visitors can buy a 1-Day Or 3-Day Singapore Explorer Bus Ticket at S$5 and S$12 respectively. It comes with a map detailing major tourist attractions and the bus services that will take you there. Your Explorer ticket will allow multiple travel anywhere in Singapore on both the red Singapore Bus Service (SBS) and the yellow Trans Island Bus Service (TIBS). Explorer Tickets are for sale at most hotels. For more details call: 287 2727.

And then there is the TransitLink Farecard for sale at S$12 at all MRT stations and bus termini. Perhaps the best alternative to hassle-free travel, TransitLink Farecard allows multiple journeys on stored-value basis, on most public buses and MRT trains.

The following table can be used as a guide when planning your sightseeing:

Buses from Orchard Road area:

Places of Interest	Bus Service & Fare
Arab Street	7 to Victoria Street, then walk (60 cents)
Bird Concert (Sunday)	123 (70 cents)
Botanic Gardens	7, 14, 105, 106, 174 (60 cents)
Bukit Timah Reserve	171, 182 (90 cents)
Cable Car Station (World Trade Centre)	65, 143, 167 (70 cents)
Changi Airport	390 (air-conditioned) (S$1.20)
Changi Prison and Village	14 (90 cents)
Chinatown	124, 167, 174, 182, 190 (60 cents)
Chinese and Japanese Gardens	198 to Corporation Road (90 cents) ; then 154 (50 cents)
City Hall	850 (60 cents)
Clifford Pier	14, 16 to Bras Basah Road (60 cents); then 97, 125, 130, 131 (60 cents)
Crocodile Farm (Upper Serangoon Road)	111 (80 cents); 118 airconditioned ($1.10)
Crocodilarium (East Coast	14 to Mountbatten Road; walk (70 cents)
Crocodile Paradise	see Jurong Bird Park
East Coast Park	16 (air-conditioned) and walk (S$1.20)
Empress Place	see City Hall
Esplanade Park	see City Hall
Haw Par Villa	143 (90 cents)
Japanese Garden	see Chinese Garden
Jurong Bird Park and Jurong Crocodile Paradise	198 (airconditioned) to Boon Lay bus interchange (S$1.20); then 251, 253, 255 (40 cents)
Kallang Theatre	see National Stadium
Kranji War Memorial	182 (90 cents)
Little India	65, 92, 106, 111 (50 cents); 64, 111 airconditioned (60 cents)
MacRitchie Reservoir	132 (80 cents)

Places of Interest	Bus Service & Fare
Mandai Orchid Gardens	171 (90 cents)
Mount Faber	143 (70 cents)
National Museum and Art Gallery	7, 13, 14, 16, 124, 167, 171, 173, 174, 179, 182, 190, 850 (50 cents)
National Stadium	14, 16 (70 cents)
Raffles City	7, 13, 14, 16, 124, 167, 171, 173, 174, 179, 182, 190 (60 cents)
Singapore Science Centre	124, 167, 174, 182, 190 (50 cents). At North Bridge Road transfer to service 197 (90 cents)
Siong Lim Temple	105 (90 cents)
Supreme Court	see City Hall
Victoria Concert Hall and Theatre	see City Hall
Tiger Balm Gardens	see Haw Par Villa
War Memorial Park	see City Hall
World Trade Centre (Cable Car Station)	65, 143, 167 (70 cents)
Zoological Gardens	171 (90 cents)

HIRE CARS: Hire cars are readily available, and cars can be hired via major hotels and travel agents, or direct from the hire car companies. All you need is a valid International Driving Licence or a current Driving Licence from home. Your car rental company will explain basic road rules and the local coupon parking system. Some of the rent-a-car agencies include:-

Hertz Rent-A-Car
280 Kampong Arang Road
Singapore 1336
Tel: 447 3388

Ken-Air Rent-A-Car Pte Ltd
Marina Square #02-200
Singapore 0101
Tel: 336 8188

Sintat Rent-A-Car Pte Ltd
207 Henderson Road #01-01

Singapore 0315
Tel: 273 2211

MRT: The fastest way to get around Singapore is by the Mass Rapid Transit (MRT) system, which makes frequent stops in the city area and also serves some tourist attractions. Trains operate from 6 am to midnight at intervals of between 3 to 8 minutes depending on time of day. There are two main routes, the north–south line from Yishun to Marina Bay and the east–west line from Pasir Ris to Boon Lay.

To travel three stops costs 60 cents and the maximum fare is S$1.40. Charts at each station show the correct fare to pay for your trip, but inner city travel generally costs no more than 60 cents. Coin-operated ticket machines are located inside the main doors at each station. Select your destination station by consulting the route map on-site, place the fare (coins only) in the machine and press the corresponding button, eg., 60 cents. The machine will give you the right change if you do not have the correct amount.

If you have no coins, money-changing machines are located opposite the ticket machines. Ten-dollar stored-value tickets are on sale at all MRT stations, for those on longer visits and planning to make multiple journeys on the train. (Also see under Buses for the TransitLink Farecard as an alternative to convenient multiple travel on the trains.)

The following table shows major attractions, the most convenient MRT station and connecting bus services as necessary.

Destination	MRT	Bus Services
Arab Street	Bugis	Walk
Bird Concert (Sunday)	Tiong Bahru	Walk
Botanic Gardens	Orchard	7, 14, 106, 174
Bukit Timah Nature Reserve	Newton	170, 171 172, 174, 179, 180, 182
Cable Car Station	Tanjong Pagar	10, 20, 30, 97, 100, 125, 180
Changi Airport	Tanah Merah	24
Changi Prison and Village	Bedok	1, 2
Chinatown	Outram Park	Walk

Destination	MRT Station	Bus Services
Chinese Garden	Chinese Garden	Walk
City Hall	City Hall	Walk
Clifford Pier	Raffles Place	Walk
Crocodilarium	see East Coast Park	
Crocodile Paradise	Lakeside	188, 240 to Jurong Bus Inter- change, then 250, 251, 253
East Coast Park	Bedok	31 and 41 (weekdays only), 401 (Sundays and holi- days)
Empress Place	City Hall	Walk
Esplanade Park	City Hall	Walk
Haw Par Villa	Tanjong Pagar	10, 30
Japanese Garden	Chinese Garden	Walk
Jurong Bird Park	see Crocodile Paradise	
Kallang Theatre	City Hall	14, 16 (after 6.45 pm)
Kranji War Memorial	Newton	170, 171, 180, 182
Little India	Dhoby Ghaut	23, 64, 65, 92, 106, 111, 118, 139, 198
MacRitchie Reservoir	Novena	104, 150, 160, 161, 163, 164, 166, 167
Mandai Orchid Gardens	see Zoological Gardens	
Marina South	Marina Bay	400
Marina Square	City Hall	Walk
Merlion Park	Raffles Place	Walk
Mount Faber	see Cable Car Station	
National Library	Dhoby Ghaut	Walk
National Museum and Art Gallery	Dhoby Ghaut	Walk
National Stadium	City Hall	14, 16 (after 6.45 pm)
Peranakan Place	Somerset	Walk
Raffles City	City Hall	Walk
Seletar Reservoir	Toa Payoh	137

Destination	MRT	Bus Services
Sentosa	see Cable Car Station	
Singapore Science Centre	Jurong East	336
Stamford Raffles Landing Site	Raffles Place	Walk
Siong Lim Temple	Toa Payoh	Walk
Supreme Court	City Hall	Walk
Tiger Balm Gardens	see Haw Par Villa	
Victoria Concert Hall and Theatre	Raffles Place	Walk
War Memorial Park	City Hall	Walk
World Trade Centre	see Cable Car Station	
Zoological Gardens	Toa Payoh	137

TAXIS: Taxis may be flagged along any road or you can wait for one at the nearest taxi stand. Designated taxi stops are found outside most hotels or shopping centres. There are several taxi companies operating different coloured fleet: blue; yellow; yellow-and-black; red-and-white; and even the cream London cabs.

Empty cabs ready to pick up passengers have their tops illuminated (only in the evenings); unilluminated taxis with a placard reading "Not for Hire" or "On Call" will not stop. Drivers who display a red destination sign on their dashboard are about to change shift, and they prefer to take passengers travelling in the same direction.

All taxis are metered, and the flagdown fare is S$2.20, which covers the first 1.5 kilometres or less. The fare then rises in stages, at 10 cents for each additional 275 metres.

Extra charges, which may not be shown on the meter, include:
• a 50 percent surcharge on the metered fare for journeys made between midnight and 6 am,
• a S$3 surcharge for any journey from Changi Airport,
• a S$2 surcharge on taxis booked by telephone (or S$3 if the booking is made half an hour or more in advance),
• a S$1 surcharge for any journey from the Central Business District (CBD) from 4 pm to 7 pm on weekdays, and from noon to 3 pm at weekends, and a S$3 surcharge on any journey into the CBD from 7.30 am to 10.15 am or 4.30 pm

to 7 pm from Monday to Saturday, provided that the driver does not already display a CBD pass. The CBD restriction does not apply on Sunday and public holidays.

The CBD system was introduced to minimize inner city traffic congestion. The restricted zone includes the city centre and some parts of Orchard Road. Taxi stands may be especially busy just before and after the CBD hours, because some passengers time their journeys to avoid the extra charges.

TRISHAWS: It seems hard to believe that once trishaws were the main mode of transportation in Singapore in the days before the advent of the automobile. The trishaw is a bicycle drawn, two-wheeled, open-air carriage that usually fits two.

If you wish to enjoy a trishaw tour:
Trishaw Tours Pte Ltd
Chow House #04-04
Robinson Road
Singapore 0106
Tel: 223 8809

Tours last for 45 minutes and start from Waterloo Street before proceeding to the Serangoon Road area. The cost is S$20 per head, which entitles each person to his own trishaw and rider.

USEFUL TELEPHONE NUMBERS

Ambulance	995
AA (Automobile Association) Road Service	748 9911
Automated Flight Enquiry	542 4422
Fire Brigade	995
Immigration Department	532 2877
International Calls Assistance	104
Police	999
Radio Taxis (24 hours)	452 5555
	250 0700
	474 7707
Time, Local	1711
Tourist Information Centre	330 0431
	330 0432
	738 3778
Weather Report	542 7788

VISA AND HEALTH REGULATIONS

Any person entering Singapore must possess a valid passport or internationally recognized travel document. The table below shows visa requirements for different nationalities.

A dash (–) indicates that no visa is required and V indicates that one is required regardless of length of stay. As regulations change from time to time, check visa requirements with your nearest Singapore embassy before departure.

Country of Origin	Visa Required If Stay Exceeds (Number of Days):
Australia	–
Austria	90
Bahrain	14
Bangladesh	–
Belgium	90
Brazil	14
Brunei	–
Burma	14
Canada	–
China	V
Denmark	90
Egypt	14
France	90
Germany, United	90
Greece	14
Hong Kong	–
India	V
Indonesia	14
Israel	14
Italy	90
Japan	90
Korea (Republic of)	90
Kuwait	V
Malaysia	–
Mexico	14
Netherlands	–
New Zealand	–
Norway	90
Pakistan	90
Philippines	14
Saudi Arabia	14
South Africa	14
Spain	90
Sri Lanka	–
Sweden	90
Switzerland	–
Taiwan	14
Thailand	14
United Arab Emirates	14
United Kingdom	–
United States of America	–
USSR	V

Any traveller who arrives from the following countries must produce a valid yellow fever vaccination certificate:
Angola
Benin
Bolivia
Brazil
Burkina Faso
Burundi
Cameroon
the Central African Republic
Chad
Colombia
Congo
Ecuador
Equatorial Guinea
Ethiopia
French Guiana
Gabon
the Gambia
Guinea-Bissau
Guyana
Ivory Coast
Kenya
Liberia
Mali
Mauritania
Niger
Nigeria
Panama
Peru
Rwanda
Sao Tome and Principe
Senegal
Sierra Leone
Somalia
Sudan
Surinam
Tanzania
Togo
Uganda
Upper Volta
Venezuela
Zaire
Zambia.

In addition, a yellow fever vaccination certificate is required if you are arriving from or have passed through any country which is either partly or wholly endemic in yellow fever within the previous six days.

DIRECTORY

AIRLINES

Aeroflot
15 Queen Street #01-02
Singapore 0718
Tel: 336 1757
Air Canada
Meridien Shopping Centre
#02–43
100 Orchard Road
Singapore 0923
Tel: 732 8555
Air France
Orchard Towers #14–05
400 Orchard Road
Singapore 0923
Tel: 737 7166
Air India
UIC Building #17–01
5 Shenton Way
Singapore 0106
Tel: 220 5277
AirLanka
PIL Building #02–00
140 Cecil Street
Singapore 0106
Tel: 225 7233
Air Mauritius
LKN Building #04-02
135 Cecil Street
Singapore 0106
Tel: 222 3033
Air New Zealand
Ocean Building #24-07
10 Collyer Quay
Singapore 0104
Tel: 535 8266

Air Niugini
United Square #01-05
101 Thomson Road
Singapore 1130
Tel: 250 4868
Alitalia
Wisma Atria #15–06
435 Orchard Road
Singapore 0923
Tel: 737 6966
American Airlines
Natwest Centre #11-02
15 McCallum Street
Singapore 0106
Tel: 221 6988
Australian Airlines
United Square #26–01
101 Thomson Road
Singapore 1130
Tel: 255 2488
Bangladesh Biman
Natwest Centre #01-02
15 McCallum Street
Singapore 0106
Tel: 221 7155
British Airways
United Square #01-56
101 Thomson Road
Singapore 0923
Tel: 253 8444
Cathay Pacific
Ocean Building #16–01
10 Collyer Quay
Singapore 0104
Tel: 533 1333
China Airlines
Orchard Towers #01-29

400 Orchard Road
Singapore 0923
Tel: 737 2211
Czechoslovak Airlines
30 Bideford Road #06-00
Singapore 0923
Tel: 737 9844
El Al Israeli Airlines
Thong Sia Building #06–00
30 Bideford Road
Singapore 0922
Tel: 733 8433
Finnair
Liat Towers #18–01
541 Orchard Road
Singapore 0923
Tel: 733 3377
Garuda
United Square #13-03
101 Thomson Road
Singapore 1130
Tel: 250 5666
Indian Airlines
Marina House #01–03
70 Shenton Way
Singapore 0207
Tel: 225 4949
Japan Airlines
Hong Leong Building #01–01
16 Raffles Quay
Singapore 0104
Tel: 221 0522
KLM Royal Dutch Airlines
Mandarin Hotel Arcade #01–02
333 Orchard Road
Singapore 0923
Tel: 737 7622

Korean Airlines
Ocean Building #01-02
10 Collyer Quay
Singapore 0104
Tel: 534 2111
Lauda-Air
PIL Building #08–03
140 Cecil Street
Singapore 0106
Tel: 223 9228
Lufthansa
Orchard Towers #05-01
390 Orchard Road
Singapore 1024
Tel: 737 9222
Malaysia Airlines
Singapore Shopping Centre
#02–09
190 Clemenceau Avenue
Singapore 0923
Tel: 336 6777
Northwest Airlines
Wisma Atria #11-03
435 Orchard Road
Singapore 0923
Tel: 235 7166
Olympic Airways
Park Mall #08-17
9 Penang Road
Singapore 0923
Tel: 336 6061
Pakistan International Airlines
United Square #01–01
101 Thomson Road
Singapore 1130
Tel: 251 2322
Philippine Airlines
Parklane Shopping Mall
#10-02
35 Selegie Road
Singapore 0718
Tel: 336 1611
Qantas Airways
The Promenade #06-05
300 Orchard Road
Singapore 0923
Tel: 730 9222
Royal Brunei Airlines
Royal Holiday Inn Crowne Plaza
Shopping Centre #01–04
25 Scotts Road
Singapore 0922
Tel: 235 4672

Royal Nepal Airlines
SIA Building #09–00
77 Robinson Road
Singapore 0106
Tel: 225 7575
Sabena Belgian Airlines
Gateway East #06-03
152 Beach Road
Singapore 0718
Tel: 291 9066
Saudia
Passenger Terminal Building
Changi Airport #031-01
Singapore 1781
Tel: 545 2041
Scandinavian Airlines System
Gateway East #23-01
152 Beach Road
Singapore 0718
Tel: 294 1611
Singapore Airlines
SIA Building
77 Robinson Road
Singapore 0106
Tel: 229 7270
Singapore Airlines
Mandarin Hotel
333 Orchard Road
Singapore 0923
Tel: 229 7294
Swissair
Wisma Atria #18–01
435 Orchard Road
Singapore 0923
Tel: 737 8133
Tarom Romanian Air Transport
Peninsula Shopping Centre
#03–07
3 Coleman Street
Singapore 0617
Tel: 338 1467
Thai Airways
Keck Seng Towers #08–01
133 Cecil Street
Singapore 0106
Tel: 224 2011
Trans World Airlines
The Plaza #09–324
7500 Beach Road
Singapore 0719
Tel: 298 9911
Turkish Airlines
Far East Shopping Centre
#02–21

545 Orchard Road
Singapore 0923
Tel: 732 4556
United Airlines
Hong Leong Building #44-00
16 Raffles Quay
Singapore 0104
Tel: 220 0488
UTA French Airlines
Orchard Towers #14–05
400 Orchard Road
Singapore 0923
Tel: 737 7166
Variga Brazilian Airlines
SIA Building #10–02
77 Robinson Road
Singapore 0106
Tel: 225 8233
Yugoslav Airlines
Liat Towers #19–02
541 Orchard Road
Singapore 0923
Tel: 235 3017

FOREIGN MISSIONS

Argentina
Tong Building #10–04
302 Orchard Road
Singapore 0923
Tel: 235 4231
Australia
25 Napier Road
Singapore 1025
Tel: 737 9311
Austria
Shaw Centre #22–04
1 Scotts Road
Singapore 0922
Tel: 235 4088
Belgium
International Plaza #09–24
10 Anson Road
Singapore 0207
Tel: 220 7677
Brazil
Tong Building #15–03
302 Orchard Road
Singapore 0923
Tel: 734 3435
Britain
Tanglin Road

Singapore 1024
Tel: 473 9333
Brunei
7A Tanglin Hill
Singapore 1024
Tel: 474 3393
Bulgaria
Thong Teck Building #09–08
15 Scotts Road
Singapore 0922
Tel: 737 1111
Canada
IBM Towers #14–00
80 Anson Road
Singapore 0207
Tel: 225 6363
Chile
105 Cecil Street #14-01
Tel: 223 8577
Denmark
United Square #13–01
101 Thomson Road
Singapore 1130
Tel: 250 3383
Egypt
75 Grange Road
Singapore 1024
Tel: 737 6613
Finland
United Square #21–02
101 Thomson Road
Singapore 1130
Tel: 254 4042
France
5 Gallop Road
Singapore 1025
Tel: 466 4866
Germany, (Federal Republic of)
Far East Shopping Centre
#14–01
545 Orchard Road
Singapore 0923
Tel: 737 1355
Honduras
Golden Wall Auto Centre
#10–08
89 Short Street
Singapore 0718
Tel: 339 8008
Hungary
United Square #22–05
101 Thomson Road
Singapore 1130
Tel: 250 9215

India
31 Grange Road
Singapore 0923
Tel: 737 6777
Indonesia
7 Chatsworth Road
Singapore 1024
Tel: 737 7422
Israel
58 Dalvey Road
Singapore 1025
Tel: 235 0966
Italy
United Square #27–02
101 Thomson Road
Singapore 1130
Tel: 250 6022
Japan
16 Nassim Road
Singapore 1025
Tel: 235 8855
**Korea, Democratic
People's Republic**
19 Fort Road #05–00
Singapore 1543
Tel: 345 3040
Korea, Republic of
United Square #10–03
101 Thomson Road
Singapore 1130
Tel: 256 1188
Malaysia
301 Jervois Road
Singapore 1024
Tel: 235 0111
Myanmar
15 St Martin's Drive
Singapore 1025
Tel: 235 8763
Netherlands
Liat Towers #13–01
541 Orchard Road
Singapore 0923
Tel: 737 1155
New Zealand
13 Nassim Road
Singapore 1025
Tel: 235 9966
Norway
Hong Leong Building #44–01
16 Raffles Quay
Singapore 0104
Tel: 220 7122
Pakistan
20A Nassim Road

Singapore 1025
Tel: 737 6988
Panama
Hong Leong Building #41–06
16 Raffles Quay
Singapore 0104
Tel: 221 8677
Philippines
20 Nassim Road
Singapore 1025
Tel: 737 3977
Poland
Shaw Towers #33–11
100 Beach Road
Singapore
Tel: 294 2513
Romania
48 Jalan Harom Setangkai
Singapore 1025
Tel: 468 3424
Saudi Arabia
10 Nassim Road
Singapore 1025
Tel: 734 5878
Spain
Thong Teck Building #05–08
15 Scotts Road
Singapore 0922
Tel: 732 9788
Sri Lanka
United Plaza #13–07
101 Thomson Road
Singapore 1130
Tel: 254 4595
Sweden
PUB Building #05–08
111 Somerset Road
Singapore 0923
Tel: 734 2771
Switzerland
1 Swiss Club Link
Singapore 1128
Tel: 468 5788
Thailand
370 Orchard Road
Singapore 0923
Tel: 737 2644
Turkey
20B Nassim Road
Singapore 1025
Tel: 732 9211
USA
30 Hill Street
Singapore 0617
Tel: 338 0251

USSR
51 Nassim Road
Singapore 1025
Tel: 235 1834

BANKS

Algemene Bank Nederland
18 Church Street
Singapore 0104
Tel: 535 5511
Ban Hin Lee Bank
Tan Ean Kiam Building #01–00
15 Phillip Street
Singapore 0104
Tel: 533 7022
Bangkok Bank
Bangkok Bank Building
180 Cecil Street
Singapore 0106
Tel: 221 9400
Bank of America
78 Shenton Way
Singapore 0207
Tel: 223 6688
Bank of China
Bank of China Building
4 Battery Road
Singapore 0104
Tel: 535 2411
Bank of India
GMG Building
108 Robinson Road
Singapore 0106
Tel: 222 0011
Bank of Singapore
Tong Eng Building #01–02
101 Cecil Street
Singapore 0106
Tel: 223 9266
Bank of Tokyo
Hong Leong Building #01–06
16 Raffles Quay
Singapore 0104
Tel: 220 8111
Banque Indosuez
Shenton House
Shenton Way
Singapore 0106
Tel: 220 7111
Chase Manhattan Bank
Shell Tower
50 Raffles Place

Singapore 0104
Tel: 530 4111
Chung Khiaw Bank
International Plaza #01–01
10 Anson Road
Singapore 0207
Tel: 222 8622
Citibank
Robina House #17–05
1 Shenton Way
Singapore 0106
Tel: 225 5225
Development Bank of Singapore
DBS Building
6 Shenton Way
Singapore 0106
Tel: 220 1111
Far Eastern Bank
Far Eastern Bank Building
#01–00
156 Cecil Street
Singapore 0106
Tel: 221 9055
**Four Seas
Communications Bank**
19 Cecil Street
Singapore 0104
Tel: 224 9898
**Hongkong & Shanghai
Banking Corporation**
Hongkong Bank Building
#19–00
21 Collyer Quay
Singapore 0104
Tel: 530 5000
Indian Bank
Bharat Building
2 D'Almeida Street
Singapore 0104
Tel: 534 3511
Indian Overseas Bank
IOB Building #03–00
64 Cecil Street
Singapore 0104
Tel: 225 1100
Industrial and Commercial Bank
ICB Building #01–00
2 Shenton Way
Singapore 0106
Tel: 221 1711
International Bank of Singapore
Overseas Union House #02–01
50 Collyer Quay
Singapore 0104
Tel: 223 4488

Kwangtung Provincial Bank
Kwangtung Provincial Bank Bldg
60 Cecil Street
Singapore 0104
Tel: 223 9622
Lee Wah Bank
Robina House #01–03
1 Shenton Way
Singapore 0106
Tel: 225 8844
Malayan Banking
Malayan Banking Chambers
#01–00
2 Battery Road
Singapore 0104
Tel: 535 2266
Malayan United Bank
55 Market Street #12–00
Singapore 0104
Tel: 535 2466
Mitsui Bank
Hong Leong Building #01–04
16 Raffles Quay
Singapore 0104
Tel: 220 9761
**Oversea Chinese
Banking Corporation**
OCBC Centre
65 Chulia Street
Singapore 0104
Tel: 535 7222
Overseas Union Bank
OUB Centre
1 Raffles Place
Singapore 0104
Tel: 533 8686
Post Office Savings Bank
POSB Building
73 Bras Basah Road
Singapore 0718
Tel: 339 3333
Security Pacific Asian Bank
50 Raffles Place
Shell Tower #01-03
Tel: 224 3363
Tat Lee Bank
Tat Lee Bank Building
63 Market Street
Singapore 0104
Tel: 533 9292
UCO Bank
Bharat Building
2 D'Almeida Street
Singapore 0104
Tel: 532 5944

United Malayan
Banking Corporation
Wing On Life Building #01–00
150 Cecil Street
Singapore 0106
Telephone: 225 3111
United Overseas Bank
UOB Building
1 Bonham Street
Singapore 0104
Tel: 533 9898

CREDIT CARD
COMPANIES

American Express
UOL Building #15–00
96 Somerset Road
Singapore 0923
Tel: 235 8133
Carte Blanche
Cathay Building #09–05
11 Dhoby Ghaut
Singapore 0922
Tel: 339 5542
Citibank Visa
Robina House #17–05
1 Shenton Way
Singapore 0106
Tel: 225 5225
Diners Club
The Plaza #03-201
7500 Beach Road
Singapore 0719
Tel: 294 4222

GOVERNMENT
AND BUSINESS

Economic Development Board
Head Office
Raffles City Tower #24–00
250 North Bridge Road
Singapore 0617
Tel: 336 2288
Fax: 339 6077
Trade Development Board
Head Office
World Trade Centre #10–40
1 Maritime Square
Telok Blangah Road

Singapore 0409
Tel: 271 9388
Fax: 274 0770

CHAMBERS OF
COMMERCE

Singapore Federation of
Chambers of Commerce
& Industry
Chinese Chamber of Commerce
and Industry Building #03–01
47 Hill Street
Singapore 0617
Tel: 338 9761
Fax: 339 5630
Singapore International
Chamber of Commerce
50 Raffles Place #03-02
Singapore 0104
Tel: 224 1255
Singapore Chinese Chamber
of Commerce and Industry
Chinese Chamber of Commerce
and Industry Building #07–02
47 Hill Street
Singapore 0617
Tel: 337 8381
Fax: 339 0605
Singapore Malay Chamber
of Commerce
International Plaza #24–07
10 Anson Road
Singapore 0207
Tel: 221 1066
Fax: 223 5811
Singapore Indian Chamber
of Commerce
Tong Eng Building #23–01
101 Cecil Street
Singapore 0106
Tel: 222 2855
Fax: 223 1707
American Business Council
Shaw Centre #16–07
1 Scotts Road
Singapore 0922
Tel: 235 0077
British Business Association
Inchcape House
450 Alexandra Road
Singapore 0511
Tel: 475 4192

Indonesian Business Association
158 Cecil Street #07–03
Singapore 0106
Tel: 221 5063
Japanese Chamber of
Commerce and Industry
CPF Building #24–04
79 Robinson Road
Singapore 0106
Tel: 2210541
Fax: 2256197
Pakistan Chamber of Commerce
Union Building #07–177
171 Tras Street
Singapore 0207
Tel: 2248562

TOURIST
INFORMATION

HEAD OFFICE
Singapore Tourist
Promotion Board
Raffles City Tower #36–04
250 North Bridge Road
Singapore 0617
Tel: (65) 339 6622
Fax: (65) 339 9423
Australia
Singapore Tourist
Promotion Board
8th Floor Goldfields House
1 Alfred Street
Circular Quay, Sydney
New South Wales 2000
Australia
Tel: (02) 241 3771
Fax: (02) 232 3658
Australia
Singapore Tourist
Promotion Board
c/o Tara Marketing Services
Suite 3
336 Churchill Avenue, Subiaco
Western Australia 6008
Tel: (09) 381 1855
England
Singapore Tourist
Promotion Board
1st Floor Carrington House
126 Regent Street
London W1R 5FE

England, UK
Tel: (071) 437 0033
France
Singapore Tourist
Promotion Board
Centre d'Affaires le Louvre
2 Place du Palais Royal
75044 Paris, France
Tel: 429 71616
Germany, Federal Republic
Singapore Tourist
Promotion Board
Poststrasse 2-4
D6000 Frankfurt am Main
Federal Republic of Germany
Tel: (069) 231 456
Hong Kong
Singapore Tourist
Promotion Board
17th Floor
United Centre
95 Queensway
Hong Kong
Tel: 527 1713
Japan
Singapore Tourist
Promotion Board
1st Floor Yamato Seimei Bldg
1-chome
1-7 Uchisaiwai-cho
Chiyoda-ku, Tokyo 100
Japan
Tel: (03) 593 3388
Fax: (03) 591 1480
New Zealand
Singapore Tourist
Promotion Board
c/o Walshes World
2nd Floor
Dingwall Building
87 Queen Street
Auckland 1
New Zealand
Tel: (9) 793 708
Switzerland
Singapore Tourist
Promotion Board
c/o Schellenberg,
Ogilvy & Mather
Werbeagentur BSW
Bergstrasse 50
CH8032 Zurich
Switzerland
Tel: (01) 252 5365

USA
Singapore Tourist
Promotion Board
Suite 510
8484 Wilshire Boulevard
Beverly Hills
California 90211
USA
Tel: (213) 852 1901
USA
Singapore Tourist
Promotion Board
Suite 1008
342 Madison Avenue
New York, NY 10173
USA
Tel: (212) 687 0385

CINEMAS

Capitol Theatre
North Bridge Road
Singapore 0617
Tel: 337 9759
Cathay Cinema
11 Dhoby Ghaut
Singapore 0922
Tel: 338 3400
Jade Theatre 1
Shaw Towers
100 Beach Road
Singapore 0718
Tel: 293 2581
Jade Theatre 2
Shaw Towers
100 Beach Road
Singapore 0718
Tel: 294 2568
Orchard Theatre
8 Grange Road
Singapore 0923
Tel: 734 2981
Prince Theatre 1
Shaw Towers
100 Beach Road
Singapore 0718
Tel: 298 4905
Prince Theatre 2
Shaw Towers
100 Beach Road
Singapore 0718
Tel: 294 2553

THEATRES

Drama Centre
40 Canning Rise
Singapore 0617
Tel: 222 9711
Kallang Theatre
Stadium Walk
Singapore 1439
Tel: 345 8488
Singapore Conference Hall
Shenton Way
Singapore 0106
Tel: 222 9711
Victoria Concert Hall
Empress Place
Singapore 0617
Tel: 337 7490
Victoria Theatre
9 Empress Place
Singapore 0617
Telephone: 3362151

NIGHTSPOTS

Live Western Music

Anywhere
Tanglin Shopping Centre
#04–08
19 Tanglin Road
Singapore 1024
Tel: 235 1041
Celebrities
Orchard Towers #B1–41
400 Orchard Road
Singapore 0923
Tel: 734 5221
The Cellar
Jack's Place
Yen San Building
268 Orchard Road
Singapore 0923
Tel: 235 7361
Club 392
Orchard Towers #01–21
400 Orchard Road
Singapore 0923
Tel: 737 7334
Europa
Block 5, #01–2011
Changi Village Road
Singapore 1750

Tel: 542 5617
International Plaza #02-02
10 Anson Road
Tel: 225 3668
Happy Days
Orchard Theatre
Grange Road
Singapore 0923
Tel: 734 3688
Saxophone
23 Cuppage Terrace
Singapore 0922
Tel: 235 8385
Top Ten
Orchard Towers #05-18A
400 Orchard Road
Singapore 0923
Tel: 732 3077

Discotheques

Chinoiserie
Hyatt Regency Hotel
10 Scotts Road
Singapore 0922
Tel: 733 1188
The Club
Omni Marco Polo Hotel
247 Tanglin Road
Singapore 1024
Tel: 471 0521
Ridley's
ANA Hotel Singapore
16 Nassim Hill
Singapore 1025
Tel: 7321222
Rumours
Forum Galleria #03-08
583 Orchard Road
Singapore 0923
Tel: 235 2466
Scandals
Westin Plaza Hotel
2 Stamford Road
Singapore 0617
Tel: 338 8585
TGIF
Far East Plaza #04-44
14 Scotts Road
Singapore 0922
Tel: 235 6181
The Warehouse
332 Havelock Road
Singapore 0316
Tel: 732 9922

Xanadu
Shangri-la Hotel
22 Orange Grove Road
Singapore 1025
Tel: 737 3644

Western Bar with Music

Bibi's
Peranakan Place
180 Orchard Road
Singapore 0923
Tel: 732 6966
Bill Bailey's Bar
Dynasty Hotel
320 Orchard Road
Singapore 0923
Tel: 734 9900
Brannigan's
Hyatt Regency Hotel
10 Scotts Road
Singapore 0922
Tel: 733 1188
Yesterday's
United Square #B1–01
101 Thomson Road
Singapore 1130
Tel: 250 8009

Western Pubs

The Cricketer
Marina Mandarin Hotel
6 Raffles Boulevard
Singapore 0103
Tel: 338 388
Excalibur
Tanglin Shopping Centre
#B1–06
19 Tanglin Road
Singapore 1024
Tel: 732 8093
The Hideout
Meridien Shopping Centre
#01–101
100 Orchard Road
Singapore 0923
Tel: 733 5806
Jimm's Pub
Negara Hotel
15 Claymore Drive
Singapore 0922
Tel: 737 0811
Mitre Hotel
145 Killiney Road

Singapore 0923
Tel: 737 3811
The Yard
294 River Valley Road
Singapore 0923
Tel: 733 9594
Live Chinese Music

Neptune Theatre Lounge
Overseas Union House #07–00
50 Collyer Quay
Singapore 0104
Tel: 737 4411

Chinese Lounges

Golden Million
Peninsula Hotel
3 Coleman Street
Singapore 0617
Tel: 336 6993
Grand Palace
Orchard Building #06–00
1 Grange Road
Singapore 0923
Tel: 737 8922
Lido Palace
Glass Hotel Shopping Centre
#05–01
317 Outram Road
Singapore 0316
Tel: 732 8855

DEPARTMENT STORES

Daimaru
Liang Court
177 River Valley Road
Singapore 0617
Tel: 339 1111
Galeries Lafayette
Liat Towers
541 Orchard Road
Singapore 0923
Tel: 732 9177
Galeries Lafayette
OUB Centre
1 Raffles Place
Singapore 0104
Tel: 535 7069
Isetan
Wisma Atria
435 Orchard Road

Singapore 0923
Tel: 733 7777
Isetan
Apollo Hotel
405 Havelock Road
Singapore 0316
Tel: 733 1111
Isetan
Parkway Parade
80 Marine Parade Road
Singapore 1544
Tel: 345 5555
John Little
Specialists' Shopping Centre
277 Orchard Road
Singapore 0923
Tel: 737 2222
Metro Grand
Lucky Plaza
304 Orchard Road
Singapore 0923
Tel: 737 6033
Metro
Royal Holiday Inn Crowne Plaza
25 Scotts Road
Singapore 0922
Tel: 733 1966
Metro
Far East Plaza
14 Scotts Road
Singapore 0922
Tel: 733 3322
Metro
The Plaza
7500 Beach Road
Singapore 0719
Tel: 297 2388
Metro
Marina Square
6 Raffles Boulevard
Singapore 0103
Tel: 337 2868
Robinson's
Centrepoint
176 Orchard Road
Singapore 0923
Tel: 733 0088
Sogo
Raffles City Shopping Centre
252 North Bridge Road
Singapore 0617
Tel: 339 1100
Tangs
320 Orchard Road

Singapore 0923
Tel: 737 5500
Tokyu
Marina Square
6 Raffles Boulevard
Singapore 0103
Tel: 337 0077
Yaohan
Plaza Singapura
68 Orchard Road
Singapore 0923
Tel: 337 4061
Yaohan
Parkway Parade
80 Marine Parade Road
Singapore 1544
Tel: 344 9011
Yaohan
Thomson Plaza
301 Upper Thomson Road
Singapore 2057
Tel: 454 6511

RESTAURANTS

Peranakan

Bibi's
Peranakan Place
180 Orchard Road
Singapore 0923
Tel: 732 6966
Nonya and Baba
262 River Valley Road
Singapore 0923
Tel: 7341382
Peranakan Inn
210 East Coast Road
Singapore 1542
Tel: 440 6195

Malay

Aziza's
36 Emerald Hill Road
Singapore 0923
Tel: 235 1130

Indonesian

Jawa Timur Permai
9th Floor
Chiat Hong Building

110 Middle Road
Singapore 0718
Tel: 337 5532
Ramayana
Plaza Singapura #07–01
68 Orchard Road
Singapore 0923
Tel: 336 3317
Sanur
Centrepoint #04–17
176 Orchard Road
Singapore 0923
Tel: 734 2192
Tambuah Mas
Tanglin Shopping Centre
#04–10
19 Tanglin Road
Singapore 1024
Tel: 733 3333

Indian

Annalakshmi
Excelsior Hotel
Shopping Centre #02–10
5 Coleman Street
Singapore 0617
Tel: 339 3007
Banana Leaf Apollo
56 Race Course Road
Singapore 0821
Tel: 293 8682
Jubilee
771 North Bridge Road
Singapore 0719
Tel: 290 8714
Keppel Restaurant
Tanjong Pagar Complex #01-05
7 Keppel Road
Singapore 0208
Tel: 222 3486
Komala Vilas
76 Serangoon Road
Singapore 0821
Tel 293 6980
Mayarani
Boulevard Hotel
#B2 Cuscaden Wing
Singapore 1024
Tel: 732 6179
Muthu's
78 Race Course Road
Singapore 0821
Tel: 293 7029

Orchard Maharajah
25 Cuppage Terrace
Singapore 0922
Tel: 732 6331
Rang Mahal
Imperial Hotel
1 Jalan Rumbia
Singapore 0923
Tel: 730 1107
Samy's Curry Restaurant
Singapore Civil
Service Club House
Blk 25 Dempsey Road
Singapore 1024
Tel: 472 2080/296 9391
Tandoor
Holiday Inn Park View
11 Cavenagh Road
Singapore 0922
Tel: 733 8333
Ujagar Singh Johal
7 St Gregory's Place
Singapore 0617
Tel: 336 1586

Cantonese

Canton Garden
3rd Floor
Westin Plaza Hotel
2 Stamford Road
Singapore 0617
Tel: 338 8585
Fatty's
Albert Complex #01–33
60 Albert Street
Singapore 0718
Tel: 338 1087
Fut Sai Kai
147 Kitchener Road
Singapore 0820
Tel: 298 0336
Golden Crown
Block 40B, #03–352
Commonwealth Avenue
Singapore 0314
Tel: 474 9255
Huan Long Court
Apollo Hotel
405 Havelock Road
Singapore 0316
Tel: 733 9677
Lei Garden
Boulevard Hotel

200 Orchard Boulevard
Singapore 1024
Tel: 235 8122
Li Bai
Sheraton Towers Hotel
39 Scotts Road
Singapore 0922
Tel: 737 6888
Majestic
31 Bukit Pasoh Road
Singapore 0208
Tel: 223 5111
Pot Luck Eating House
199 East Coast Road
Singapore 1542
Tel: 344 8190
Prawn House
Marina Square #04–401
6 Raffles Boulevard
Singapore 0103
Tel: 338 3988
Ru Yi
Hyatt Regency Hotel
10 Scotts Road
Singapore 0922
Tel: 733 1188
Shang Palace
Shangri-la Hotel
22 Orange Grove Road
Singapore 1025
Tel: 737 3644
Tsui Hang Village
Asia Hotel
37 Scotts Road
Singapore 0922
Tel: 737 3140
Wah Lok
Carlton Hotel
76 Bras Basah Road
Singapore 0718
Tel: 338 8333
Xiang Man Lou
Bras Basah Complex #01–79
231 Bain Street
Singapore 0718
Tel: 338 7885

Hakka

Moi Kong
22 Murray Street
Singapore 0207
Tel: 221 7758

Hokkien

Beng Hiang
20 Murray Street
Singapore 0207
Tel: 221 6684
Beng Thin Hoon Kee
5th Floor OCBC Centre
55 Chulia Street
Singapore 0104
Tel: 533 7708

Szechuan

Charming Garden
Novotel Orchid Inn
214 Dunearn Road
Singapore 1129
Tel: 251 8149
Cherry Garden
Oriental Hotel
5 Raffles Avenue
Singapore 0103
Tel: 338 0066
Dragon City
Novotel Orchid Inn
214 Dunearn Road
Singapore 1129
Tel: 254 7070
Golden Phoenix
Equatorial Hotel
429 Bukit Timah Road
Singapore 1025
Tel: 256 0431
Liu Hsiang Lou
Tai-Pan Ramada Hotel
101 Victoria Street
Singapore 0718
Tel: 336 0811
Long Jiang
Crown Prince Hotel
270 Orchard Road
Singapore 0923
Tel: 734 9056
Omei
Grand Central Hotel
22 Cavenagh Road
Singapore 0922
Tel: 737 2735
Pine Court
Mandarin Hotel
333 Orchard Road
Singapore 0923
Tel: 737 4411

Westlake
Block 4, #02–139
139 Queen's Road
Singapore 1026
Tel: 474 7283

Taiwanese

Goldleaf
Orchard Point #04–01
160 Orchard Road
Singapore 0923
Tel: 737 7830

May Garden
Orchard Towers #02–01
400 Orchard Road
Singapore 0923
Tel: 235 1829

**Mosque Street
Steamboat House**
44 Mosque Street
Singapore 0106
Tel: 222 9560

Teochew

Ban Seng
79 New Bridge Road
Singapore 0105
Tel: 534 1402

Chao Zhou Garden
6th Floor
UIC Building
5 Shenton Way
Singapore 0106
Tel: 225 6355

Lim Seng Lee
38 South Buona Vista Road
Singapore 0511
Tel: 472 1019

Swatow
DBS Building #B1–15
6 Shenton Way
Singapore 0106
Tel: 223 5473

Swatow
Plaza by the Park
Bras Basah Road
Singapore 0718
Tel: 339 2544

Tai Seng Gourmet Corner
6 Murray Street
Singapore 0207
Tel: 222 1413

Dim Sum

Fook Yuen
Pidemco Centre #01–01
95 South Bridge Road
Singapore 0105
Tel: 532 7778

Fook Yuen
Paragon Shopping Centre
#03–05
290 Orchard Road
Singapore 0923
Tel: 235 2211

Garden Seafood Restaurant
Goodwood Park Hotel
22 Scotts Road
Singapore 0922
Tel: 737 7411

Seafood

Ng Tiong Choon
59 Lorong Chuntum
Singapore 2775
Tel: 754 1991

Orchard King Prawn
UOL Building #01–05
96 Somerset Road
Singapore 0923
Tel: 734 4079

Seafood International
902 East Coast Parkway
Singapore 1646
Tel: 345 1211

Singa Inn
920 East Coast Parkway
Singapore 1646
Tel: 345 1111

Stamford
6 Raffles Avenue
Singapore 0103
Tel: 339 8058

UDMC Seafood Centre
East Coast Parkway
Singapore 1646
Tel: 241 5173 (Bedok Sea View)
444 7967 (Chin Wah Heng)
448 2020 (East Coast Park)
448 1894 (Golden Lagoon)
442 3435 (Jumbo)
442 2690 (Kheng Luck)
344 7722 (Ocean Park)
442 3112 (Red House)

Chinese Vegetarian

Buddhist's Banquet
760 Upper Serangoon Road
Singapore 1923
Tel: 286 7559

Fairway
611 Geylang Road
Singapore 1438
Tel: 748 6108

Fo You Yuan
20 Lorong 11 Geylang
Singapore 1438
Tel: 744 8009

Fu Sai Kai
147 Kitchener Road
Singapore 0820
Tel: 298 0336

Kwan Im
Southeast Asia Hotel
190 Waterloo Street
Singapore 0718
Tel: 336 2389

Thai

**Chao Phya Thai
Food Market & Restaurant**
Block 730, #02–4272
Ang Mo Kio Avenue 6
Singapore 2056
Tel: 456 0118

Haadyai Beefball
467 Joo Chiat Road
Singapore 1542
Tel: 334 3234

Her Sea Palace
Forum Galleria #01–16
583 Orchard Road
Singapore 0923
Tel: 732 5688

Parkway Thai Restaurant
Parkway Parade #02–08
80 Marine Parade Road
Singapore 1544
Tel: 345 8811

Japanese

Kampachi
World Trade Centre #04–02
1 Maritime Square
Singapore 0409
Tel: 273 0230

Nadaman
Shangri-la Hotel
22 Orange Grove Road
Singapore 1025
Tel: 737 3644
Shima
Goodwood Park Hotel
22 Scotts Road
Singapore 0922
Tel: 734 6281
Suntory
Delfi Shopping Centre #06–01
402 Orchard Road
Singapore 0923
Tel: 732 5111
Unkai
ANA Hotel Singapore
16 Nassim Hill
Singapore 1025
Tel: 732 1222
Yamagen
20th Floor
Yen San Building
268 Orchard Road
Singapore 0923
Tel: 235 0481

Korean

Han Do
Orchard Shopping Centre
#05–01
321 Orchard Road
Singapore 0923
Tel: 235 8451
Kam Han Kguk
Golden Mile Complex #02–95
5001 Beach Road
Singapore 0719
Tel: 296 2522
Korean Restaurant
Specialists' Shopping Centre
#05–35
277 Orchard Road
Singapore 0923
Tel: 235 0018
Seoul Garden
Parkway Parade #02–56
80 Marine Parade Road
Singapore 1544
Tel: 345 1339

American

New Orleans
Holiday Inn Park View
11 Cavenagh Road
Singapore 0922
Tel: 733 8333
Nutmegs
Hyatt Regency Hotel
10 Scotts Road
Singapore 0922
Tel: 733 1188
Trader Vic's
New Otani Hotel
177 River Valley Road
Singapore 0617
Tel: 337 2249

Mexican

Chico's and Charlie's
Liat Towers #05–01
541 Orchard Road
Singapore 0923
Tel: 734 1753
El Felipe's
Orchard Towers #B1–01
1 Claymore Road
Singapore 0922
Tel: 733 3551
El Felipe's
34 Lorong Mambong
Holland Village
Singapore 1027
Tel: 468 1520

Continental European

Belvedere
Mandarin Hotel
333 Orchard Road
Singapore 0923
Tel: 737 4411
Casablanca
7 Emerald Hill Road
Singapore 0922
Tel: 235 9328
Chateaubriand
Pan Pacific Hotel
7 Raffles Boulevard
Singapore 0103
Tel: 336 8111
Fourchettes
Oriental Hotel

5 Raffles Avenue
Singapore 0103
Tel: 338 0066
Hubertus Grill
ANA Hotel Singapore
16 Nassim Hill
Singapore 1025
Tel: 732 1222
Le Vendome
Dynasty Hotel
320 Orchard Road
Singapore 0923
Tel: 734 9900
Restaurant 1819
Tuan Sing Towers #B1–00
30 Robinson Road
Singapore 0104
Tel: 223 4033
The Stables
Mandarin Hotel
333 Orchard Road
Singapore 0923
Tel: 737 4411

English

Foster's
Specialists' Shopping Centre
#02–38
277 Orchard Road
Singapore 0923
Tel: 737 8939

French

Harbour Grill
Hilton Hotel
581 Orchard Road
Singapore 0923
Tel: 737 2233
La Brasserie
Omni Marco Polo Hotel
247 Tanglin Road
Singapore 1024
Tel: 474 7141
Latour
Shangri-la Hotel
22 Orange Grove Road
Singapore 1025
Tel: 737 3644
L'Escargot
Imperial Hotel
1 Jalan Rumbia
Singapore 0923
Tel: 737 1666

Le Restaurant de France
Meridien Hotel
100 Orchard Road
Singapore 0923
Tel: 733 8855

Italian

Bologna
Marina Mandarin
6 Raffles Boulevard
Marina Square
Singapore 0103
Tel: 338 3388
Grand Italia
Glass Hotel
317 Outram Road
Singapore 0316
Tel: 733 0188
La Taverna
DBS Building #08–17
6 Shenton Way
Singapore 0106
Tel: 221 0375
Mamma Mia Ristorante Italiano
Orchard Towers, #02–21
400 Orchard Road
Singapore 0923
Tel: 732 0977
Prego
Westin Stamford Hotel
2 Stamford Road
Singapore 0617
Tel: 338 8585

Swiss

Chesa
Equatorial Hotel
429 Bukit Timah Road
Singapore 1025
Tel: 256 0431
Le Chalet
Ladyhill Hotel
1 Ladyhill Road
Singapore 1025
Tel: 737 2111
Movenpick
Scotts Shopping Centre #B1–01
6 Scotts Road
Singapore 1025
Tel: 235 8700
Movenpick
Standard Chartered Bank Building #B1–01

6 Battery Road
Singapore 0104
Tel: 221 0340

Russian

Balalaika
York Hotel
21 Mount Elizabeth
Singapore 0922
Tel: 737 0511
Shashlik Restaurant
545 Orchard Road #06–19
Far East Shopping Centre
Singapore 0923
Tel: 732 6401/734 3090

Vietnamese

Pare 'Gu Vietnamese
Seafood Restaurant
150 Orchard Road
#01–24/34
Orchard Plaza
Singapore 0923
Tel: 733 4211
Saigon Restaurant
15 Cairnhill Road
#04-03 Cairnhill Place
Singapore 0922
Tel: 235 0626

HOTELS

$ – less than or equal to S$100
$$ – S$100-150
$$$ – S$150-200
$$$$ – S$200-300
$$$$$ – S$300 upwards

The rates quoted are for standard single rooms only and are subject to a 10% service charge and a 4% government tax.

Amara $$$
165 Tanjong Pagar Road
Singapore 0208
Tel: 224 4488
350 rooms
Ana $$$$
16 Nassim Hill
Singapore 1025

Tel: 732 1222
456 rooms
Apollo $$$
405 Havelock Road
Singapore 0316
Tel: 733 2081
317 rooms
Asia $$$
37 Scotts Road
Singapore 0922
Tel: 737 8388
146 rooms
Bayview $$$
30 Bencoolen Street
Singapore 0718
Tel: 337 2882
117 rooms
Boulevard $$$$
200 Orchard Boulevard
Singapore 1024
Tel: 737 2911
528 rooms
Broadway $
195 Serangoon Road
Singapore 0821
Tel: 293 6788
62 rooms
Cairnhill $$
19 Cairnhill Circle
Singapore 0922
Tel: 734 6622
220 rooms
Carlton $$$$
76 Bras Basah Road
Singapore 0718
Tel: 338 8333
420 rooms
Cockpit $$
6 Oxley Rise
Singapore 0923
Tel: 737 9111
182 rooms
Crown Prince $$$$
270 Orchard Road
Singapore 0923
Tel: 732 1111
303 rooms
Duke $
42 Meyer Road
Singapore 1543
Tel: 345 3311
170 rooms
Dynasty $$$$
320 Orchard Road

Singapore 0923
Tel: 734 9900
400 rooms
Equatorial $$$
429 Bukit Timah Road
Singapore 1025
Tel: 732 0431
224 rooms
Excelsior $$$
5 Coleman Street
Singapore 0617
Tel: 338 7733
300 rooms
Furama $$$$
60 Eu Tong Sen Street
Singapore 0105
Tel: 533 3888
352 rooms
Garden $$$
14 Balmoral Road
Singapore 1025
Tel: 235 3344
216 rooms
Glass $$$
317 Outram Road
Singapore 0316
Tel: 733 0188
509 rooms
Golden Landmark $$$
390 Victoria Street
Singapore 0718
Tel: 297 2828
392 rooms
Goodwood Park $$$$$
22 Scotts Road
Singapore 0922
Tel: 737 7411
231 rooms
Grand Central $$
22 Cavenagh Road
Singapore 0922
Tel: 737 9944
365 rooms
Great Eastern $$$
401 Macpherson Road
Singapore 1336
Tel: 284 8244
155 rooms
Harbour View Dai-ichi $$$
81 Anson Road
Singapore 0207
Tel: 224 1133
420 rooms

Hilton $$$$
581 Orchard Road
Singapore 0923
Tel: 737 2233
435 rooms
Holiday Inn Park View $$$$
11 Cavenagh Road
Singapore 0922
Tel: 733 8333
320 rooms
Hyatt Regency $$$$$
10 Scotts Road
Singapore 0922
Tel: 733 1188
738 rooms
Imperial $$$
1 Jalan Rumbia
Singapore 0923
Tel: 737 1666
600 rooms
International House $$
RELC Building
30 Orange Grove Road
Singapore 1025
Tel: 737 9044
128 rooms
King's $$$
430 Havelock Road
Singapore 0316
Tel: 733 0011
319 rooms
Ladyhill $$
1 Ladyhill Road
Singapore 1025
Tel: 737 2111
171 rooms
Lion City $
15 Tanjong Katong Road
Singapore 1543
Tel: 744 8111
163 rooms
Mandarin $$$$
333 Orchard Road
Singapore 0923
Tel: 737 4411
1,200 rooms
Marina Mandarin $$$$
6 Raffles Boulevard
Singapore 0103
Tel: 338 3388
557 rooms
Meliá at Scotts $$$$
45 Scotts Road
Singapore 0922

Tel: 732 5885
241 rooms
Meridien $$$$
100 Orchard Road
Singapore 0923
Tel: 733 8855
407 rooms
Meridien Changi $$$$
1 Netheravon Road
Singapore 1750
Tel: 542 7700
280 rooms
Metropole $
41 Seah Street
Singapore 0718
Tel: 336 3611
54 rooms
Ming Court $$$
1 Tanglin Road
Singapore 1024
Tel: 737 1133
300 rooms
Miramar $$$
401 Havelock Road
Singapore 0316
Tel: 733 0222
346 rooms
Mitre $
145 Killiney Road
Singapore 0923
Tel: 737 0222
19 rooms
Negara $$
15 Claymore Drive
Singapore 0922
Tel: 737 0811
104 rooms
New Otani $$$$
177 River Valley Road
Singapore 0617
Tel: 338 3333
408 rooms
New Park $$$
181 Kitchener Road
Singapore 0820
Tel: 291 5533
525 rooms
New Seventh Storey $
229 Rochor Road
Singapore 0718
Tel: 337 0251
38 rooms
Novotel Orchid Inn $$$
214 Dunearn Road

Singapore 1129
Tel: 250 3322
457 rooms
Omni Marco Polo $$$$
247 Tanglin Road
Singapore 1024
Tel: 474 7141
903 rooms
Orchard $$$
442 Orchard Road
Singapore 0923
Tel: 734 7766
350 rooms
Oriental $$$$$
5 Raffles Avenue
Singapore 0103
Tel: 338 0066
515 rooms
Pan Pacific $$$$$
7 Raffles Boulevard
Singapore 0103
Tel: 336 8111
800 rooms
Paramount $$
30 Marine Parade Road
Singapore 1544
Tel: 344 5577
250 rooms
Peninsula $$$
3 Coleman Street
Singapore 0617
Tel: 337 8091
315 rooms
Phoenix $$$
Somerset Road
Singapore 0923
Tel: 737 8666
300 rooms
Plaza $$$$
7500 Beach Road
Singapore 0719
Tel: 298 0011
353 rooms
Premier $$
22 Nassim Hill
Singapore 1025
Tel: 733 9811
29 rooms
Raffles $$$$
1 Beach Road
Singapore 0718
Tel: 337 8041
106 rooms

Regent $$$$
1 Cuscaden Road
Singapore 1024
Tel: 733 8888
441 rooms
River View $$
382 Havelock Road
Singapore 0316
Tel: 732 9922
476 rooms
Royal $$
36 Newton Road
Singapore 1130
Tel: 253 4411
313 rooms
**Royal Holiday Inn
Crowne Plaza $$$$**
25 Scotts Road
Singapore 0922
Tel: 737 7966
495 rooms
Seaview $$
26 Amber Close
Singapore 1543
Tel:345 2222
435 rooms
Shangri-la $$$$$
22 Orange Grove Road
Singapore 1025
Tel: 737 3644
821 rooms
Sheraton Towers $$$$$
39 Scotts Road
Singapore 0922
Tel: 737 6888
407 rooms
Southeast Asia $
190 Waterloo Street
Singapore 0718
Tel: 338 2394
51 rooms
Strand $$
25 Bencoolen Street
Singapore 0718
Tel: 338 1866
107 rooms
Supreme $
15 Kramat Road
Singapore 0922
Tel: 737 8333
86 rooms
Tai-Pan Ramada $$$$
101 Victoria Street

Singapore 0718
Tel: 336 0811
500 rooms
Victoria $
87 Victoria Street
Singapore 0718
Tel: 338 2381
50 rooms
Westin Plaza $$$$
2 Stamford Road
Singapore 0617
Tel: 338 8585
796 rooms
Westin Stamford $$$$
2 Stamford Road
Singapore 0617
Tel: 338 8585
1,253 rooms
YMCA $
1 Orchard Road
Singapore 0923
Tel: 337 3444
111 rooms
York $$$$
21 Mount Elizabeth
Singapore 0922
Tel: 737 0511
400 rooms

SHOPPING CENTRES

Albert Centre
271 Albert Street
Singapore 0718
Albert Complex
60 Albert Street
Singapore 0718
Blanco Court
585 North Bridge Road
Singapore 0718
Bras Basah Complex
231 Bain Street
Singapore 0718
Centrepoint
175 Orchard Road
Singapore 0923
Chinatown Complex
Smith Street
Singapore 0105
Chinatown Plaza
34 Craig Road
Singapore 0208

Colombo Court
1 Colombo Court
Singapore 0617

Cuppage Plaza
5 Koek Road
Singapore 0922

Delfi
402 Orchard Road
Singapore 0923

Far East Plaza
14 Scotts Road
Singapore 0922

Far East Shopping Centre
545 Orchard Road
Singapore 0923

Fortune Centre
190 Middle Road
Singapore 0718

Forum Galleria
583 Orchard Road
Singapore 0923

Fu Lu Shou Complex
149 Orchard Road
Singapore 0718

Funan Centre
109 North Bridge Road
Singapore 0617

Golden Landmark
390 Victoria Street
Singapore 0718

High Street Centre
1 North Bridge Road
Singapore 0617

High Street Plaza
77 High Street
Singapore 0617

Hill Street Centre
Hill Street
Singapore 0617

Hong Lim Complex
531 Upper Cross Street
Singapore 0105

International Building
360 Orchard Road
Singapore 0923

Liang Court
177 River Valley Road
Singapore 0923

Liat Towers
541 Orchard Road
Singapore 0923

Lucky Plaza
304 Orchard Road
Singapore 0923

Marina Square
6 Raffles Boulevard
Singapore 0103

Midlink Plaza
122 Middle Road
Singapore 0718

Midpoint Orchard
220 Orchard Road
Singapore 0923

Ming Arcade
21 Cuscaden Road
Singapore 1024

New Bridge Centre
New Bridge Road
Singapore 0105

North Bridge Centre
North Bridge Road
Singapore 0718

Orchard Emerald
218 Orchard Road
Singapore 0923

Orchard Plaza
150 Orchard Road
Singapore 0923

Orchard Shopping Centre
321 Orchard Road
Singapore 0923

Orchard Towers
400 Orchard Road
Singapore 0923

**Overseas Union
Shopping Centre**
Collyer Quay
Singapore 0104

Paradiz Centre
1 Selegie Road
Singapore 0718

Paragon
290 Orchard Road
Singapore 0923

Park Lane Shopping Mall
35 Selegie Road
Singapore 0718

Peace Centre
1 Sophia Road
Singapore 0922

Pearl's Centre
100 Eu Tong Sen Street
Singapore 0105

Peninsula Plaza
111 North Bridge Road
Singapore 0617

Peninsula Shopping Centre
3 Coleman Street
Singapore 0617

People's Park Centre
101 Upper Cross Street
Singapore 0105

People's Park Complex
1 Park Road
Singapore 0105

Pidemco Centre
95 South Bridge Road
Singapore 0105

Plaza
7500 Beach Road
Singapore 0719

Plaza by the Park
Bras Basah Road
Singapore 0718

Plaza Singapura
68 Orchard Road
Singapore 0923

Promenade
300 Orchard Road
Singapore 0923

Raffles City
252 North Bridge Road
Singapore 0923

Rochor Centre
1 Rochor Road
Singapore 0718

Scotts
6 Scotts Road
Singapore 0922

Selegie Centre
189 Selegie Road
Singapore 0718

Selegie Complex
257 Selegie Road
Singapore 0718

Shaw Centre
1 Scotts Road
Singapore 0922

Shaw Towers
100 Beach Road
Singapore 0718

Sim Lim Square
Bencoolen Street
Singapore 0718

Sim Lim Tower
10 Jalan Besar
Singapore 0820

Singapore Shopping Centre
190 Clemenceau Avenue
Singapore 0923

Specialists' Shopping Centre
277 Orchard Road
Singapore 0923

Supreme House
9 Penang Road
Singapore 0923
Tanglin Shopping Centre
19 Tanglin Road
Singapore 1024
Tong Building
302 Orchard Road
Singapore 0923
Waterloo Centre
261 Waterloo Street
Singapore 0718
Wisma Atria
435 Orchard Road
Singapore 0923

HOSPITALS

East Shore Hospital
321 Joo Chiat Place
Singapore 1542
Tel: 344 7588
Gleneagles Hospital
4 Napier Road
Singapore 1025
Tel: 473 7222
Mount Alvernia Hospital
820 Thomson Road
Singapore 1129
Tel: 253 8844
Mount Elizabeth Hospital
3 Mount Elizabeth
Singapore 0922
Tel: 737 2666
National University Hospital
5 Lower Kent Ridge Road
Singapore 0511
Tel: 779 5555
Singapore General Hospital
7 Outram Road
Singapore 0316
Tel: 222 3322
Thomson Medical Centre
339 Thomson Road
Singapore 1130
Tel: 256 9494

POST OFFICES

General Post Office
Fullerton Building
Fullerton Square

Singapore 0104
Tel: 533 8899
Comcentre
31 Exeter Road
Singapore 0923
Tel: 733 7899
Tanglin Post Office
60 Tanglin Road
Singapore 1024
Tel: 733 8899
Orchard Post Office
Tangs Superstore
320 Orchard Road
Singapore 0923
Tel: 732 8899
Orchard Point Post Office
Orchard Point #B1–16
160 Orchard Road
Singapore 0923
Tel: 732 7899
Rochor Post Office
Rochor Centre #01–560
1 Rochor Road
Singapore 0718
Tel: 296 8899
Raffles City Post Office
Raffles City Shopping Centre
#01–32
252 North Bridge Road
Singapore 0617
Tel: 339 8899

PLACES OF WORSHIP

Buddhist or Taoist Temples

**Kong Meng San
Phor Kark See Temple**
Bright Hill Drive
Singapore 2057
Kwan Im Thong Temple
Telok Blangah Drive
Singapore 0410
Long San See Temple
Race Course Road
Singapore 0821
**Sakaya Muni Buddha
Gaya Temple**
Race Course Road
Singapore 0821
Siong Lim Temple
Jalan Toa Payoh
Singapore 1231

Tan Si Chong Su Temple
Magazine Road
Singapore 0106
Thian Hock Keng Temple
Telok Ayer Street
Singapore 0106
Wak Hai Cheng Bo Temple
Phillip Street
Singapore 0104

Churches

Armenian Church
Hill Street
Singapore 0617
Bethesda Church
Bras Basah Road
Singapore 0718
**Cathedral of the
Good Shepherd**
Bras Basah Road
Singapore 0718
Church of St Peter and St Paul
Queen Street
Singapore 0718
Church of the Sacred Heart
Tank Road
Singapore 0923
St Andrew's Cathedral
Coleman Street
Singapore 0617
St Joseph's Church
Victoria Street
Singapore 0718

Hindu Temples

Sri Krishnan Temple
Waterloo Street
Singapore 0718
Sri Mariamman Temple
South Bridge Road
Singapore 0105
Sri Srinivasa Perumal Temple
Serangoon Road
Singapore 0821
Sri Thandayuthapani Temple
Tank Road
Singapore 0923
Sri Veeramakaliamman Temple
Serangoon Road
Singapore 0821

PHOTO CREDITS

Al-Abrar Mosque
Telok Ayer Street
Singapore 0106
Bencoolen Mosque
Bencoolen Street
Singapore 0718
Hajja Fatimah Mosque
Beach Road
Singapore 0719
Jamae Mosque
South Bridge Road
Singapore 0105
Johor Mosque
Telok Blangah Road
Singapore 0409
Malabar Jama-ath Mosque
Victoria Street
Singapore 0719
Melaka Mosque
Keng Cheow Street
Singapore 0105
Nagore Durgha Shrine
Telok Ayer Street
Singapore 0106
Sultan Mosque
North Bridge Road
Singapore 0719

Synagogues

Chesed-El Synagogue
Oxley Rise
Singapore 0923
Maghain Aboth Synagogue
Waterloo Street
Singapore 0718

Antiques of the Orient: 6 (top & bottom)
Marcus Brooke: backcover (top right); x (right); xi (left & right), 24, 28, 43, 52, 55, 56, 66 (top), 75, 84, 100, 103 (bottom), 116, 118, 122, 128, 130, 132 (top & bottom), 164, 170, 171, 177, 186, 195, 197, 198, 200, 206, 207, 240, 256, 260, 262, 272, 273
Wendy Chan: endpaper front, xiii, xvi, 50/51, 58, 66 (bottom), 74, 77, 86, 93, 94/95, 102, 125, 134, 138, 139, 142, 143, 145, 147 (right), 156, 159, 162/163, 178, 179, 180, 264/265, 276
ERA-Maptec: 32/33
Alain Evrard: cover, backcover (top left), vi, viii, viii/ix, ix, xii, xv, 31, 54, 57, 59, 60/61, 73 (right), 104, 106/107, 109 (right), 131, 151, 152, 173, 191, 196, 224, 247, 268, 270, endpaper (back)
Hard Rock Café: 246
Hideout: 251
J. Hutchison/M. Pfeiff: 126
The Image Bank: 90
The Image Bank/Andy Caulfield: 103 (top), 226
The Image Bank/Wendy Chan: 68/69, 96, 97, 194, 231, 261
The Image Bank/Chong Chuen Wei: 205
The Image Bank/Jean Claude Conninges: 80
The Image Bank/Kevin Forest: 220/221
The Image Bank/Robert Holland: 203 (right)
The Image Bank/Ingo Jezierski: 94, 140/141
The Image Bank/S.F. Lam: 89
The Image Bank/Anne Rippy: 204 (bottom)
The Image Bank/Steve Satushek: 266/267
The Image Bank/Kim Steele: 37, 258
The Image Bank/Nevada Wier: 11, 78/79, 202/203, 204 (top)
Joe Lynch Photography: 81, 88, 113, 114, 117, 119, 120/121, 135, 136, 137, 166/167, 169, 172, 176, 192, 193, 217, 218, 222/223, 228, 230, 232, 238, 248, 252/253, 254/255, 263
Geoff Kirby, 242/243, 244
Gilles Massot: 26, 38/9, 92, 115, 150, 185
Fiona Nichols: xii/xiii, 30, 129, 214
R.C.A Nichols: 70, 146/147
R.Mohd Noh: 274, 275
Pro(file) Library/Alberto Cassio: 208/209
Pro(file) Library/Neil Farrin: 22/23, 184
Pro(file) Library/Pat Lam: 2/3, 36, 95
Pro(file) Library/Dominic Sansoni: vii, 34, 45, 64, 87, 91, 148, 158, 160/161 (4 pictures), 168, 210, 212, 215, 220 (left), 234/235, 236, 239, 241, 249, 250
Allan Seiden: 144
Singapore Ministry of Information & the Arts: 13, 14/15, 16, 19
Singapore National Archives: 4/5, 7, 10
Singapore Symphony Orchestra: 82/83
Morten Strange: 40, 42, 44, 46, 48/49 (7 pictures)
Trans Globe Photo Agency: backcover (bottom), x (left), xiv, 20, 21, 62/63, 72/73, 79 (right), 108/109, 112, 123, 140 (left), 149, 154, 155, 160 (top extreme left), 189, 216, 219, 221 (bottom)

INDEX

NOTES

NOTES

NOTES

NOTES